GLOSSA?

CW00539739

AGI	ARMOURGROUP IRAQ
AGW	ABU GHRAIB WAREHOUSE
HQ	HEADQUARTERS
LN	LOCAL NATIONAL (IRAQIS)
TCN	THIRD COUNTRY NATIONALS (NON-COALITION NATIONALITIES)
MSR	MAIN SUPPLY ROUTE
PSD	PERSONAL/PRIVATE/PROTECTIVE SECURITY DETAIL
PSC	PRIVATE SECURITY COMPANY
PMC	PRIVATE MILITARY COMPANY
CET	CONVOY ESCORT TEAMS
MST	MARITIME SECURITY TEAMS
LMCC	LOGISTICAL MOVEMENTS CO-ORDINATION CENTRE
CP	CLOSE PROTECTION
UQ	UMM QASR
TL	TEAM LEADER
2 I/C	SECOND-IN-COMMAND
ROF	RULES OF FORCE (CONTRACTORS)
ROE	RULES OF ENGAGEMENT (MILITARY)
DFAC	DINING FACILITY
SUV	SPORTS UTILITY VEHICLE
EOD	EXPLOSIVE ORDINANCE DISPOSAL
PX	POSTAL EXCHANGE (US MILITARY BASES)
OPS	OPERATIONS

PLATE CARRIER	ARMOURED VEST
IP	IRAQI POLICE
ING	IRAQI NATIONAL GUARD (ARMY)
SOFA	STATUS OF FORCES AGREEMENT
CPA	COALITION PROVISIONAL AUTHORITY
LOAC	LAW OF ARMED CONFLICT
CEFO	COMBAT EFFECTIVE FIGHTING ORDER
PRR	PERSONAL ROLE RADIO
LI	LIGHT INFANTRY
3 RIFLES	3RD BATTALION THE RIFLES
QM	QUARTER MASTER
NCO	NON-COMMISSIONED OFFICER
WO	WARRANT OFFICER
RSM	REGIMENTAL SERJEANT MAJOR (APPOINTMENT OF WARRANT OFFICER CLASS I)
NCO	NON-COMMISSIONED OFFICER (LANCE CORPORAL UP TO COLOUR SERJEANT)
O GROUP	ORDERS
IRA	IRISH REPUBLICAN ARMY (TERRORIST GROUP OF NORTHERN IRELAND)
NAAFI	NAVY, ARMY, AIR FORCE, INSTITUTION
SLA	SIERRA LEONE ARMY
DPM	DISRUPTIVE PATTERN MATERIAL (CAMOUFLAGE)
RMP	ROYAL MILITARY POLICE
NI	NORTHERN IRELAND
VCP	VEHICLE CHECKPOINT
PVCP	PERMANENT VEHICLE CHECKPOINT

SEVEN POINT SIX TWO

THE TRUE STORY OF SOLDIERS FOR HIRE IN IRAQ

GARY ROBERTS

STEEL CITY PRESS

This first edition published in 2019 by Steel City Press
9 Ravenscroft Close, Sheffield, S13 8PN, United Kingdom.

ISBN 978-1-913047-08-5

Copyright © 2019 Gary Roberts

All rights reserved. This book or any portion thereof
may not be reproduced or used in any manner whatsoever
without the express written permission of the publisher
except for the use of brief quotations in a book review.

Proudly printed in the United Kingdom.

SVCP	SNAP VEHICLE CHECKPOINT
RQMS	REGIMENTAL QUARTERMASTER SERJEANT (APPOINTMENT OF WARRANT OFFICER CLASS 1)
GPS	GLOBAL POSITIONING SYSTEM
IZ	INTERNATIONAL ZONE (FORMERLY THE GREEN ZONE, FORMERLY THE AMERICAN ZONE)
FOB	FORWARD OPERATING BASE
IED	IMPROVISED EXPLOSIVE DEVICE
EFP	EXPLOSIVELY FORMED PENETRATOR
SAF	SMALL ARMS FIRE
IDF	INDIRECT FIRE (MORTARS/ROCKETS/ ARTILLERY ETC.)
CIVVI/CIVVY	CIVILIAN
CIVVIES	CIVILIAN CLOTHING

Note: throughout this book, we use the traditional spelling of Serjeant. This spelling dates back to the days of the British Light Infantry, and is still in common usage in the Rifles today.

For Daniel and Georgia.

PROLOGUE

2017...

The room is grey: grey furniture, grey walls, grey door. A grey table separates the room; two grey chairs stand either side.

I'm sat facing two grey suits, both men sit in silence. One of the men makes a show of unwrapping the plastic from three blank DVDs and holds them up for me to see. I nod my assent before he places them in a DVD recorder at one end of the table. I glance at the black-lensed cameras in the corners of the room. As the video screen flashes into life, I see the back of my head along with that of Alice's sat next to me.

Suit number-one clears his throat and asks the three of us if we're ready to start. Alice nods and gives the okay. Suit number-two leans over and hits the record button. After brief introductions, suit one goes straight into his spiel…

"Gary Roberts. You do not have to say anything. But it may harm your defence if you do not mention when questioned something which you may later rely on in court. Anything you do say may be given in evidence. Do you understand…?"

"Yes", I reply.

"And are you aware of why we'd like to talk to you today, what we want to ask you questions about?"

I nod…"Iraq".

PART I

"Convoys are probably the most dangerous job in Iraq right now..."

Paul Bremmer (Head of the CPA - Coalition Provisional Authority)

IRAQ

2003...

Chaos. There is no government, no law, and no effective infrastructure. Thousands of Iraqis are dead. Thousands are displaced. Buildings lie in disrepair or ruins.

And so begins the long period of military occupation and reconstruction. In the Green Zone (a four-square-mile area of central Baghdad that was the administrative centre for Saddam Husain's Ba'ath Party) the Coalition forms a transitional government, the CPA (Coalition Provisional Authority). Western companies are contracted to rebuild the country's infrastructure.

Resistance gains ground. Angry insurgents use guerrilla tactics - small-arms, mortars, missiles, car bombs, improvised explosive devices, rocket-propelled grenades, suicide attacks - all aimed at damaging the reconstruction efforts and taking out Coalition forces and those aiding them. Their attacks claim more coalition lives than those lost during the war. This is the war after the war, the real war.

On an unprecedented scale, war is outsourced. Tasks once undertaken by the military are hired out privately. Private military contractors are brought in to protect key people, places, organisations, convoys; to face explosives and gunfire on a day-to-day basis; to engage with the enemy, not under a flag, but as private contractors in a war without regular rules, a war without lines, a war without fronts; and to - if so required, give their lives in the line of doing their jobs.

This is *their* war: a clandestine war, an unknown war, a war with no official record or death toll. They are soldiers for hire.

I.I

2006...

The man hanging out of the bus is dead, judging by his stillness, the amount of blood all over him and the woman wailing hysterically by his side - his mother, I think.

My team is in northern Baghdad, on Route Senators (named by the Americans; they've renamed all the roads in the city, often after sports teams, staking their claim). Two security trucks, ten lorries, and then two more security trucks at the back. No idea what the cargo is we're protecting; boxes of something. Can't be majorly valuable, like ammo, or we'd have an American chopper escort.

I'm commanding the front vehicle, an F350 gun truck, with my LN (Local National) driver and two LN gunners in the back, open-topped, 'the bucket'. We hire LNs because they're cheap compared to us ex-pats, not because they're good. My job is simple: be the eyes of the convoy – pick a path through, weaving us around debris and potholes and vehicles; flag upcoming checkpoints; scout for suspicious activity; radio comms back to the boys behind, giving a constant commentary and brief on what's ahead. As usual, I'm geared up: M21 rifle, Glock 17 pistol, ammo, plate-carrier and a helmet, because I'm just as likely to die of a knock on the head after a road-side bomb as a gunshot.

I've been building up a track ahead through the traffic, but there's a jam upcoming. We're on a dual carriageway with a central reservation barrier, so there's no chance of just crossing to the other side and bypassing the build-up by driving up the wrong side, the usual protocol.

'Slow, slow,' I radio to my team – Irish Steve (second vehicle), Greg (a Kiwi) and Marc (a Yorkshireman) at the back – so that they can keep their distance. Better to be four small targets than one big one.

The lorry drivers decelerate too. They don't have radios; their instructions are simple: follow the vehicle in front. When he stops, you stop. When he goes, you go. Leave a space. Match the speed. You've got to take them thinking for themselves out of the equation.

I peer ahead, through the piercing glare of the sun that reflects off the dusty concrete buildings all around – the city of beige – and command my driver to fight through the traffic.

'Push to the left. Static ahead. Go round it, mate, round it!'

I'm uneasy at being hemmed in by vehicles full of locals, amid high buildings. Any could house someone with an AK or RPG or worse, and the usual response of driving through a contact at speed won't work here.

With a couple of cars in front of me I call, 'Stop, stop.'

Now I can see the source of the jam – a checkpoint. Two Iraqi guys in combat camouflage stand on the road, AKs low down, scanning the traffic. They look jittery, ready for trouble. They stare their onlookers down, daring anyone to question their authority. Behind them, the cause of their nervousness: a minibus, shot to shit, riddled.

The dead guy hangs limp from the door of the bus, face down, legs on the steps, head on the floor. Judging by his dark hair and Western dress – trousers and a now-bloody shirt – he's pretty young. I see no weapon; no reason for the killing. Looks to me like he was trying to get off. It was totally innocent, I decide, nothing sinister in it; the bloke just wasn't looking where he was going and he pushed the guards' buttons. He paid with his life: blood everywhere – across his body, up the side of the bus, puddle on the floor around his head.

The old woman is making a God-awful racket. I know this because I can hear her inside my armoured vehicle; the thick glass and metal shell of the armour strip out all but the loudest exterior noises. She's dressed from head to toe in a voluminous black burqa that's more tent than cloak, to conceal her massive size. As she staggers about, moaning and shrieking, the burqa shifts and I catch a glimpse of her full face. This is a woman in agony. There are guards grabbing her arms, trying to steady her and get a firm enough grip to lead her away from the grisly sight she's fixated on, but she shakes them off. She will not be moved. Just another day in sunny Baghdad.

11

We're stuck there for a while, waiting in our vehicles. I pass the time talking to Ahmed, my driver, while eying up the surrounding streets, buildings, vehicles, people, and potential firing points. He's a young lad with an air of the unkempt about him – thin as a roll-up, chin perpetually stubbled, sticking-out hair that's begging for a comb. But it's his teeth that you most notice – uneven, mustard-yellow gnashers thanks to many years of chain smoking. Dental hygiene isn't exactly a priority for Iraqis.

He looks at me now, grins and decides to try his luck.

'I have cigarette while we wait, Mr Gary?'

I eyeball him.

'Hmmm…Fuck no.'

Ahmed rolls his eyes but says nothing. It's one of my rules for drivers: no smokes in the vehicle. On a six-to-seven-hour mission, I don't want to be stuck with that. It's unprofessional, it stinks and it's not going to help my fitness (not much point exercising with the guys one day only to breathe in lungfuls of acrid tar fumes the next). Plus, in operational terms I think it's useful to see out of the window rather than driving in a fog of smoke. But all the drivers smoke, so my rule isn't popular.

Ahmed's knees are jiggling – nicotine withdrawal. Tough, I think.

'I never have cigarette?' he asks me.

'Not while we're driving. Maybe if something really bad went down – after, if we've got through it, then I might be soft and let you have one. One, mind.'

Ahmed's pinched face lights up. He's positively glowing at the thought of us getting into serious shit. Now it's my turn to roll my eyes.

We sit quietly for a while, watching the world not go by.

Then the gunfire starts.

Time slows as I hunt out the source. It's the Iraqi guards, shooting from the hip at buildings towering over us. I whip my head around to see the targets. Insurgents, nine o'clock, laying down small-arms fire directed at the road.

I hit the button on the radio that puts me in touch with our convoy. 'Contact, left! Contact, left! Small arms!' I say loudly but coolly. No point shouting. It makes the words indecipherable over the radio and stirs everyone into a panic. Our guys start shooting; I hear the tat-tat-tat-tat-tat of the machine guns behind me in the bucket and the empty brass clunking to the floor by their feet. I look to the left, past Ahmed, who is sitting in the left-hand front seat, the driver's side in Iraq. Continued gunfire from the buildings around, firing indiscriminately at the checkpoint, the civilian cars, us. I see insurgents bouncing between the alleyways with AKs. I think they're wearing blue boiler suits. Which is odd, because our guys wear boiler suits.

I'm giving instructions over the radio when Ahmed kicks open his door and starts shooting his AK from the hip at the insurgents in the alleyways. He's obviously been in this position a few times. The LNs have had more contacts than the rest of us, and some of them have got balls, I'll give them that.

'What the fuck are you doing!' I shout at him. Yeah, now I'm shouting.

I'm pissed off that he's opened the door – without telling me anyway. The armoured truck protects us from small-arms fire - in fact, even under fire I feel relatively safe inside. But now he's opened us right up to taking a hit. He's meant to do as I say; he's the driver, not the leader. Still, this isn't like PSD - it's not set in stone.

But then I clock the baddies, and decide there are more pressing matters than bawling him out.

I roughly grab Ahmed and push his skinny frame forward to make room for me to fire my M21 from the shoulder. In less than a second I have my weapon up, eye focused through the optical sight (my own, smuggled in from the UK; always makes for a fun trip through UK and international airports), and am firing.

My British Army training has kicked in – I'm putting down single shots, not automatic. More accurate. But more to the point, it saves wastage on ammo, and it's not like we have a QM on call who'll chopper us up an ammo replen on request. It's a joke that I do this now – in private contracting no one's going to slap me on the wrist for pounding out a whole heap of ammo, and the guys behind me in the gun bucket certainly aren't worrying, judging by the incessant pounding of their weapons. But how I fire comes automatically to me now. No thought required.

I focus on the insurgents on the ground, running between buildings. They're not firing at us, but they're holding weapons, and I figure our gunners and the Iraqi guards have the guys in the buildings covered. I miss the first couple of insurgents, then I start getting through. I catch one guy in the hip, and he falls through a door, out of sight.

As I focus on firing, I know one of the team will have pushed the panic button (our nickname for the transponder) to let the ops room know we're in contact. Back at the Baghdad Villas, the base for the company I'm working for, the ops commander and watch-keeper follows the call signs going around Iraq via GPS. Now, his screen will be bleeping.

The gunfire is relentless – the insurgents are having a whale of a time. Ammo discipline is a foreign concept. They'll keep the heat on until they've run out of bullets.

Civilian drivers around us are panicking, trying to do U-turns and get out of the action. They're bashing into each other, shunting people out of their way. It's like a deadly game of dodgems.

The guards who were trying to rein in the old, grieving woman have joined the battle, firing up at the buildings. Abandoned amid the carnage, the dead man's mother continues to sway and wail.

Steve – the team leader – has had enough. His job is to get us out of danger, not engage in kill-the-bad-guy missions. He comes on the net and tells us to stop fucking around and push through.

I agree. Time to get the hell out. Not our job to deal with the shooters. We're not here to change the world, just to get the convoy through.

'Shut the fuckin' door,' I instruct Ahmed. 'We're going.'

He does as he's told.

The ops room calls on the mobile – one of three strapped to the dashboard, because there are three networks in Iraq covering different parts of the country. 'Call you back,' I say shortly.

We push through. Ahmed honks the horn at the cars in front of us while the gunners on-top do a bit of crowd control, shouting at the civilian drivers to move. One of the vehicles right in front of the checkpoint is frozen, and has come to rest at an angle that's blocking forward flow of traffic. It's just a little civilian car – an Iraqi piece of shit from the eighties. So we touch up behind it and push it out of the way. As we pass, I look down from the height of our truck into the tiny car. I see the driver's legs. Slack, no movement. Either dead or getting there, I think. Just a civvy on his way to work caught in the crossfire, another victim of the trigger-happy checkpoint guards.

There'll be no comeuppance for the guards. This is Baghdad. The war may be over, but no one's safe.

The path ahead is clear and we push on. We pass the shot-up minibus. The woman is on her knees beside the dead man now, rocking and chanting, stroking his hair. God knows how she's survived the bullets. Perhaps she doesn't care. Perhaps she wants to be with him.

A minute later I hear 'Contact, left, small arms' as Marc and Greg, bringing up the rear of the convoy, hammer through the hot zone. Then, finally, quiet.

'Mr Gary?'

I know what's coming.

'Mr Gary? I have cigarette now, yes?' Ahmed's eyes glint as he bares his yellow teeth at me in a hopeful smile.

'No fucking chance, Ahmed,' I say wearily.

'But Mr Gary! We nearly die!'

'Get a grip fuck-face. We were fine mate. The only time we were at risk was when you - fucking shitbreath - opened the door.'

Ahmed looks glum. 'Few more hours and we'll be at the drop-off,' I console him. 'Then you get a break and you can do what the fuck you like.'

The rest of our journey north is uneventful, and we drop off the cargo. Ahmed has a cig. I have a can of Coke with my team.

It's a good job I boosted my blood sugar because on the way back I'm burning through my reserves fast. Four rolling contacts – small-arms ambushes that we drive straight through. The armor of our gun-trucks take some hits and the top-gunners burn through belts of ammo as we push on. The radio's hot from use as I relay a running commentary on what's ahead to the convoy:

'Static car, left.'
'Slow, slow.'
'Huge pothole. Push right.'
'Push left.'
'Push right.'
'Road merging right. Traffic holding.'
'Vehicle Three, up to front. Block junction on the right.'
'Checkpoint ahead.'
'Clear checkpoint.'
'Cut speed.'
'Checkpoint clear.'
'Bend in road. Slow, slow.'
'Contact right, small arms.'
'Contact left, small arms.'
'Contact right, small arms.'

'Contact right, small arms.'

Finally, we come to an American call sign near a village called Al Mushada, which is really hot for convoy guys; everyone knows about it. There are a couple of AFVs: an Abrahams tank and a Bradley APC with an American soldier sticking out of the top hatch of the Bradley.

I radio: 'Slow, slow. Green call sign ahead.'

We always slow right down when we see American call signs – it can be a dangerous game to bomb past, and there's always the worry that a young soldier might misjudge us and think we're enemy.

This time, I direct Ahmed to stop the truck. I jump out, get one of the top gunners to take charge and go over to the APC.

'Look,' I say to the soldier on top, who looks pretty friendly, 'we've just been ambushed. Half a K that way. Just to let you know.'

I'm not too bothered from my point of view – I'm fine – but I want to deal with it because the next call sign that comes along might lose somebody, one of our lads.

As I expected, the American is itching for a fight. For him, every insurgent attack is personal. For him, the guys who've fired at me are the 9/11 bombers, masterminds, supporters.

'We'll get that sorted right away, sir,' he booms at me, then jumps on the radio.

I head back to my vehicle and watch as the two AFVs turn around and head back up the way we've come, looking for a fight. Good on them, I think. I remember a time when that was me, jumping into the fray. But it's not in my job description to do that right now. My job's to get from A to B alive.

That night, I lie in my bed and run through the day in my head. Dead man on bus. Dead man in car. Men I've wounded – killed? Ahmed flinging open the door and leaving us vulnerable. The Americans off for glory.

This is my first rotation on convoys, after a year in PSD, and I've gotta say, it's not too bad. Some PSD guys say, 'Never do convoys. You get fucking shot to shit every day.' PSD get contacts, and yeah, some are pretty heavy. But it's not like it is here. Now, in a two - to three-day mission, I know I'll have one contact; and today, it's been five. But I'm ok with it.

It's doesn't turn me on, but neither do I cry myself to sleep at night. I don't go out to seek action, but it doesn't put me off either.

Lots of people say, 'I wouldn't do that convoy contract because the living conditions are shit.' I say, 'Pay me enough money, I'll sleep in a skip.' Convoys isn't just about moving the cargo; it's about ruling the roads.

Yes, I think. Convoys are going to suit me just fine.

1.11

I'm working for the American government - well, for a British company contracted by the US Defence Department. They're known. Professional. Well respected. Been around a good while, since the early eighties.

The companies operating in this industry like the terms 'private security' or 'private military' to describe what they do. Check out their websites and you'll see smiling people holding clipboards or sat around boardroom tables having smiley conferences: the corporatisation of military work. There's a sense of professionalism, control. They use pleasant-sounding terms like 'risk management' and 'secure support services'.

On the other hand, you have those who apply the term 'mercenary' to private companies in Iraq. Basically, a mercenary is someone who's paid to take part in an armed conflict who isn't a party in the conflict. Mercenaries have been used for hundreds of years. But in the past fifty years' popular culture has brought a new meaning to the term, and it's often synonymous in people's minds with cold-blooded killers. Some private contractors are happy to be defined as mercenaries. But some dislike the connotations.

Personally, I think the name is meaningless. I know what my job is. I know what I'm paid to do. I'll kill if I have to. But I'm not hired to kill.

The company I work for are one of the top firms with convoys contracts. So we're busy all the time, moving around Iraq - stuff for the US military like weapons, ammunition and vehicles, lots of vehicles for the Iraqi Police and Army.

We work solidly, with a visit home every two to three months. There are no set hours; a mission takes as long as it takes. We get the odd day off, but the contract is busy and we're mostly out on the road. Doesn't bother me working so hard. It's not like there's much to do in Iraq on your day off.

Speak to some PSD or CP guy and you may come away thinking we on the convoys are Mad Max wannabes. Cowboys. Convoy is like a dirty word to some PSDs.

Certainly, convoys are a bit rougher around the edges - you've no client to mind your p's and q's in front of, no company that's contracted you that you have to work closely with. Yeah, you come across some blokes who aren't cut out for the job - they lack reality, they can't take the heat. And yeah, there's the odd 'Action-man' who's out for glory and swaggers about gripping his rifle like it's an extension of his dick.

But most are professionals. We've been in the military. We know this is a job, not a load of schoolboys playing war. Plus, it cuts both ways: plenty of convoy guys think PSDs are in need of a reality check. All that time off, sleeping in your own bed each night, journeys that pass without a rain of 7.62mm bullets peppering your vehicle…it's easy for a lot of guys to jump on that bandwagon, but I know PSDs have it just as tough as us – we run the same roads, after all, and unlike us they're working with clients, which restrains them in ways that we aren't.

I.III

We're heading up to Mosul on Route Tampa North, north of Baghdad. The further north you go, the more the city falls away and you're in open countryside – arid, sandy plains framed by sweeping hills and outcrops of rock. Only the grey road breaks up the endless pale landscape, a long stretch of tarmac ahead with the odd barrier next to the road to signify a rocky drop.

In such an open space, I'm wary, and I keep the LNs on a short leash. I'm in the front, directing Ahmed and map-reading. (You can't trust an LN to map-read from one end of the country to the other. Fuck knows what would happen to your cargo if you did.) It's a drizzly day, rare for Iraq, but I easily spot the convoy in the distance. I recognise the vehicles: although they're a mismatch and some have different weapons, at this time pretty much every PMC convoy in Iraq is Armorgroup. They're static, changing a tyre.

We slow down; it's customary to tip your hat at a fellow call sign. Could be anyone – there are plenty of call signs from the company based down south in Umm Qasr, not out of Baghdad. Then Steve, in the vehicle behind, comes on the radio to say he knows these guys. We pull up alongside, and Steve and I jump out to see if they need any help.

Steve introduces me to the two ex-pats supervising the LNs as they put on a new tyre: a Kiwi bloke by the name of Steve Gilchrist and a Brit lad called Lofty. I notice at once that the vehicle that's immobilised is damaged. Explosive, I think.

Sure enough, when Steve and Lofty give us a quick heads-up on the contacts they've just had in Mosul, it involves some small-arms fire and an IED. They've driven through, but the damage from the explosion to the vehicle that took the brunt of it has meant they couldn't limp far without stopping to fix it.

They show us the contact points on the map. We thank them and head back to our vehicles. I look at the map, try to work out another route to dodge around the areas they've pinpointed. But there's no other sensible route to take, so we press on.

It's ages since we've done a run to Mosul, and even by Iraqi standards it looks terrible – bombed-out shells of buildings, like some post-apocalypse scene. The roads are falling to bits, so it's not like you can speed your way through. And the place is deserted – which is a combat indicator: when people get the hell out, you know trouble's imminent.

It's no surprise when we hit the first contact. Small arms. The Iraqi-police-slash-insurgents at the checkpoint a mile back no doubt tipped them off we were coming through. Because insurgents aren't just crazy kufiyah-wearing outsiders. They're also in the police, the Army, the organisations running the country – the insiders.

Foot down, we drive through the rain of bullets. We make the drop-off, then head back out of the city – if you can call the ruins that – and get stuck behind an American military convoy. In the last vehicle a rear gunner is holding traffic back, not that there's much traffic in Mosul on this road because it's so dangerous. We know the drill: they've probably found a suspicious vehicle ahead. Static ones are the most worrying – they too often contain a suicide bomber or a vehicle-borne IED.

We've pulled up behind their truck, and their gunner in the back is eyeballing me, so I get my flag out, a little a4 sized American flag on a clipboard, and put it on the dashboard just to say, 'Don't shoot, we're on your side.' A lot of Americans don't have the pre-deployment training the Brits have, and they just haven't seen contractors before. Some of them seem to live in a bubble where anyone not in a US military uniform in a US military vehicle is enemy.

The bloke starts waving his hands about, trying to communicate something to me. I haven't a clue what he's on about. So I tip my door open and poke my head up, over the top. He starts gesturing wildly, shouting something at me – but he's too far; I can't hear him. Then he lifts up a square of cardboard on which he's scrawled in marker pen - *Sniper, keep down.* Like I was saying, the Yanks know the score and are well-trained, decent guys.

Eventually, we move on. We pass a static Iraqi vehicle which I suspect is the cause of the holdup. They must have decided it was harmless. The Americans turn off at a roundabout, and we carry on back to base along the same route on which we encountered the contact on the way in. And yes, it's the same shit on the way out. Another rain of bullets.

We're pretty much constantly under fire; the soundtrack to the journey is the rhythm of brass shells falling in the bucket at my rear as the LNs go for it. The convoy through the murky grey day is a plethora of disco lights: red for the brake lights, white for the muzzle flashes. In my wing mirror I see Steve's gunners struggling with the pivot arms on their weapons to get them angled high enough to counter the fire coming from the high buildings. As the slow-moving convoy bottlenecks through the rubble-strewn road I catch a glimpse of either Marc or Greg out of his vehicle putting some accurate fire down.

We get through unscathed (the vehicle armour has taken hits, but as long as the gunners and tyres are okay and we're moving then we're pretty much masters of our own destiny and can make decisions not based on wheel changes and first aid because the Iraqis are shit shots. 'Spray and pray' is their motto. With trained soldiers like us on their side, it would be a different story.

I.IV

A couple of days later, I'm lying on my bed taking a breather when one of guys comes in to tell me there's an O Group outside on the kerb. No big deal; we have these meetings all this time. Admittedly not in the morning on the kerbside, though. I head out and stand with the other guys. I'm chitchatting about football with one of the lads – the Premiership - when John, the OPs managers, comes out.

A hush falls straight away. From John's serious expression, we can tell something's wrong.

'A call sign's been hit on Route Dover,' he says. 'It's one of the Umm Qasr teams. They've hit the transponder; struggling to extract themselves.' He pauses. Then: 'There's a fatality.' We take that to mean an ex-pat fatality, one of us.

While I was on the PSD contract, contact was a big deal – loads of meetings and analysing and talking to agents about it. But on convoys, people get contacts twice, three times a week or more. It's no big thing. You go out for two or three days on a mission and then come back, and people don't even know about what shit you've seen. You have a cup of tea back at the compound and tell the tale. It's just a given that people are getting whacked all over the place. Serious injury or death - it's not unusual, but it *is* news.

John tells us to be ready to move out, just in case. That's not enough for us lads. It's one thing driving through a contact; it's another when a man's down and three others are at risk. When you have a good team and lads you trust, you're happy to risk yourself, to take them out. So we decide we'll get going – just ex-pats, though; no time to get LNs set up. It's what we'd hope people would do for us if we were stuck in a contact.

John gives us the okay. He gets a map and shows us where the call sign is. We quickly delegate jobs. A couple of guys pore over the map, planning a route. A couple more head off for vehicle keys. We organise who'll do what – driving, directing, manning the guns in the rear buckets. Then we hurry back to our rooms and grab our plate-carriers and weapons. We're all but ready to leave when John emerges from the office again and calls a halt.

'Stand down, guys. Ops room says they've managed to extract themselves. I'm still going to need one team to go out to… well, to transport…'

The company's responsible for transporting the body back to the family; in this case, to Australia. They use military assets, so we need to move the body to another American camp, Victory, the main base in Baghdad.
Steve volunteers our team. John agrees.

'Who the fuck is it…?' one of the blokes asks.
He doesn't need to finish; we all know he means, 'Who's dead?'
'It's Steve,' says John. 'Steve Gilchrist. With the amount of damage, looks like an EFP.'

Explosively formed penetrator. Fucking hell.

IEDs are what the journalists write about. In 2007, the Washington Post called them 'the single most effective weapon against our deployed forces'. Yeah, there are plenty around. They're homemade bombs. The Iraqi insurgents learnt in ten months what it took the IRA ten years to master. That said, IEDs aren't hard to make. Your average Iraqi could be taught to put an IED together in ten minutes so. They leave them beside the road, in abandoned cars, in dead animals. There are several ways to trigger them – most commonly we see them run off a command wire leading back to an insurgent with a trigger or detonated by phone. Unlike the military, we don't have the luxury of electronic countermeasures like jammers.

But the EFP blows the IED out of the water. They're ridiculously powerful; they can blow a tank off the road. The insurgent packs a short tube with explosives, caps one end, places a detonator on the capped end and sticks a concave copper plate on the open end. When it detonates, the explosives melt the copper and form a slug projectile that's fucking lethal. Can penetrate armour even when fired from some distance, and then breaks up inside the vehicle to spray out metal fragments. They're often placed at window-level, to do maximum damage to occupants of vehicles, and at choke points, where vehicles slow, to allow a greater degree of accuracy. They're pretty new to guerrilla warfare, and while they're not common, they're all over Iraq.

Detonation may be by command wire or radio or phone, but the insurgents have come up with a seriously deadly method as well: infrared. They lie in wait, and when the last of the civilian traffic passes they switch on a machine that sends an infrared beam across the road. Once the front of your vehicle breaks that beam, the device, hidden at the side of the road, goes off. Boom. Dead.

Beyond being vigilant, your only defence against EFPs is the beam breaker. Some of our vehicles have them – a bit of metal that protrudes in front of the grill, so that it breaks the beam first, and then the explosive goes off course and hopefully misses the cab. But they keep getting blown off by IEDs, so they're not on every truck.

EFPs are quite a talking point amongst the guys. In my head I can justify the risk-to-vulnerability equation. When it comes to IEDs or being shot up in the armoured vehicles, I feel relatively safe. But EFPs, they're another matter. Rarer. Bad news.

I think back to the road to Mosul just a couple of days back, to Steve Gilchrist, having survived an IED, giving me the lowdown on the contacts lying ahead, looking out for us. I didn't know him that well, but he seemed like a nice bloke, a professional. Of course, he knew the risks; we all do.

While the rest of the blokes stand down, talking in hushed tones as they take off their kit, our call sign – Steve, Marc and Greg at this point – prepare to move out to transport Steve Gilchrist. His team's holed up at Fort Apache, a little American base in the heart of Baghdad.

Steve and I will go in one vehicle, Marc and Greg behind in another. We put our heads together to plan the route – we come up with a primary and a secondary route and Steve gives a quick 'actions on' brief.

As for the plan once we link up with Lofty's team in Fort Apache, that's not so clear. 'Let's just get to Fort Apache and take it from there,' suggests Steve. It's a quiet journey, uneventful. We're all deep in thought.

At Fort Apache Marc and Greg wait in the courtyard and I sign the paperwork for Steve and me to enter. As we pull into the yard in front of the medical centre, I see that even the LNs are sombre, puffing away on their cigarettes in the yard. By all accounts they had a hell of a firefight – small-arms fire on top of the EFP. Lofty, Steve's mate who was with him in the vehicle, is there. He's all right, pretty cool, but he's just lost his mate so he's gutted. He tried to save him; picked him up and put him in the back of a truck while under fire. But he was dead when the EFP hit.

An American doctor meets us on the steps. Young, confident, smooth.
'If you'd like to follow me…' he says carefully.

No, I wouldn't *like* to follow you, mate, I think. Who wants to go into these places?

I step through the door and am hit by a stink of disinfectant that makes my stomach roll. We're shown into a treatment room. My first impression is that it's bright, clean and well-equipped – plenty of fancy medical equipment that's not much use to Steve now. It crosses my mind to start asking what kit is going spare, but I decide to put that thought to the back of my mind for now.

A nurse inside the room is zipping up the body bag as we enter. I try to focus on the doctor instead as he hands me a transparent plastic bag containing Steve's personal effects – his phone, his ID, his wallet. From the ease with which the doctor handles us I can tell this is no new experience to him. This little FOB in the middle of Baghdad has seen a lot of death.

The doctor gestures to the table on which lies the body bag, as if to say, 'He's all yours.'

Steve and I step forward to look. The nurse has zipped the bag up to conceal his body and the fatal wounds, but as she zips him up we can see his head and hair, covered in dust. He looks asleep. No, not asleep. Dead.

Do I feel anything? No. Not really. If I'm going to have an emotional reaction, this is neither the place nor the time. I've still plenty of roads to drive down in Baghdad. Focus is key.

I.IV

We zip up the bag, go back out the front and recruit two LNs to carry him, one at each end. Steve and I hold the doors open. The others watch silently.

When we get to the truck, I say, 'Steve, it's not right, putting him in the back. Let's put him on the back seat. He can ride with us.'

Steve agrees, and we carefully slide the body in.
I get in the front in the driver's seat. Steve goes off to sign some papers. When he gets back he gets in, looks over his shoulder at the body bag and says simply, 'Fucking Stevie, eh.'

We head out of Fort Apache, hooking up with Marc and Greg, and take the body to FOB Victory. We're directed to the mortuary where an Army medic meets us. The last we see of Steve Gilchrist is his body being wheeled away.
Steve pulls out his phone and calls the ops room.
'Job done.'

As we drive back into AGW, I think about Steve Gilchrist. I wonder whether he had kids, but I don't dwell on it.

Better him than me.

Team Basra

Team Baghdad

Author talking to pilot > Tikrit

Iraqi police & army checkpoint > Haji

PMC gun truck communications including red 'panic button'

(Author) Weapon test, Baghdad

Iraqi security forces > Baghdad

Low-profile PMC > Baghdad 2008

Author firing .50 Barrett rifle

PMC convoy > Southern Iraq

Convoy Protection > Southern Iraq

A gun truck after a roadside IED > Fire would often take hold after the explosion

I.V

Our job is to get the convoys out of danger. It would be a damn sight easier without the insurgents. We're not in the military now, we're PMCs, but old habits die hard, and there's a reason they employ soldiers.

In the military, we operate according to Rules of Engagement. They lay down the grounds for what's legal and illegal; who you can kill, in what circumstances. Break the rules and your neck (potentially) is on the line. Inquiry. Court martial. The PMCs issue us with Rules of Force, based on the Military Rules of Engagement. They lay down the following rules for contractors:

- *You are a noncombat and may not engage in offensive operations with Coalition forces.*

- *Cooperate with Coalition and police/security forces and comply with theatre force protection policies. Do not avoid or run Coalition or police/security force checkpoints. If authorised to carry weapons, do not aim them at Coalition or police/security forces.*

- *Deadly force is that force which you reasonably believe will cause death or serious bodily harm. You may use necessary force, up to and including deadly force, against persons in the following circumstances:*
  In self-defence
  In defence of facilities and persons and Coalition-approved property as specified in your contract
  To prevent life-threatening offenses against civilians

- *Use the reasonable amount of force necessary. The following are some techniques you can use, if their use will not unnecessarily endanger you or others:*
  Shout verbal warnings to halt in native language
  Show your weapon and demonstrate intent to use it
  Shoot to remove the threat only where necessary

- *If you must fire your weapon:*
  Fire only aimed shots
  Fire with due regard for the safety of innocent bystanders
  Immediately report incident and request assistance

- *Treat civilians with dignity and respect. Make every effort to avoid civilian casualties. You may stop, detain, search, and disarm civilian persons if required for your safety or if specified in your contract*

- *Treat humanely all who surrender or are captured. Do not torture or harm someone who can no longer fight. Turn detainees over to the police/security or Coalition forces as soon as possible*

- *Possession and use of weapons must be authorised and must be specified in your contract*

- *Collect and care for the wounded:*
  Treat all wounded equally
  Prioritise - injured are treated first
  Proper treatment of the dead (i.e. no booby-trapping, burning or mutilation

- *Destroy no more than the mission requires:*
  Return fire with aimed fire
  Limit/eliminate collateral damage to innocent civilians

- *Respect private property and possessions:*
  Do not steal property
  Do not destroy, or threaten to destroy, property of others

- *Nothing in these rules limits your inherent right to take action necessary to defend yourself*

Most of it's pretty obvious, of course. Mutilating bodies? Gunning down innocent bystanders? Looting property? Pointing your weapon at Coalition soldiers? Joining up with an Army for a mission? Clearly not going to win Brownie points with any PMC company.

But some of it's less clear-cut. We're not going to treat wounded insurgents, we're going to leave them where they drop. And then there's the grey area of the point at which an insurgent stops being a legitimate threat you can meet with lethal force. When he's standing in a field bashing out rounds on his AK in the hope of killing me, it's within the rules for me to shoot to kill. But if, in a matter of split seconds, he stops shooting and angles his weapon away from me, then I'm supposed to stop shooting? Not likely when he's been doing his utmost to take us out. And what if he turns? Walks away? He made his choice to come at me. We're in the middle of fucking nowhere. Who's to know what goes down?

At this point, we have the guidelines, the Rules of Force, but we're not accountable under Iraqi law for our actions. This country is a fucking mess, and there's no report to file after an incident, no investigation. No Military Police officer is going to demand an explanation for the dead Iraqi in the ditch with an AK at his side.

We don't go out to get them. But if they get in our way, we'll move them. And if they come at us, we'll fight back, hard.

We won't cross the line. We won't use the fact we can get away with murder to get away with murder. We won't gun down random Iraqis for the fun of it. But if they shoot at us, we'll fucking shoot to kill.

The worst that will happen if I move into the grey area? I lose my job. And that won't stop me getting another as a private contractor.

Still, even contracting, I consider myself a soldier. A soldier is something you are, not something you do. You can't just put green kit on and join the reserves and call yourself a soldier. I don't think a soldier's job is just to kill people, but his job is to put himself in a situation where lethal force maybe necessary.

I don't want to die or anything, but I accept that I might get my legs blown off. And the insurgent firing at me should accept that too. He should accept that if he's going to walk that path, he's going to die, and I'm going to kill him, because if not, he might kill me.

I get why he's fighting. I'd be pissed if some country invaded Britain. But if he takes me on, I'll respond with force…without hesitation and without emotion. In the Army, you fight under a flag, for a cause. Now, I think I'm on the right side, but I don't lie awake thinking, thinking I'm doing something good for the world here, sorting Iraq out. I just do what I do best, where the money is.

I.VI

The work rotation system means plenty of us are in Iraq for Christmas. (You can't apply for leave; you'd fuck up the rotation.) It doesn't bother me working Christmas day, though I know it bothers my family. Still, I'd rather not attempt some half-arsed celebration here. Sticking some tinsel up in the ops room and getting some Iraqi to burn a chicken for you isn't Christmas.

It's 25th December. Most people think of Iraq as hot, but in winter it gets pretty cold. Jackets and heaters on in the vehicle today. I'm attached to another team for this mission: Aussie Gaz is team leader, riding in front (team leader gets to ride wherever he sees fit), I'm in the second gun truck and South African Nick and English Steve are bringing up the rear (yes, another Steve and another Gaz; you see why nationalities become part of names to help you differentiate). Between us is the usual fleet of trucks. No idea what they're carrying.

We've driven down Route Tampa, the north–south road that bisects the country, to the south, made the drop-off and stopped for a break at the American FOB Scania. It's a convoy support centre, 150 miles south of Baghdad, and a common stop-off for us. It's pretty jolly here – turkey dinner on offer in the DFAC, tinsel hanging from the roof and a tree with fake wrapped presents underneath.

These places are like oases in the desert and they bear testament to the might of American logistics. Good food, video games, pool tables, decent TV – even coffee shops and Burger Kings. The shops are good: you can buy anything from food and drink (bottled water is essential) to Oakley's, magazines and DVDs – even TVs. You have to pay in dollars, and you don't get change, just cardboard tokens you have to spend in the shop.

The reception we get at the bases is mixed. Some know of private security and are friendly, interested even in what we do ('What's the pay?', 'What's the job?', 'What's the leave?', 'Do you have to be ex-Special Forces?', 'Do you have to be able to skin a bear to join?'). Others haven't a clue who we are, and don't appreciate us sharing their resources.

Refuelled, we leave Scania, heading north on the dual carriageway. We're surrounded by open desert, and it's pretty deserted. We pass a Bedouin herder with his camel and a young boy smacking sheep on the arse with a stick. What do animals graze on in the desert? I wonder.

There are no vehicles in sight. The American call signs have the day off. The isolation makes me edgy. I'm happier in Baghdad, even with the constant attacks there – with hundreds of roads and hundreds of call signs moving about, I figure the odds are with me there that I'll escape a contact. But here, in the middle of nowhere, one convoy on one road is conspicuous, and there's so little traffic that it's easy for an insurgent to target us.

The sound of the EFP exploding is deafening – so much more quick and loud than the IEDs I'm pretty used to hearing. It comes from the central reservation and goes straight into Gaz's car ahead of mine, black smoke shooting across horizontally and enveloping the vehicle.

The noise, the colour, the direction – I know at once it's an EFP. An image of Steve Gilchrist in a body bag springs to mind.

My driver – not my usual one as I'm filling in – panics and instinctively slams on the breaks to avoid plunging into the smog ahead.

'Go, go, go!' I shout in Arabic. 'Push through! Drive!'

This is why I've been working to learn Arabic from the LNs – so that in a highly charged situation I can instruct in their mother tongue, meaning less chance of a misunderstanding and a quicker reaction time. (Well, that and because I like to curse in Arabic, and learning it allows me to engage in a bit of banter with drivers.)

The driver quickly puts his foot back on the accelerator. By now visibility is nil; we're in a dark cloud.

'Contact; central reservation. Front vehicle. IED,' I radio. Then: 'Gaz, radio check. Gaz, radio check.'

No reply.

Fuck, I'm thinking, he's dead.

The smoke clears, and I see the front truck has rolled to a stop.

'Nick, move up. We'll need spare wheels.'

We push up behind, and I jump out, gesturing to the driver to park in front of Gaz's vehicle. Gaz is kicking his door out from the inside of his truck, which is a wreck of torn metal and smashed glass. He stands back and looks at his truck. To a non-professional, you'd think he was having a 'Jesus, look at the state of this' moment', but I know he's working out how to extract it. How many new wheels does he need? Can it be salvaged at all?

'I'm all right,' he shouts, shaken but not stirred. 'But fucking hell is Allah hurt.' Allah is the interpreter. Most convoys have one, to allow us to converse with the LNs.

I go to the rear passenger door. It's a mass of contorted metal, but with a bit of effort and my foot against the side of the truck, I'm able to pull it open.

My first thought is that it's like I'm looking at a crime scene that's a month old. The inside of the vehicle is a mess, reeking and covered in blood and bits of flesh that look like chicken. Must be the temperature of the EFP that's caused everything to dry out so fast.

My second thought: Allah's dead. He's taken the brunt of the EFP, which has come through his section of the cab at window height and rebounded inside by the looks of the mess. His legs are mincemeat; the fleshy bits are missing, and all I see is tendons and bones amid the shreds of his trousers and boots. His hair, usually neat-ish and styled in a centre parting, is dishevelled. His face is white. His eyes are closed.

I reach across to feel his wrist for a pulse, at my touch he rolls his head round and looks at me. Fuck me, I think, you're alive.

'Get me a stretcher!' I shout to an LN standing about beside the vehicle. 'You!' I shout at another. 'Get the med bag.'

Then the shooting starts. We're under fire. Rounds skim off the tarmacked road next to us, more rounds hit the vehicle, some just inches away from me.

I spin around and bang out half a mag of rapid single shots. My hope is to at least keep the enemies' heads down, if not kill them outright.

Turning back to Allah, I pull him from the truck and onto the stretcher laid on the ground. His legs are sickeningly floppy, hanging on by threads of who-knows-what. At least there's not blood everywhere. Looks like the EFP heat has cauterised the wounds somewhat.

All around I hear weapons firing as the LN gunners take on the insurgents. We're not getting targeted heavily – as the explosion went off we rolled through and passed it. But the end of the convoy has stopped further back, near the explosion site, where the bad guys are lurking.

I look back and see red smoke: Steve, at the back, is in a heavy firefight and is throwing smoke grenades to confuse the insurgents. I drag the stretcher around the other side of the vehicle, away from the firing line, and to my truck, which my driver has parked in front, ready to tow Gaz's. In PSD, the client usually owns the vehicle. In convoys, the trucks belong to the company, and they want them brought back to base at all costs. Gaz supervises LNs putting new tyres on the fucked truck, sufficient to allow us to pull it to the next American base, FOB Kelsu, up the road.

I'm surprised to see an Iraqi truck driver from the convoy bring his lorry up and park it between mine and the source of the gunfire, to act as a buffer. Usually, the LNs sit tight during a contact and let us deal with it. The insurgents aren't interested in LNs; it's the Westerners they want to hurt, piss off. Most of the LNs don't even duck down in their cabs; they're blasé by now about gunfire. This guy gives a shit. So he should. I'm helping his fellow national.

Above me, in the gun bucket, one of the LNs throws his helmet on the floor, swears in Arabic and then starts praying while crying. He's sick of seeing his mates injured, I think. Some of the LNs have been on since the start of the contract in 2003 – they're tired, jaded. This kind of contract is hard to sustain. If you go through an area you know is hot, your eyes are on stalks and it wears you down; those levels of weariness can't be simulated in training.

Another LN shrieks that he's been shot in the hand; I glance up and tell him to shut the fuck up. He'll live.

Nick has come from the back now to help me out. I put tourniquets on Allah's legs, just loosely because he's not bleeding profusely but I want them there in case. We haul him into the back seat of my truck. I put some rounds down in the general direction of the contact then jump in the back with him.

Allah is remarkably calm; in shock, I think. This is a tough guy – he fought in the Iraq–Iran war. Rumour has it in one battle his was the only tank that survived. I remember him taking the piss out of us before we set off that morning:

'This Christmas day, yes? Your holiday. This'll be the day you're all getting killed.' Then he turned to me with a yellow-toothed grin, gestured to my dark complexion and added, 'You be all right. You have the face of an Iraqi.'

Now, he stares up at me and says, 'I think I lose my legs.'

'No, no,' I say calmly, 'you'll be okay. They're just broken, you'll be fine.'

His black eyes are sharp, understanding. He knows alright. The best he can hope for is some decent stumps, but given that they amputate above the bloody mess, I don't think he's got much chance of even that.

We're moving now, but slowly because we're towing Gaz's truck. I stuck an LN in the truck at the wheel and told him to steer it, but he's getting a hell of an arm workout. We move out of the contact, then half a minute later we're back under fire, this time from the right.

Allah's turning white; I work on putting in an IV. During my medical training, back as a young lad in the Army, it would take me several attempts. No such luxury now; this is life and death, not a drill. I get the IV in first time, in a moving vehicle, under fire.

Finally, it's quiet.

A few miles on we meet another Armorgroup call sign freewheeling in the opposite direction heading to the company's base in Umm Qsar – four trucks, no convoy. Kiwi Jeremy and Scottish Bob in the other call sign stop now. We fill them in, and they offer to take Allah on to FOB Kelsu, because they're fast moving, while we're towing a wrecked gun truck and have a convoy of lorries. We can meet them there.

We pull Allah out of the truck and haul him over the central reservation. His IV falls out and his legs flop at an unnatural angle. He's dosed up on morphine now, though, and remains calm. That's the last I see of Allah that day as the other call sign rushes him off for the medics.

We slow-move to FOB Kelsu and mount Gaz's truck onto a flatbed so we can move it back to base more easily. A group of Americans in civilian clothing come out to see the state of the vehicle – it's fucked, and quite a talking point. Turns out they're Delta Force. They're operating locally. Covert, trying to clear cells in the area, I think – though of course they can't tell us what they're doing.

One of the 'Unit' analyses the damaged vehicle, trying to work out the angle of the EFP. He tells me he was an Army engineer prior to joining Delta. 'Clever,' he says. 'Targeted to kill an occupant, not just do damage. Did you see a wire?'

'No. Nothing,' says Gaz. 'Remote detonation then. Quite rare - especially in the area.' The Americans promise to get the bastards who set the EFP. Then they invite us to their compound.

That night I ring my girlfriend on my piece-of-crap Iraqi mobile. I ring most days, but the signal's shit and sometimes we have to give up if the line's terrible. Email on the laptop is just as unreliable with the fluctuating Wi-Fi signal.

Tonight, I wish Nikki a merry Christmas and ask about her day. Turkey and the Christmas movie. I feel a long way from home.

When she asks about mine, I don't tell her about the EFP, or the smashed-up vehicle, or the man whose legs hang by a thread. I tell her that I spent Christmas day evening drinking beer, and playing computer games with the Americans.

I.VII

I was still a soldier in the British Army when the US 1st Brigade Combat Team of the 4th Infantry Division joined forces with Task Force 121 to mount Operation Red Dawn in ad-Dawr, Iraq. Six hundred soldiers to root out one man: Saddam. They found him lying in a spider hole. An easy capture in the end; no resistance. As Donald Rumsfeld put it, 'Here was a man who was photographed hundreds of times shooting off rifles and showing how tough he was, and in fact, he wasn't very tough, he was cowering in a hole in the ground, and had a pistol and didn't use it, and certainly did not put up any fight at all. In the last analysis, he seemed not terribly brave.'

How they must have itched to shoot, the soldiers who stood over him as the shabby, red-faced old man lay at their feet.

It was impossible not to be aware of the trials that took place in 2005 and 2006. The media were, understandably, obsessed. And we were frequently stuck in traffic jams in the Green Zone as they closed off roads to ferry Saddam around the city.

Come November 2006, the verdict is in. The Iraqi Special Tribunal has found him guilty of crimes against humanity (as defined by the Rome Statute of the International Criminal Court: 'particularly odious offenses... [that] constitute a serious attack on human dignity or grave humiliation or a degradation of one or more human beings'). Now, he's sentenced to death by hanging.

The date is set for 30th December, and in the compound, death of a dictator is the hot topic of conversation amongst the lads.
'Hanging's too good for the fucker.'
'Slow torture. Bring back the rack. Keep him hurting.'
'Where are they hanging him? They should sell tickets. I'd go see that, bro'.'
'Fucking dance on his dead body.'

The BBC is reporting mixed reactions from Iraq: 'The verdict is unfair – Saddam has not committed any of the crimes that he has been accused of,' complains a computer programmer from Al Anbar Province.

'Saddam and those around him deserve this end for the crimes they committed against the Iraqi people,' says a Baghdad civil servant.

'I feel cautious and anxious because of the expected reaction from terrorist groups who wished to see Saddam returned to power,' says a student in Basra.

You'd expect the West, at least, to be united and jubilant. Bush is certainly on cloud nine. But plenty are bickering. There are critics who quibble about how fair the trial was. There are those, like Prime Minister Tony Blair, who oppose the death penalty. But really, how hard are you going to push that point for a bloke who killed that many people?

The most hated man in the Western world (bar Bin Laden) goes to the gallows at the crack of dawn on the 30th of December. The world watches news reports that contain the official video of the lead-up to the execution. He seems calm in the clip as the masked hangmen put the noose around his neck. He's handcuffed and clutching the Koran, and he refuses the hood to conceal his face as he dies. But newsreaders report on witness statements that it was more chaotic than the clip reveals. That he struggled with those who escorted him from his cell. That the witnesses and guards shouted insults at him as he died. That they took photos with him as souvenirs, to humiliate him.

But a canny guard has gone a step further and videoed Hussein's last moments on his mobile phone. The film goes viral, and we see that there was no dignified end for Saddam. We watch the jeering as he goes to the gallows. Then we see the trapdoor open and the dead man's face as he hangs, sightless eyes staring.
The next day, the BBC News website publishes an English transcript of the final exchange between the condemned and those assembled:

Saddam: Oh God.
Voices: May God's blessings be upon Muhammad and his household.
Voices: And may God hasten their appearance and curse their enemies.
Voices: Moqtada (Al-Sadr)... Moqtada... Moqtada. [Moqtada is a radical Shia cleric – Saddam was a Sunni.]
Saddam: Do you consider this bravery?
Voice: Long live Muhammad Baqir al-Sadr. [Moqtada's father, who was murdered by Hussein's agents.]

Voice: To hell.
Voice: Please do not. The man is being executed. Please no, I beg you to stop.
Saddam: There is no God but Allah and I testify that Muhammad is the messenger of God. There is no God but Allah and I testify that Muhammad...
... Silence

The next day in Taji, just north of Baghdad, as we're sitting in my vehicle waiting for cranes to unload a convoy, I ask my driver Ahmed-Al-Shit-Breath what he thinks.

'Saddam's dead. Good or bad thing?'
Ahmed shakes his head. 'This is bad.'

'Why?' I know many Iraqis are glad to see the back of the dictator, and I'm sure Ahmed was never an ardent fan.

'Because the bad guys loved Saddam,' says Ahmed. Then: 'Are we going to be back in time for lunch?'

The mentality seems to be: I didn't know Saddam, so it's nothing to do with me. Plus, the LNs are usually more interested in their next meal than politics, in my experience.

The other ex-pats are in agreement: the insurgents aren't going to like this; we'd better watch our backs.

Mind you, I think, how much hotter can it get?

I.VIII

Explosions and machine-gun fire ring in my ears. A convoy trip without enemy contact is a rarity. The teams are averaging twenty contacts per rotation; that's two to three a week.

Saddam's execution *has* pissed off the insurgents. But what really pushes them over the edge is the troop surge. In his January State of the Union address, Bush announces:

'The Iraqi government must stop the sectarian violence in its capital. But the Iraqis are not yet ready to do this on their own. So we're deploying reinforcements of more than 20,000 additional soldiers and Marines to Iraq. The vast majority will go to Baghdad, where they will help Iraqi forces to clear and secure neighbourhoods, and serve as advisers embedded in Iraqi Army units. With Iraqis in the lead, our forces will help secure the city by chasing down the terrorists, insurgents, and the roaming death squads. And in Anbar Province, where al-Qaeda terrorists have gathered and local forces have begun showing a willingness to fight them, we're sending an additional 4,000 United States Marines, with orders to find the terrorists and clear them out. We didn't drive al-Qaeda out of their safe haven in Afghanistan only to let them set up a new safe haven in a free Iraq'.

With another wave of Americans swarming into the country and such a declaration of war against the insurgents, you can't really expect they'd take it lying down. Weren't 'Down with the Americans' among Saddam's last words to his people? The insurgents want American blood.

Sure, I'm not American, and neither are the lads working with me on the convoys. But we're working for a company that's working for the Americans.

I don't think the insurgents think that hard. They look at us - our skin colour, our stubbly, not massive-beard-boasting chins, our combats and t-shirts and baseball caps - and think 'Westerner', 'Coalition'...'Enemy' and that's enough.

Westerner, bad. Kill them when you can. Every little helps.

Reports in the news indicate that there are now more private military contractors in Iraq than troops. The Los Angeles Times reports in July that there are 'at least 21,000 Americans, 43,000 foreign contractors and about 118,000 Iraqis – all employed in Iraq by U.S. tax dollars, according to the most recent government data'. And that's without a full count of private security contractors.

The Defence Department guy who oversees contractors says, 'The only reason we have contractors is to support the war fighter. Fundamentally, they're supporting the mission as required.' I have to laugh at the last line of the article: 'But critics worry that troops and their missions could be jeopardized if contractors, functioning outside the military's command and control, refuse to make deliveries of vital supplies under fire.' Not likely.

The more pressing concern for most is that we 'hired guns' lack discipline. Who's policing us? Are we swaggering, cocky outlaw types with poor experience and trigger control to rival an overexcited virgin lad in a whorehouse?

Beyond the questions of accountability and control there are those about finance. Who's paying for all this? Is it costing more than using soldiers? Contracting is a shady business. It's not shouted about by those who hire us. And it's only since Blackwater in 2004 – more on that later – that the public have got interested.

But now, with the troop surge, they need us for support. More troops means more convoys. And more convoys means more targets and more attacks and more risk to us. In July, USA Today reports that attacks on supply convoys protected by private security companies in Iraq have more than tripled, with 869 such attacks from the beginning of June 2006 to the end of May 2007. It's crazy – 100-odd IEDs going off across the country in one day alone.

In view of the rising heat, the company changes policy: for any run North of Baghdad – to Fallujah or Mosul, for example – instead of four security trucks per convoy, we're now in teams of six. The company's priority is the cargo reaching its destination intact, so now it's prepared to up the expenditure for another two ex-pats per run, plus two vehicles and LNs to crew them.

I move teams, and teams come to us and we work with a range of blokes. Teams are pretty much thrown together now, and I find myself working with different guys a lot.

We see so much action that a quiet day is a rarity; boring, almost. My mate Mick, an ex-Marine, ex-boxer, Scouser, I train with at the gym, comes up with a plan early on in the convoys: we only get dessert ('duffs' to Mick in Marine lingo) at the American bases if we've had a contact. Key lime pie. Cheesecake. Chocolate brownie. British Army food is basic; American Army food is decent. Pretty soon, we're overloading on treats, and have to add extra sets and reps at the gym, and we get disappointed on days we're not shot at.

Often, we get through unscathed. But now and again someone gets hurt, or you realise how close you've come.

We're going through Mosul on Route Tampa. We've split the security trucks up two, two, two – two at the front, two in the middle and two bringing up the rear. Tom, in front, takes the brunt of the IED. He limps through even though his truck's in such a state he's pretty much driving it sideways. Mick calls, 'Contact right, contact right,' and we roll through small-arms fire, the gunners in the back on the case.

There's an ominous rattle coming from my vehicle's engine, and a funny smell. 'Drive on,' I command when my driver starts complaining that he's losing power. Last thing I want is to end up static in the middle of small-arms fire. I feel pretty safe in the armoured vehicles, but that's when we're moving. Being stuck in one, stationary, is another matter entirely.

We limp on, and my vehicle waits until we roll into the yard of the drop-off point to give its final juddering gasp and die.

The Iraqis are pretty handy under the bonnet – I guess you have to be in a place where there aren't garages all over – but fixing the problem is beyond them. Bullets have ricocheted into the engine, and it's going to need new parts.

We stick the truck on a flatbed in the convoy, and I ride back with Mick, through another round of small-arms fire, grateful I'm not driving a death trap.

It makes me think. Given that I'm shot at on a daily basis, I feel pretty safe. An armoured car that's in motion does that for you. But my staying alive basically relies on a whole heap of glass and metal and plastic and wires to tick along, doing the job they're set up to do.

Put that way, my life is in the hands of the Iraqi mechanic back at base. Not a comforting thought.

I.IX

Now that the number of Americans in Bagdad has shot up, we often take convoys into the Green Zone. What was once Saddam's seat of power is now effectively a massive American base (four square miles) covering a whole area of Baghdad. There's no place on earth like it: a weird mix of military and civilians. Buildings abandoned during the war are squats for the poor, but there are other Iraqis there too with better fortune.

It's metropolitan – decent roads, offices, bridges, flyovers, tunnels – but there's a lot of waste ground due to the air strikes from the war. Still, there are some beautiful buildings. The Republican Palace, spared during the invasion because it was believed to house valuable documents, is imposing, with a curved façade overlooking a leafy green square and two mammoth bronze busts of 'Saddam the Warrior' (later removed) looking down at each side from the roof.

The Green Zone is self-contained, cordoned off from the rest of the city by high concrete blast walls, T-walls and fences topped with barbed wire. It's one of the safest places in the country for Westerners, and has earned the nickname 'The Bubble'. Still, insurgents have a go now and again with mortars and rockets, and suicide bombings aren't unheard of and at times are common place – like in April of 2007 when a bloke blows himself up in the Iraqi Parliament cafeteria, killing a Member of Parliament and injuring twenty-two others.

Entry is via checkpoints. There's one entry point designated for convoys at the bottom of the Green Zone, which is guarded by soldiers from the Romanian Army.

One sweltering day, Marc and I are taking our time at the checkpoint, getting some air before cramming back into the vehicles. Air-con is hit and miss. Some are like sitting in a fridge. Others are like an old man blowing at you with a straw. We're chatting to the Romanian guards. There's a lot of rivalry out here between nationalities, between men doing different jobs – military or civilian. One of the Romanians is bigging himself up.

'I was professional soldiers back in Romania. I sniper. Many wars,' he says proudly. Then he points to the phosphorous grenade on Marc's rig and says, 'What's that?'

Oh yeah, many wars, mate. Doesn't even know a smoke grenade when he sees one. Makes me glad the lads around me know the difference.

On the way out we're stopped, waiting for trucks to manoeuvre through the chicanes, when I see a group of street kids hanging about on the street. They're filthy, thin, with eyes that look like they've seen it all. Most of them have no parents. I have some cookies in the truck, and I get them out now, rifle at my side, and move towards the kids. They don't seem frightened of me, but they don't come forward.

I take out a cookie, break it in two, and offer half to a little boy. He scampers up and takes it, then rushes back. Now they all approach eagerly, holding out grubby hands, clamouring in Arabic. I hand them all out. Some cram them straight in their mouths, some nibble them slowly, some shove them in a pocket – for later, or for a younger sibling perhaps.
'*Shukran*,' says one. 'Thank you.'

Back at the compound the lads want to know where their cookies are – the ones I promised I'd bring back.

'Gave them to some kids,' I say.

'*You fucking what?*'

I.X

When we go out of northern Baghdad we always cut up on Route Tampa. Kiwi Greg christens it the 'chicken run', because on it we regularly face rolling ambushes. In places the road narrows to just a single-track road leading through farmland and we're easy game. The guards at the checkpoint are usually corrupt. After you pass through they call up their bad guy mates and say, 'Convoy on its way. Ten minutes out.'

So Kiwi Greg comes up with an approach that takes some of the heat off (literally). He stops at checkpoints on Route Tampa and says, 'Hot day, guys. Here, have some water.' And he hands over a case of bottled water. Not much, you might think, in the way of a bribe. But anything that stops us getting whacked is worth a try, and the Iraqis could easily go, 'Okay, let these guys through. We'll tip off after the next lot.' There are always plenty more to come.

Corruption is rife – not just among the Iraqi Army guards, but also in the police force. When we're further afield, outside of Baghdad, one of the worst places to pass through is Al Mushada. You hear a lot about places like Basra and Baghdad, but not much about this tiny village north of Baghdad that seems to be a breeding ground for insurgents. Every time we pass through we get shot up. Often, the gunfire comes from the police station.

On one trip the firefight gets pretty heavy. We follow the standard procedure – push through while the gunners retaliate. But as we do for some reason Ibrahim, my driver on the mission, goes to pieces and decides to duck down.
'Jesus, man!' I shout. 'Get up! Drive!'

He's driving blind, foot on the pedal, hand on the wheel, head in my fucking lap. I shove him back up. I don't know what his problem is - as long as we're driving, we're safe.

The LNs firing in the back, they're the ones at risk. Sure enough, a gunner gets injured – a ricochet has hit his body armour, square in the chest, he's fallen and cracked his head open. We push through (Ibrahim pulls himself together enough to look where he's going) and drive to the next FOB, Speicher, to get the

LN some medical attention.

Before I get out of the vehicle, I give Ibrahim a rollicking. He takes it. He knows he's fucked up. His reaction was strange – he's usually a hard bloke, really quiet, thousand-yard stare. The first time I met him, he could hardly speak English. His mate said to me, 'This Ibrahim. He has no family. All Dead'. I don't know how his family got wiped out. Don't want to know. Perhaps something in that contact triggered a memory. He won't last long on the job in any case. One day he just won't turn up. Lifted by the police for killing some people, so the rumours go. Leaving Ibrahim to stare vacantly out of the windscreen, I head inside. The medical centre is hectic – helicopters go out every day and bring in more casualties. The LN's head wound is nothing compared to the horrors you see here.

I get chatting to an American doctor, after a while he says to me, 'Hey, man. Wanna see something fuckin' freaky?'

'Ok, sure', I reply.

He shows me into a hospital ward. It's crowded, full of Iraqi men. They look up at us as we come in, then return their attention to the man on the bed.

Can I call him a man? He has no arms. He has no legs. He has no face to speak of – no obvious mouth or ears or nose, he must have lost half his face and it looks like they've grafted skin right across it. Just one eye, looking at me. Could be glaring with annoyance, could be regarding me sadly. Impossible to tell without his face to give an idea of expression. He's just a torso and a head. And a dick? I wonder.

I keep a poker face, and head out of the room.

'Pretty gross, huh? It's a miracle he's alive. He's Iraqi Army, caught in an explosion.' His own countrymen did this to him then.

'Worst I've seen,' continues the doctor. 'Poor guy. Couldn't lose much more. Your arms and your legs and most of your face...'

... And your dignity and your independence and your freedom and your future, I think. It's something you talk about with the lads – in the Army, and now, in the contracting work.

What's your limit for living? When wouldn't you want to be saved? This half-man is my worst fear embodied.

'If I ever end up like that,' I tell the doctor, 'I'd rather one of the lads put me out of my fucking misery' – the guy can't even hang himself.

When you're in the moment, and it's a choice between an agonising, drawn-out death – burning, for example – or a nice, cold, quick nine-mil round in the brain, I know what I'd pick. But even if the choice is life or death, and the life is some kind of living death where you can't speak or hear or move or shoot a fucking rifle, I'd choose the bullet. And so would plenty of soldiers – for hire and military.

I'd like to think I'd shoot a mate if necessary. Or an enemy. If it were the *merciful thing to do*.

PART II

"*It is not the critic who counts; not the man who points out how the strong man stumbles, or where the doer of deeds could have done them better. The credit belongs to the man who is actually in the arena, whose face is marred by dust and sweat and blood, who strives valiantly; who errs and comes short again and again; because there is not effort without error and shortcomings; but who does actually strive to do the deed; who knows the great enthusiasm, the great devotion, who spends himself in a worthy cause, who at the best knows in the end the triumph of high achievement and who at the worst, if he fails, at least he fails while daring greatly. So that his place shall never be with those cold and timid souls who know neither victory nor defeat.*"

– *Theodore Roosevelt*

II.XI

Three thousand-odd miles away from the hot, arid, dusty land that will become my life lies home.

SHEFFIELD, SOUTH YORKSHIRE

Home to two inventions that changed the world: stainless steel and football. The site where the Magna Carta was signed. Industrial city, giant in steel production. City of hills, with the highest tree-to-inhabitant ratio of any European city. The most CCTV'd city in Europe. Gateway to the Peak District. Location of two major universities, Sheffield and Hallam.

Hometown of Sean Bean (actor and Blades supporter); Michael Palin (traveller and Monty Python legend); Jessica Ennis (golden girl of the 2012 Olympics); champion boxers Kell Brook, Paul Jones, Johnny Nelson, Herol 'Bomber' Graham, Clinton Woods, Naseem Hamed, and Ross Burkinshaw (a former Rifleman); England footballers Gary Cahill, Kyle Walker, Kevin Davis, and 1966 World Cup winner Gordon Banks; and not forgetting that studliest of studs - politician David Blunkett.

Birthplace/home of bands and artists including The Human League, Heaven 17, Joe Cocker, Pulp, Def Leppard, The Longpigs, The Beautiful South, Moloko, and the Arctic Monkeys.

Location of giant shopping mall Meadowhall, built on a massive area of wasteland, of which there are heaps following bombings in World War II and the closure of steel works. Reportedly, if it failed as a shopping centre, there were plans to turn it into a prison. Urban myth, probably.

Most importantly, Sheffield is the home of the world's best (albeit underachieving) football club, dating all the way back to 1889: The Blades, Sheffield United. Also home to their rivals Sheffield Wednesday, and the little known Sheffield FC, the first football club in the world.

George Orwell called it 'The ugliest town in the Old World'. Harsh? It's no Venice, that's for sure. But it's no Baghdad either.

The problem is war. The first records mentioning Sheffield go back to the battle of Dore in the 8th century, and since then Sheffield's too-often been a battleground. Once, it boasted a classic motte-and-bailey castle, built after the Norman Conquest. That didn't survive the thirteenth-century Second Barons' War. A new castle was erected, and it was there that Mary-Queen of Scots was held between 1570 and 1584. Held by the Royalists during the Civil War, it was given up to the Parliamentarians, who razed it to the ground. No one bothered to build a third castle - tempting fate for another war, it would seem.

Fast-forward to the twentieth century and, with Sheffield's steel industry churning away, during World War I the city was at the forefront of armaments production, much of this industrialisation was enabled my mass Irish Immigration. By 1917 Sheffield produced 90 per cent of the world's steel, the world! One steel factory even employed an elephant because it could do the work of three horses.

Cue the arrival on 25 September 1916, under cover of cloud and darkness, a German Zeppelin loaded with bombs. People were killed in their beds as the city had its first encounter with the destruction wrought by an air raid.

It was a taste of things to come for World War II. Once again, steel factories ramped up production of armaments, and once again enemy forces targeted the city - but this time with planes and weapons infinitely more powerful and precise. The worst days for the city were between 12th and 15th December 1940, three solid nights of bombing. In the Luftwaffe operation 'Crucible', Sheffield was all but destroyed off the map. The result: thousands dead, injured and homeless. Records released by Germany in 2006 show that the target for the attacks was indeed the suburbs of Sheffield, where a million workers lived, and not the steelworks themselves. Hitler's aim was to destroy the will of the Sheffield people. He did not succeed, but the decimation of the city would leave long-term scars.

1978

Born in spring, I arrive just in time for the 'Winter of Discontent'. Like any northern city in the seventies, Sheffield is in decline. Steelworks are closing; poverty rife. There's an air of depression all around. Pay cuts. Job losses.

Homelessness. Out on the streets, the vivid neon spikes of punk rockers mingle with the fury of football hooligans.

When I'm three years old, Peter Sutcliffe, the Yorkshire Ripper, is picked up a few streets away from our house in Broomhill with a prostitute. He's pulled in for having false number plates. The unwitting copper lets him pop off into the house whose drive he's been caught in for a piss. Next day, shrewd police officers who match Sutcliffe's looks to the man they want for the murder of several women go back to the house and find a knife, a hammer and a rope. He's later arrested, charged, found guilty, and banged up in Broadmoor for thirteen murders.

As soon as I can walk, my life's ambition is to be a footballer, like Linekar or Maradona (without the nonce haircuts). I go to the matches at Bramall Lane when possible, wear my red and whites. United is down in the doldrums of football. Lots of crowd trouble; but if not for them there wouldn't be much of a crowd. At 8-year-old we move from Broomhill to High Green.

1986

The goalkeeper throws the ball out to one of his defenders. With deft control, he turns on his heel and threads the ball skilfully through to a tall lad in the centre of midfield. The tall kid dwells on the ball, I turn my steady jog into a sprint, covering 25 meters in a few seconds. I slide into the mud about 5 feet from him with my studs up. For a split second my vision becomes a blur of twisted legs, ankles and studs. I emerge the other side of the tall kid and use my momentum to slide back onto my feet - I've got the ball and I'm on the move. A quick glance to my rear and I see the tall kid lying in the mud, he had no chance. Its 0-0 and we're coming up to the end of the game. I run with the ball at my feet, zig-zagging every few metres, the two central defenders are hammering it toward me, and we all know this is the last attack of the game. The kid with the deft touch is going to be on me first, I've seen that he's good, and that if I let him, he'll end my little dash for glory. I slow down slightly and push the ball toward him, for a split second it looks like I've given him the ball but I know his momentum is too much and the space he's in will be empty in a second's time. I'm right, my sudden change of direction sends him flying past me. In a 25 years' time a young footballer called Messi will explain how the first yard of any run against an opponent is in your head.

I keep running, it's raining hard now and the pitch is just a mass of wet mud sucking at my boots every time I step. The ball keeps getting stuck in the mud every time I push it forward. I'm on the edge of the penalty-box now, and have a clear run at the goalkeeper, I've got space and time - which is when I usually fuck things up; with too much thinking time my brain is conjuring up images of me kicking the ball, missing it, and falling flat in my face. I know I'm at my best when I'm playing on instinct without time to think. I decide it's too muddy to just wildly whack the ball in the general direction of the goal. Without thinking I chip the ball up to head height catch it on my knee then lob the ball with my right boot. The ball loops over the goalkeeper and into the back of the net. 1-0. They quickly kick off again from the centre spot and the ref blows his whistle a couple of seconds later, we win. Revenge. My team, Chapletown Juniors, had just beaten Dronfield Contact, the team at the top of the league; less than a year ago they'd murdered us 7-0. Result.

Later that afternoon I'm sat on our living room floor with two of the other boys from the team. We're still in our muddy - but now dry - kit, shin-pads an-all. We've watched the live Division 1 match on the BBC and we're waiting for the other results to be shown from around the country. My dad comes in and passes out three portions of fish and chips for us to get stuck into.

I'm 8 years old and it's well before the time of smart TVs and instant results on alert. Upon realising we have to suffer the BBC news before the scores are shown we break into casual football conversation as we eat, the news remained on in the background.

Gradually my attention is drawn back to the TV, the BBC news showing footage of a place called Beirut. Men in war-torn streets, firing machine guns in a street battle. I'm hypnotised by the sights and sounds of these fighters, and soon the noises around me are unheard as my fascination of these images from another world ignite my minds imagination. I'm confused, are the men fighting on the TV soldiers? I'm not sure, they're wearing civilian clothes with scarfs around their heads. There's the odd one wearing an old army jacket. My perceptions of war at that young age had built up in me a narrowly defined vision of Army versus Army, movies and documentaries about World War Two had formed pre-conceptions about what war was meant to be; as kids, when large groups of us played war, it'd be us versus the Germans. I listen intently to the reporter, but I don't understand much of what she says. She refers to these fighters as 'Gorillas', but to my eight-year-old brain I'm wondering why she's suggesting they're something from the ape family.

An initial spark in my brain, that was the first time I began to think of the wider world. Did I automatically think they were baddies? Probably. But from that day on I had an interest in the news that was unusual for a lad of my age. Certainly, it was the attraction of a sense of adventure that seemed to exist in a palpable reality, this wasn't a comic or a movie. It was real.

In bed that night I asked my dad why they were called Gorillas. He laughed and explained that they were actually called 'Guerrillas' and that they are men living and fighting amongst their own homes. More confusion.

Real action on the news became an interest to me, I began to watch the news, and not just for the football results, anything that exhibited adventure inspired my imagination, and the fact that it was real made it even more gripping. I soon realised that adventurous situations on the news seemed to be centred around wars and fighting. After a given news report I'd often bombard my dad with questions, automatically expecting him to know all the answers - looking back, he probably had to do a lot of quick thinking and have some answers ready when he saw the cogs turning in my mind as I was watching TV.

I became friends with a lad at school called Steve who was a year above me at St. Mary's. We spent a lot of time mountain biking around the woods and streets around High Green. He often talked about how he was going to join the Army, and we'd often take our .22 air-rifles with us on our mountain bike outings to practice our so-called marksmanship. We used to walk his dogs all day long, and to this day I still know every track, path, trail, and genel around High Green.

Steve told me his dad had been a PTI (Physical Training Instructor) in the Army. I didn't know there were different jobs in the Army, I thought you were a soldier and that's that. He also told me that when he joined they probably wouldn't let him go to Northern Ireland because he was half-Irish, and they *definitely* wouldn't let him go because he was half-Irish and Catholic - I didn't know what he meant at the time.

1988

Aged 10, I was stood in Castle Market next to my mum and younger brother, she was haggling with a stall owner over the price of meat. They agreed on a price and after she paid I asked her for the change to get some sweets; to my surprise she handed it over. I quickly gave them the slip and I went off to hunt down some goodies. I found the stall I was looking for and after I handed my money over to a big Jamaican bloke with dread-locks he passed over my change and a brown paper bag of sweets. I walked around the outside of Castle Market because it was less crowded, and I thought I'd have a better chance to see my mum if I looked from the outside in. I walked around to the front of the market that was on the main road and came face-to-face with the Army recruiting office. The cogs were turning.

I stuffed the sweets into my trackies, and slowly walked toward the entrance. I was shitting bricks as I opened the doors and stepped in the office. Two blokes with camouflage trousers, black boots, and green woolly jumpers turned around from their desks eyeing me up. They both had two stripes sown onto their sleeves. The soldiers were drinking tea and smoking. One thing that stuck in my memory was that they both had long hair, not long like a woman but definitely long for a soldier, it was down past the tops of their ears. Don't soldiers have to have shaved heads?

'Can I help ya fella' said one of the troops.
'Errr…' my mouth went dry.
They just stared at me.

I took a deep breath and blurted it out - 'Can you join the Army even if you're a Catholic?' I asked.
Both men cracked a smile.

'Course you can mate, all are welcome'.
'Ok, it's just my mate said…'
'Don't listen to that horse-shit' the soldier interrupted.
'How old are you anyway?'.
'Ten' I replied.
'Well ok mate, come back in a few years. The Army will still be here', he said.

I rushed out the door and let out a deep breath. I saw my mum and brother coming out of a shop and ran over to join them. So it tuned out Steve was wrong. But who could blame us, we were only 10 and 11 years old after all. Besides, in those days there was little culpability towards schools, and as we both attended a Catholic primary school the teachers were free to ram all sorts of religion-based opinions down our necks. Opinions that often overlapped with contemporary politics. War is just mass killing - that was the implication, and therefore, by default, a soldier's job is to indiscriminately kill - a default that automatically breaks the Ten Commandments. While that part about war may be true, I would later discover 99% of ground operations that applied the use of soldiers are about preserving and saving life - peacekeeping, security operations, defensive operations, and delaying operations; even the Rules of Engagement are about preserving life to the best of circumstances in the worst possible settings. The situation in Northern Ireland was largely misunderstood by the general population in mainland Britain. Many years later, whilst at a patrol base in Northern Ireland, I would mention these points to a priest in the army (Yes, you can join the Army as a 'man of the cloth' - from any religion). He pulled out a small pocket bible and showed me a few references to soldiering in the book; every one of the passages he showed me illustrated soldiering as a noble profession, a profession of dignity, and a profession of cause. We chatted a while, and my thoughts on soldiering as being something you are - and not something you do - became cemented in my consciousness; this strengthened my opinions that you don't need to be a part of a standing regular army to be a soldier.

Conversely, the priest went on to tell me, there are many people in the Army who have no concept of what it means to be a soldier - 'You can't just put some green kit on and a call yourself a soldier, it must be part of your psyche, a state of mind'. He continued 'That's why National Service doesn't work, it's a load of bull'.

I learned as much as I could about Northern Ireland, which at 10 years old meant watching the TV. Later that year I sat watching a news report from a place I'd never heard of called Gibraltar. Some British soldiers had shot and killed some IRA members who were planning to blow up an Army parade or something. I was starting to realise that these 'guerrilla' types could be a lot closer to home. Still, I was too young to connect the dots and understand that the different types of labels these organisations were given by the media had overlapping connotations. The hazy TV images showed empty streets in Gibraltar, and some tape to cordon off the area. I watched intently expecting to be shown footage of the shootings. There wasn't any footage; and I'm not sure if I was relieved or disappointed. This was also the first time I heard the phrase 'Shoot to kill' on TV, a phrase I would here many times in the future.

However, a few months later there was footage. Again, I sat in front of the news as the TV showed me pictures from the funeral of one of the men who was killed by a grenade attack at the funerals of one of the IRA members shot in Gibraltar. A lone car had mistakenly driven into the tight road where the funeral procession was led. At that age I could name any make and model car on the road - my bedroom walls were covered in car and football posters. I instantly clocked the VW Sorocco skidding to a halt and trying to reverse out of the small road, no chance. Black taxis blocked-in the car from either end (I would later learn about the context black taxis had in Norther Ireland), the camera showed two soldiers in civvies desperately trying to U-turn the car. The crowd swarmed. Then they withdrew suddenly, as one of the soldiers pulled a pistol and pointed it at the crowd. But this was an IRA funeral, a republican crowd, an anti-British crowd, and emotions of hate ran high. The crowd re-grouped and swarmed around the two soldiers; they were dragged off to some nearby waste ground, stripped and beaten, thrown into a waiting black taxi, driven two hundred yards away and executed. They were shot several times. One was shot six times, twice in the head and four times in the chest. He was also stabbed four times in the back of the neck and had multiple injuries to other parts of his body; the cameras (filmed by local republican supporters) were not allowed to follow them. A Catholic priest, Father Alec Reid, tried to intervene and save the two soldiers but he was dragged away and threatened. Nevertheless, he followed the taxi to the waste grounds and gave the two soldiers, David Howes and Derek Wood, the last rites. Again, when I went to Northern Ireland myself years later I would learn that the two soldiers weren't just executed, they were noxiously tortured. Eyes cut out, stabbed dozens of times with all sorts of random objects, and one int. officer told us they'd had their genitals cut off. All this before being shot in the head. It also turned out there was footage of this, an Army helicopter captured it from high above. But of course, the film has never been realised to the general public.

~

It's my birthday weekend and I'm turning eleven years old. I'm chuffed with the new England shirt I've been given. So me and some mates scrape together some bus fare and head down to Hillsborough park for a kick about. The streets are absolutely rammed with pedestrians, cars are at a standstill, the park is full of people, and the police are out in force. Its April 15th 1989, and Sheffield is hosting the FA Cup semi-final - Liverpool v Nottingham Forest.

It's hard to get a proper game going in the park with so many people, so we just find a small corner and knock the ball around a while. Occasionally the odd Scouser or two (usually wearing Adidas Sambas') would come and join in with us, trying to do kick-ups while holding a can of larger. The sun is out and it's a good-natured atmosphere. It's coming up to 2pm so we decide to head back up to High Green, none of us has the money to get in the ground, and besides, this is a massive game and therefore it's been deemed an all-ticket match - meaning people can't pay on the turnstiles, a rarity back in the '80s.

Back home, I turn on the TV and watch the match kick off. Within minutes there are people on the pitch, climbing over the pens. Was this crowd trouble? Surely not, fans stagger onto the grass and sit down. Some lie down - gasping for breath. These aren't hooligans. After fifteen minutes the ref calls a halt to the game. The stadium is in chaos by now, fans climbing to the upper tiers, as the players rush for the tunnel.

The national news that night is dominated by the events in my home city. Ninety-six Liverpool fans were crushed to death in the stadium. Over the next twenty-five years there would be analysis, inquests, and legal wranglings over who was to blame. The atmosphere in Sheffield changed over the next few days and weeks. Graffiti popped up all over the city, blaming the likes of Thatcher and the establishment in general. The police conduct that day came in for particular scrutiny. South Yorkshire Police had an infamous reputation in the 1980s amongst the football hooligans of England. Many 'old-boys' would attribute their toughness to solid organisation in their retrospective years, they just didn't have a chance to do anything. Away fans were shepherded from the stations to the matches and back again with little chance to get away with anything; many fans would point out that they'd probably honed their public-order skills during the miners' strikes a few years earlier. Not everyone blamed the police though, I remember some graffiti painted on the side of Kelvin flats espousing - 'Police are not to blame 15/4/89' - that graffiti was there for years, right up until they knocked the flats down.

~

In September 1989 I moved up to Notre Dame Catholic High School in the leafy Fulwood area. It took ages to get there and back from High Green every day, and during the winters I would arrive home well into the dark hours. I liked Notre Dame, and for the first time I had friends from all over the city - they took in pupils from all the Catholic primary schools in Sheffield - and before long I'd be spending the weekends and half term breaks transiting all over the place on the bus to meet up with my group of mates; little adventures into uncharted territory. I got to know lads from middle-class areas such as Millhouses or Crosspool, expensive areas such as Fulwood or Greystones, and tough areas such as Southey or Pittsmoor. It wasn't lost on me, and I felt lucky that I knew people from all over the city. Most high schools worked on local catchment areas so the pupils would be from relatively close areas.

By the end of the school year the TV held only one interest for me and that was the approaching world cup in Italy. England had been disappointing in the last competition, Euro '88, but I was looking forward to it with excitement. The best footballers in the world weren't accessible like they are today and you basically had to wait every four years to see them; the very best was going to be playing in the opening game - Diego Maradona, against some country I'd never even heard of: Cameroon.

Argentina won the coin toss as both captains stood in the centre circle. A few seconds before the game was due to start Maradona flicked the ball up, caught it on his head, and started doing keep-ups on his shoulders. I was in awe.

Unbelievably Argentina - the reigning champions - were beaten 1-0, and Cameroon gained a lot of admiration from then on.

The World Cup produced some new household names for me and my friends to talk about and emulate. Players like Roger Miller, Scalachi, and Paul Gascoigne became world-famous in the space of one month. England got to the semi-final and were beaten on penalties by Germany. As Chris Waddle walked from the centre circle to the box, my dad said 'He looks shaky'. Waddle skyed it, and I was gutted.

~

I watched the news, mainly because my dad watched the news and we only had one TV. Most of the news stories were boring to me - as a twelve-year-old I didn't really care what percentage of GDP was being spent on agricultural subsidies. I wasn't long into my second year at Notre Dame, and one evening I was sat in-front of the TV eating dinner when the headlines were read out by the news reader. I was gripped…

'Iraq invades and annexes the small sovereign state of Kuwait'.
'Leaders around the world condemn the invasion'.

More headiness followed, all to do with the Iraqi assault on Kuwait. I watched the whole news from start to finish, I didn't eat a thing. I knew of Iraq, but it was the first time I'd heard about this bloke Saddam Hussain, they'd recently just had an eight-year war with their neighbours, Iran.

The invasion was massive news, every night after school or after football training I'd settle down in-front of the TV to watch the latest updates. Even school was in on it, Mr McNerney, the history teacher, talked about it loads during class and he even conducted full lessons on what was going on, I was chuffed.

One day he gave us an informal written test on recent wars. One of the questions was 'Where was the last time the Americans fought?'. I wrote down my answers and handed in the paper. Mr McNerney read out his answers for us to tick off; to my disbelief, he marked my answer to that question as wrong - he said the answer was Vietnam. I was well pissed off. I shot my hand into the air, but I didn't wait for him to acknowledge me - 'Didn't the Vietnam war finish in nineteen-seventy-five sir?…And didn't the Americans fight in Granada in nineteen-eighty-three sir?…And in Panama in nineteen-eighty-nine, sir?' 'Errr…' was his initial reply.

He pulled himself together - 'The answer is Vietnam' he said staunchly. 'No, the answer is Panama' I retorted defiantly. The whole class swivelled their heads back and forth as if engrossed in some macabre game of ping-pong. He stuck to his guns, 'Give yourself one point if you wrote down Vietnam' he exclaimed to the class as if trying to pretend I wasn't there. The heads all turned back to me - 'Are you fucking kidding me' I said loudly in frustration. After a few seconds of silence, I was sent to the exclusion room (a classroom with office dividers between the desks so people couldn't talk) to spend the rest of the lesson in isolation, funny thing is there was no one there to keep an eye on whoever got sent there, I guess they all thought some other teacher would be there.

I sat alone in the room, staring at the walls for about ten minutes - then, the door cracked open. It was Steve, my mate from High Green who was in the year above me. He looked around the room, and when he realised there were no teachers about he grinned at me, I grinned back. We exchanged stories about how we'd been excluded from class.

The bell rang and we began to make our way toward the school gates for the busses home. 'Hey, I've got an idea' Steve said, 'Let's get kicked out of our classes tomorrow and meet up again in the exclusion room, same time'. 'OK' I replied, without putting much thought to it, and so we did. Again, there were no teachers there to watch us, nor were there all the other times we arranged to meet up in the exclusion room, bonus. Steve, being a year older than me, had been invaluable when I left St Marys because he gave me load of inside information about going up to Notre Dame, a School with about a thousand students. The same thing would happen a few years later, when - again being older than me - he joined the Army first, passing on loads of advice for when I was old enough. Steve had all the reasons in the world to be a fuck-up - rough upbringing, skint, and an alcoholic dad, but he remains one of the most positive and pro-active people I've ever met.

From that day on I realised that a lot of supposed authority was based on the supposed ignorance of one's subordinates. I'd lost my respect for school and for teachers by my second year of Notre Dame. I realised that as much as they were trying to teach us and education us in points of study, there was an educational sub-text that said - don't question the narrative, don't think analytically, don't think for yourself, we're correct and that's that.

The build-up to the Gulf War continued in earnest, and I watched with relish. I learned all about the hardware I saw on the TV, everything from A-10 Tank busters to Warrior APCs. America and Britain were now the two largest contributors to the build-up that produced a coalition made of dozens of countries. British 'Tornado' aircraft were shown off to the media by the RAF, and the media lapped it up.

When the air-war started we were told that the American pilots were doing day runs, and the British the night runs. I spun my head round toward my dad, he didn't wait for me to ask the question... 'It's because the British are better pilots, and the night runs are harder' he said matter-of-factly.

At some point during the war, the Prime Minister was holding a war-cabinet meeting at no.10. Unbeknownst to them, the IRA had parked a few streets away in a van that had a detachable roof. They'd mounted some Mortars in the back, removed the roof and fired them toward Downing street. Fortunately, they missed the meeting but the attack would come to be considered a PR win for the IRA. With the UK and world's media obsessed with the Gulf-war, the IRA must have been feeling a little starved for attention. This was their way of saying - 'Just to let you know, we're still here, don't you go forgetting about us'.

The ground war started in early 1991 and was over within hours, and by all media accounts it was nothing less than awesome. And, at 12 years old, watching with awe as the British Challenger Tanks and Warrior APCs blasted their way across the desserts of Kuwait and southern Iraq, I had to agree. As the Iraqi convoy columns withdrew from Kuwait back to Iraq along the main highway the coalition missiled the shit out of it to the point of devastation. Kuwait was liberated and Saddam was contained. In later years George Bush Senior would espouse regret of a missed opportunity, saying that we should have continued the offensive all the way to Baghdad and toppled Saddam.

How my life would've been different if that had happened! But with a coalition of some 40 nations and over half-a-million troops, Bush would have had a nightmare controlling that amount moving parts (both militarily and politically) in an invasion.

One point that stuck with me at that age was a new term I had heard on the TV coverage - 'Friendly Fire', also known as 'Blue on Blue'. I watched the aircraft footage with an American pilot's voice as he destroyed some enemy APCs on the ground. Only thing was, those 'enemy' APCs were friendly APCs, and those friendly APCs were Warrior-APCs, and those Warrior-APCs were British. Years later, whilst on the PMC circuit I would be teamed up with one of the APC commanders who was there that day, a Highlander, he was in the next Warrior-APC over from the ones that got hit. He said the blast was devastating and they were dead instantly, a small gratuity I guess.

Indeed, American munitions had reached cult-status as a result of the Gulf War, phrases such as 'Smart-Bomb' and 'GPS-guided' were bandied about the media as if they were going out of fashion. This war was dubbed the first televised war, and it was easy to see how. I tuned in every night to get an update on the coalition's progress that day. Again, I was too young to realise that I was only getting one side of the story.

The tech that had been demonstrated by aircraft in the first major war since the end of the Cold War also gave rise to many an observer proclaiming that the Infantry were a redundant concept of the past. Wars could now be fought remotely and from a safe distance. Again, my dad answered the question before I asked it - 'How do you hold ground without ground troops?'.

1992

Officially a teenager, I entered a stage in my life that sociologist and psychologist scholars may term as - 'Couldn't give a fuck'. I gave up on school work, I gave up on homework, and I had already decided I wasn't going to turn up for my GCSEs, even though they were still three years away. I truanted a little bit, but not much. I still enjoyed the school environment, my group of mates, and the little bit of sport we did. I smoked a little bit, and on weekend nights our group would meet up in parks, and bus stops, and after we'd combined our meagre amounts of money together, we'd decide who looked the oldest and send him in to buy some alcohol from the off-licence. Each week our group would expand in numbers, and - as we passed around cigarettes and bottles of Mad Dog 20/20, having a couple of puffs and sips each, I noticed that we'd started to include a few girls from school into our fold. This was good news - not just because they were easier to look at, but because they'd often turn up wearing make-up and jewellery and they dressed a bit older than their years would suggest. The cogs were turning. I decided to put my theory to the test. I pooled my money with a couple of the boys and we sent one of the girls off to buy some alcohol; five minutes later, she came back with a bottle of some shit called 'White Lightning'.

Result. My sociological experiment had worked. It tasted like dog-piss but now we knew that we'd have a much better chance of being served if we had a girl go in for us. We all became good friends and Friday nights became a 'thing' for our group as we met up in various parks and streets around Sheffield. We always made sure the girls got on their buses first, before going for ours. We were very protective of the lasses in our group and looked out for them in our own immature way.

Later that year - unknown to me - I glimpsed a first sight of my future regiment. I sat in front of the TV again and listened intently as the news report showed troops and helicopters in a small Northern-Irish town called Crossmaglen. The solders had swarmed the village, taken up fire positions, overlooking roads, in ditches, and in hedgerows, no one was mooching, and they all looked purposeful. Policemen with dogs were all over the place, every single car was stopped and checked. Lynx helicopters dropped off more soldiers in the fields - as they dismounted and ran for cover in the hedges, the choppers barely touched the ground and were gone as soon as the last soldiers boot left the landing skid.

'The soldier was killed whilst on patrol beside the town square by a single sniper's bullet' the reporter said. 'Soldiers from the Army's Second Battalion, the Light Infantry are securing the area as the investigation gets underway'. This incident would turn out to be the first success of the IRA's infamous South Armagh sniper team. Unlike many inaccurate news reports, where they would refer to someone being randomly shot as the result of a sniper, this actually was a sniper, he was using a .50 calibre Barret, a devastatingly powerful and accurate weapon that killed the young soldier instantly, going straight through his body-armour plates. It would take years for the full facts to come out, and many of those facts still only reside within our battalion folklore. I would later learn that the lad who'd been shot was only 18 and on his first operational deployment with the Army. His name was Paul Turner.

Some years later whilst on patrol myself in Crossmaglen square I would take up a fire position where Paul Turner had been shot and look up toward the firing position, the local Catholic church. It was an easy shot, and Paul wouldn't have stood a chance. Although, I must admit, the shooter's escape route was poor

- and risky at best, but nevertheless, extremely well planned. I was the patrol commander, and therefore was able to call a halt to the team over the radio, the lads around me took up fire positions in doorways and between walls. It was the second week of November. I ordered one of the satellite teams to move through us toward Dundalk road, where they could cover our team - the primary team - as we moved across the square. It took the satellite team a few minutes to move up. I seized my opportunity - I pulled out a remembrance-day poppy from behind my fist-mic and placed it on the small white wall next to where he'd been shot. I'd studied old photos of Crossmaglen back in the patrol base and concluded the wall hadn't been there in 1992. I placed a stone on the stem of the poppy so it didn't blow away. I then clicked the presell on the team radio - 'Prepare to move'.

1993

By my fourth year at Notre Dame I'd upped my game from *couldn't give a fuck* to *really couldn't give a fuck*. I was in the bottom sets for everything, not because I was thick but because I really couldn't give a fuck. Our gang of school friends were still meeting up on Friday and Saturday nights. It was a 'thing' at the time for loads of teenagers to hang out in Endcliffe park at the top of Ecclesall road. Some nights there were hundreds of kids there, all drinking and smoking. Kids from all different schools started to turn up, and inevitably, fights would break out between boys from all the various schools.

One Friday night, aged 15, I was leaning against a brick wall on Rustlings road next to Endcliffe park with two of my mates, Si and Adam. We were waiting for our friend Lisa to come out of the off-licence. I watched as she pushed open the glass door and stepped onto the pavement. Immediately three lads walked up to her and tried to 'tax' her bag of drinks. We were over like a shot. Si, who was short and stocky, hooked the first lad in the jaw and he stumbled to the pavement. Within seconds the six of us were in a tangled blur of fists, arms, and legs as we tried to fight them off. After about 30 seconds they started to back off. I noticed the kid on the pavement had a Stone Island coat on - expensive kit. I pulled a Stanley knife out of my jeans pocket and slashed at his jacket several times. I then quickly threw the blade into the pocket of my trackie-top. We decided it was time to leave the artificially-lit road and head to the darkened park across the street. Just as we turned on our heels, I paused, reached down to the lad with the slashed-up jacket and unbuttoned the Stone Island badge from his sleeve, I stuffed it into my back pocket. Si and Adam were clearly full of adrenaline as we headed for the unlit park. Lisa didn't move. I wrapped my arm around her shoulders and ran her across the road, cars and buses beeping and flashing at us as we weaved between the traffic, I aimed her through a small gate in the green metal fence. It was instantly dark as we ran across the grass, we headed for the tarmacked path next to the children's playground and came to a stop. Somehow me and Lisa had gotten separated from the other two, we stood in the dark alone. She was out of breath, not surprising after running in her girly platform shoes - I was wearing Nike Air 1-80s.

Eventually, Lisa turned to me, grinned, and held up the bag of drinks - mission accomplished. She cracked open one of the bottles, took a drink and passed it to me. For five minutes, we stood in silence as we shared the small bottle of booze.

'Thanks' she eventually muttered to me. 'Errr, ok', I replied throatily. We smiled at each other. Then she stepped towards me; we were within an inch of each other. Standing on her tip-toes, she gave me a two-second kiss on the side of the mouth. She then pulled away and stepped backwards. Still smiling, she held up the Stanley knife she'd just lifted out of my pocket - unbeknownst to me. She walked over to a nearby bin and dropped it in. 'You don't want this, Gary' was all she said. She put her arm through mine as we walked down the path, and we soon found the rest of our schoolfriends. I watched Lisa intently as she divvied up the remaining drinks and counted out everyone's change.

Later that night our gang of about sixteen kids rode the bus back towards the city centre, from there we'd all be getting different buses back to our various parts of Sheffield. We made sure all the girls got on their buses ok, and I walked through the Hole-in-the-Road to catch the 77 back up to High Green. I got on the bus and climbed the stairs to the top deck, at this late hour the bus was empty - except for two lads sat at the back. I instantly recognised them as Notre Dame kids, they were in the year above me. One of the lads was covered in dry blood. He explained the story of how they'd been in Endcliffe park and his gang had gotten into large running battles with the kids from High Storrs school, knives and metal bars had been brought, and he'd been stabbed in the neck by a broken bottle. I leaned over to have a look at his wounds, they looked more like big scratches than stab wounds, but still, they'd produced a fair amount of blood. They told me they were going to spread the word and go back next week, hopefully with larger numbers. The date was April 23rd, 1993.

The next Friday, I was sat in a classroom with Mrs. Rowan - an English teacher, and three other kids. There was Michael, he was a black kid from Shirecliffe and was known for being hard, he was also very aggressive and a bully, many other kids used to tip-toe around him a lot. There was Adam - my mate, and a girl called Siobhan. We sat in a line of four, facing Mrs. Rowan. We were in remedial English class, but a more apt label would have been - 'Get these kids out of the fucking way class'. We were supposed to practice our reading; Mrs. Rowan had a book which she wanted us all to take turns in reading aloud. She held the book out to Michael, who flat refused to take it. Next, she tried to pass it on to Adam, he shook his head. Obviously Siobhan was going to be next in line, I looked at her as Mrs. Rowan held the book out for her to take. She clammed up, and with her arms folded she just stared down at the floor, she was petrified. I don't know why but it made me angry. I reached across and quickly snatched the book from Mrs. Rowan's hand. 'I'll read it', I said with a pissed off tone; Mrs. Rowan was visibly relieved. For over an hour I read the book aloud so Siobhan didn't have to. By the end my voice was hoarse, and when the bell rang for the end of school I went straight to the water fountain before heading for the bus. Years later I would find out that Siobhan had severe dyslexia. She said the letters would dance around on the page whenever she tried to read. No one diagnosed it, no one gave a fuck. She's a teaching assistant now - brilliant.

That night our gang all met up at the gates to Endcliffe park, the busses were packed with groups of kids from various schools, I recognised a few groups of Notre Damers walking about. We all stood around, waiting for everyone to arrive. We were standing in a loose kind of circle and I was listening to some of the chat, when I felt someone's hand around my wrist. I was surprised and quickly spun around. It was Lisa, I gave her a throaty 'Hi'. Smiling, she asked me if I had a drink, I said I didn't. She then offered to share one with me but only if I walk her up to the off licence. We walked up and I waited outside while she went in. When she came out we walked up the road a little way and took a seat on someone's garden wall next to a bus shelter. We shared the drink and conversed easily. Once we'd finished the bottle, I stood up and walked over to the small bin that was attached to the bus stop and dropped it in. When I turned around Lisa was stood right in front of me - this time she gave me a proper kiss. We spent the rest of the evening in the bus shelter with our mouths locked together. We didn't see any of our friends for the rest of that night, or anyone else for that matter, nor did we know what had happened in Endcliffe park.

The next morning, I scored a goal, and missed a penalty, but we still won 2-1. One of the dads from the football team had arranged to take me and a couple of the other lads to Nottingham that afternoon to watch the Blades play Forrest. United won 2-0. Chuffed. We stopped off for fish and chips on the way back to Sheffield, and it was past 7pm when I finally got dropped off at home. That night Adam called me on the house phone.

'Where were you last night?' he asked.
'Errr…'
'Never mind, have you seen the news, someone was murdered in the park last night' He said.
'What, who?'
'I dunno' he said, 'But I don't think its anyone from our school'.

I'd been out all day so I'd heard nothing. But the story was big, and it was carried in the ITN local news and the Sheffield papers that weekend.

At school on Monday everyone was talking about it, and it soon became common knowledge that the murder had been committed by Michael, the lad from my class who I'd been in remedial English with on Friday. I was sceptical of all these so-called facts that everyone seemed to know. At dinner-time I saw Lisa smoking in the tennis courts (she was in all the top sets, so I never saw her in class), I walked over and we chatted, she told me it definitely was Michael who'd committed the murder. In the end, it turned out she was right.

Like me, he was a fourth-year at Notre Dame. On Friday night, with a large group he'd gone down to Endcliffe Park specifically for the gang fights, I don't think he'd been down there prior. Grant Jackson, a 17-year-old from High Storrs school, was fought to the ground and stabbed three times with a 2ft-long bayonet. He died of shock and haemorrhaging that night in hospital. On Saturday he'd apparently talked about the stabbing, and when the police found the bayonet in his room, had claimed he was keeping it for a friend and denied all knowledge of the battle. Michael Errol Donaldson, who initially claimed manslaughter on the grounds of diminished responsibility, received a life sentence at Sheffield Crown

Court on 24th of November 1994. He was released in 2008. The school never acknowledged the killing, and nothing was ever said to the pupils in general, I guess no one cared if or how the remaining students would process the incident - or not.

~

I didn't see out my final year at school. I sat in the headmaster's office, slouched in a chair, staring at the wall, while he summed up the details of my latest transgression. The office has become a familiar setting over the years I've been at the school. I could probably recite the titles of the books on the shelf in order, so often have I scanned them.

Mr Lawrence, the head, is on a roll. 'Respect… GCSEs… do well… make something of yourself… buck up your ideas…'

I get what he's saying. I understand his point. But at that age, I knew school wasn't the place for me.

Mr Lawrence's an alright bloke, and I know he's looking out for me, but nothing he can say will make me become the model pupil this Catholic school prides itself on creating. I did receive an education from Notre Dame, just not the one they had planned for me. I was reasonably aware of the world, I watched the news, and I read books. Although for some reason I was ashamed of the fact that I read, and kept it a secret.

'I'm talking to you!'

I meet Mr Lawrence's glare. He's a firm, in-control sort of bloke but his expression makes it clear he's pretty close to losing it. He thinks I'm stupid, that I've no interest in learning. He's misunderstood me, but I'm not prepared to tell him that.

'I'm sorry, Roberts, but that's it. Your list of misdemeanours could fill a book. You're expelled.'

I shrug.

It's quiet outside the school now, in the middle of the day. The streets are eerie; Fulwood is devoid of the hustle and bustle you see at the start and end of school. I've never been a skiver, and it feels odd being out here in the day.

To get home I had to go into the city and then catch another bus out. On the city-bound bus I retrieve my walk-man from my backpack and put it on - Biggie Smalls blares into my ears: Ready to Die. I pull out a book too, The Shankill Butchers: A Case Study of Mass Murder. I read a bit then give up; the bus has a shitty suspension and I'm vibrating about like a rabbit on speed. In the city centre the bus pulls up at Castle Market, and my wandering gaze settles on the Army recruitment office on the street below.

My grandad and his brother were in the thick of World War I, both serving in the Gallipoli campaigns and the battles of Gaza during the Palestine campaign, but no one in my immediate family has military experience. And none of my mates seemed interested in current affairs or wars of the past.

III.XII

PART III

"*Without the Infantry nothing can be done, nothing at all. The Infantryman cannot be replaced upon the battlefield. He may have more aids, better transport and better weapons, but as never before he must be constantly fit, have the guts and stamina to carry his weapons across country, to* **run, dig, march, crawl** *and fight when* **tired, hungry** *and* **exhausted.**

He must be well led and have high morale, his training must be realistic, tough and develop his initiative and individuality.

Throughout the ages 'experts' have predicted the demise of the Infantryman. But he is still with us essential as ever. It is only he who can fight in all conditions, by day and night and can adapt to every terrain.

He is not halted by **mud, sand, jungles, deserts, heat, cold, fog** *or* **snow.** *He is not affected or jammed by electronic countermeasures.*

It is the Infantryman and him alone who must eventually 'close the deal'."

British Army Instructor

80

III.XII

Before long I was bored. Then, one day I caught a second glimpse of my future regiment on the news, again unbeknown to me. This time it was Bosnia; the TV showed soldiers from the Light Infantry's Second Battalion on patrol - some on foot, others in the armoured Warrior-APCs I'd seen during the Gulf War. The news report made light of the fact that these troops were the first 'Green Troops' to be utilised in Bosnia, meaning that they didn't wear the blue UN head-dress and badges, neither were their vehicles painted white with blue UN signs on the side. They wore the traditional green berets of the regiment, or camouflaged helmets, and their Warriors were Army green, as they were supposed to be. The news report had a jovial tone to it, and explained that Army policy was for all soldiers when outside to wear combat helmets at all times.

The soldiers had rigged up an old bath in the open air at a makeshift patrol base. A group of lads all stood waiting for their turn in the bath, all undressed with just towels wrapped around themselves but wearing their helmets. Even the lad in the bath had his helmet on. At the end of the report he stood up, showing his arse to the camera while the other guys laughed. I'd later find out from the lads that this scene was staged for the benefit of the female news reporter.

~

I made a pact with myself that I'd be gone from Sheffield (one way or another) by the time I was 18, which was some months away. On Monday morning, I walked into Castle Market Army careers office and was met by Serjeant Bob Parker, who I'd later find out was also from my future regiment, he was the Serjeant of Machine Guns Platoon in the second battalion. He didn't put too much effort into recruiting me that day, instead he gave me some leaflets and told me to come back if I wanted. I came back the next day.

That day he put a bit more effort in. He asked me if I knew what job I fancied doing in the Army. I told him I wasn't sure, but I knew I didn't want to be in a support role. He gave me some forms to fill in and explained that I'd need to do an intelligence test on the computer, and that he'd book me in next week for it. Before I left, he gave me a book with some basic fitness programmes, so I could prepare for the three-day selection.

Before leaving the office I clocked a poster on the wall, the title said, 'Light Infantry', but what caught my attention was the beret badges that the guys on the picture were wearing - a silver bugle. I recognised those badges from a TV show that was showing in the mid-90s called Sharpe's Rifles. I asked Serjeant Parker who they were, and he said that's the Light Infantry, *my* regiment. He opened a desk drawer and showed me his green beret complete with silver bugle badge, the same as the old-fashioned Riflemen from the TV. He went on to explain - with restrained patience - that Sharpe's Rifles were a real regiment and the stories were based on actual events. He told me where the regiment was, and what they were doing, and I was glad to hear that one of the battalions had just been sent to Belfast.

~

In 1755, at war with the French in North America, the British Army was struggling to use conventional war tactics in the trackless forests and mountains of the American terrains. The French, meanwhile, turned to Native Americans and used them to devastating effect. In Canada a column of British troops led by General Braddock was decimated by an inferior force. Dressed in bright red coats and in close formation, the French-Canadian and the native sharp shooters had little trouble defeating the British soldiers.

The British recognised the need for specially trained Infantrymen who could scout and skirmish, move about quickly and quietly, and use individual initiative without waiting for orders; troops who in times of danger would not look to a Serjeant or officer but would know from their training just what to do. The Light-Armed Troops were formed, comprising of soldiers that were handpicked from their regiments for their efficiency, toughness and high level of intelligence - chosen men. They were lightly equipped and their dress modified in brown and russet green to blend with the natural countryside.

In 1777, the Light Infantry attacks a detachment of 1,500 dug-in Americans in the forest of Paoli, defeating them quickly - inflicting over three hundred kills and capturing one hundred at a cost of only three killed. As a result of this action, the Americans vowed vengeance on the Light Infantry. In turn, the Infantrymen sent word to the rest of the British troops that they would stain feathers in their caps red to differentiate them from other soldiers, so that no other regiment would pay the price. The Americans never got their revenge.

By the early 1800s the green-clothed troops were using the Baker rifle rather than the musket used by their red-tunic wearing counterparts - the first native British regiments to use rifled (grooved) barrelled weapons for greater accuracy. In 1809, they gained cult-fame within the British Army as the fastest marching troops. To make it to the Battle of Talavera Light Infantrymen marched fifty hilly miles in twenty hours, arriving in good order, weapons primed, and launching straight into the attack - they decimated the enemy troops. They went on to gain dozens of battle honours against Napoleon during the Napoleonic and Peninsular Wars and in every major war since then. Eventually, they evolved into our current regiment - The Rifles.

The Green Berets make up the toughest combat force in the British Army and have more battle honours and operational tours to their name than any other regiment. Staying true to the original ethos of 'thinking soldiers' and 'chosen men'.

~

I passed the computer test and was sent down to Pirbright training centre for Army selection. This consisted of a lot of PT (Physical Training) sessions, usually indoor circuits or trainer runs, and some briefs about the Army. These briefs ranged from the interesting: how great Army life was, and what adventure training and extracurricular activities were available - to the boring: pension structures and dental plans. There were some tests to pass; starting with a medical examination, hearing and sight tests, some fitness tests, and an interview. I don't know how well I did, but the final interview lasted about three-minutes, the officer behind the desk gave me a piece of paper with my personal Army number on it and told me to memorise it before my start date.

Back in the Sheffield Army careers office I was given a train ticket and swore my allegiance to the Queen, and I was surprised when they gave me a certificate for that. I was sent to Winchester Army Training Regiment - the home of the Light Division - to be trained up by solders from the four sister battalions of the Light Infantry and Royal Green Jackets. The first week was spent filling out forms, more medicals, PT tests, and getting us to march in unison. A lot of time was spent teaching us personal admin, washing, shaving (although most of us had barely a need to shave), making our beds, ironing and preparing our uniforms, and cleaning and arranging our lockers and barrack rooms. There were 56 lads that started the course.

The instructors were shouty, and they weren't shy when it came to dishing out punishments, often accompanied by the odd whack. This didn't bother me one bit, to me it was part of the course, part of the curriculum. I was ready for it, it was to be expected no matter how well (or not) you performed. Many of the boys in the platoon took it to heart, took it personally, and felt they were being unfairly treated. I knew we were being tested all the time in our skills and in the assessments they conducted, but I knew they weren't testing us at being punished - how do you score being punished?

Within a couple of weeks the pace started to pick up, we were introduced to all the weapons used by Combat Infantrymen in a rifle company; mainly the personal assault rifle - the 5.56mm L85 A1 SA80, and the support weapons we were taught included; the LSW (Light Support Weapon), the GPMG (General Purpose Machine Gun), the 51mm Mortar, the 94mm Anti-Armor rocket, the RGGS (Rifle Grenade General Service), the L2 Hand Grenade, and the HP Browning Pistol. Before we could complete the course we'd have to show competency in all these weapons with a dry (no ammunition) weapon handling test, followed by and a live fire test. All the tests were scored and certain pass-marks had to be attained.

The Light Division has never been big on Parade-Square Drill, but it was part of the curriculum so they had to teach it. We were a fucking shamble of shit on the drill-square. Before long our platoon was spending its evenings on the parade-square doing remedial drill sessions. We soon got to a passable standard (although they weren't going to put us in front of the Queen anytime soon). Our platoon instructors didn't want us to get too comfortable once our remedial drill lessons came to an end, so instead, they began to take us out onto the football pitch every night for a 'Beasting Session' (PT session, often associated with harshness or punishment), to atone for our supposed wrongdoings that day, we did press-us, sit ups, stress-positions, ran, crawled, duck-walked, and all sorts of imaginative and fucked-up PT.

We also had to do block-jobs in the barracks, these jobs rotated round the platoon members every week and ranged from mopping the corridors, to cleaning the toilets and shower rooms.

One morning I was in the instructors staff room doing my block-jobs, it was a doddle as I only had to tidy up their brew area and wash out some coffee mugs. 'Ready for yer beasting tonight?' asked Corporal Richardson, as he lounged in a scruffy arm-chair drinking his morning brew.

'Err… yeah, but we haven't fucked up yet, Corporal', I replied.
'Don't worry about that son, you will, I guarantee it' he said with the sardonic grin of a mystic fortune-teller.

We were beasted that night - *he really could predict the future.*

Before long room inspections, locker inspections, and block inspections took to the back-burner and we started spending most of our weeks in the field. Cammed-up, kitted-up, we'd be taught and practice all the tactics of a Combat Infantryman and where we fitted in within a fire-team, section, platoon, company, and battalion. Our time in the field was interspersed by days on the firing range, or days in the classroom learning weapons and field tactics, every morning started with PT, usually a run or a TAB (weighted forced march), but sometimes it would be circuits, the assault course, or swimming. Our training continued to include other skills such as, battlefield first-aid, radio and telecommunication, map reading, and compass work, everything we did was scored and tested and we'd receive personal feedback from the instructors last thing every Friday.

By the time our final exercise finished, we were down from the 56 that started the course to just 18 members of the platoon. There were the odd few that had failed and been sent home, but I would say that 95% of the platoon that didn't pass *actually* failed themselves. They couldn't process being shouted at, or they would find things hard and give up, maybe some were just too young and missed their mum's cooking, or their girlfriends back home. Either way it was their fault and no one else's, those guys would have passed if they'd manned-up and stuck it out. After one lad left, our Platoon Serjeant, Serjeant Nichols, imparted on us some of his pearls of wisdom whilst we stood on parade - 'Never make a life decision based on a woman' was all he said.

We 'Passed Off' the drill square, and some old officer stood on a plinth and told us how awesome we were. He went on for fucking ages. After the weekend, we were sent to Catterick Garrison in North Yorkshire for Phase Two training. This course continued in much the same vein, as the curriculum was preparing us for our role as Combat Infantrymen. The course was more narrowly focused, and concentrated a lot more on the field-craft and the operational aspects of conventional soldering. We'd spend most weeks in the field on exercise, learning and then practicing many of the various phases and operations of warfare, including attacks - of varying sizes from individual up to company level, defence ops, delaying ops, reconnaisance, FIBUA (Fighting in Built Up Urban Areas), and patrol ops. All these skills culminated in live fire exercises, live ranges, and battlefield tests.

We were allowed out some weekends. Last thing on a Friday Before 'Falling-out' and being left to our own devices, we'd receive a security brief. We were not to wear uniform out of camp, or to show ourselves as military in any way. No regimental T-shirts, no G-10 watches - nothing, not even Army-issued socks. A few of us with cropped hair were even told to let it grow out a bit. This was due to the threat of the IRA, and in particular their 'Dickers' (lookouts and spies for their intelligence network). In fact, we were told upon arrival at Catterick that a Dicker had been lifted at Darlington train station the year before. I now knew why those soldiers in Castle Market were allowed long hair all those years ago.

On a Friday, after that week's field exercise, in the evening we'd conduct platoon admin, and be told to have all our personal kit clean and ready for inspection by Monday morning, before we went back in the field. I had an ace up my sleeve, Sheffield was just over an hour away from Catterick, I'd gather up all my kit, pack it into a civvi bag, and nip home on the train. Everything that was metal, magazines, mess tins, BFA (Blank Firing Attachment), even the wire brushes and pull-throughs from of my weapon-cleaning kit were shoved into my mum's dishwasher. They came out gleaming. My mum worked at the Northern General hospital and she'd managed to procure one of their big industrial washing machines that was going to be thrown out anyway. I'd shove all my muddy kit into the machine, clothes, Webbing (Belt-Kit), Bergan (Army Rucksack), Bivvie-bag, even boots, and wash those too. I'd sit back have a cup of tea, eat some dinner, watch the football scores, then get my kit, and head back up to Catterick.

On Monday morning, I stood to attention with all my kit laid out neatly on the floor. A Green Jacket Corporal began inspecting our equipment in minute detail, picking up objects and holding them to the light. Lads would have their kit thrown back at them and told they would be re-inspected at a later time. Some lads had shit-loads to re-show, others just one or two items.

Eventually, he came to me and started sifting through my kit and equipment. The corporal was fair and he didn't pick lads up for nothing. But the longer he inspected my kit, the harder he tried to find fault with my stuff. Getting eager he told me to open-up my weapon's cleaning kit, which I duly did. He picked out one of the wire brushes and held it up. It was gleaming gold and looked like it had never been used. He pulled out another one...

'How 'ave you got these so clean?' he asked, with a hint of suspicion.
I played dumb - 'I dunno corporal, you told us to clean them, so I did'.
I guess he couldn't argue with that.

He duly moved along to the lad next to me and proceeded to tear his 'pathetic excuse for a kit' to shreds.

III.XIII

Belfast. Aged 18. I took a seat in the corner of the small waiting room. Sitting on the moulded plastic chairs in my Jeans and Track-suit top I stared around the quite room, I read a small sign on the wall - 'Smith Air'. Occasionally, someone would come in and wait a while before getting picked up. I leaned my head back and closed my eyes, listening to the clock ticking away on the wall. Eventually, after about an hour, the door swung open. A large bloke stood in the door frame checking a bit of paper in his hand...

'Roberts... Second Battalion?'
'Yeah' I nod.
'I'm Slug, grab ya bags mate, follow me'.

Slug had a thick Geordie accent, and was wearing civvies too. I followed Slug to the car-park and loaded my gear into the boot of an old Ford Sierra. Before I got in the car Slug looked me up and down, 'Take that watch off, put it in yer pocket, it looks too military'. I did as I was told, thinking back to when I was a ten-year-old kid and seeing the news of two solders getting caught out at a funeral before being dragged off to their execution. I got myself into the front passenger seat and began to put my seat-belt on, Slug quickly put an end to that - 'Leave it off, in case we have to do a quick bug-out from the car'.

I was expecting an actions-on brief from Slug. Instead, he just reached over to my side of the car, opened the glove-box and pulled out a Browning 9mm pistol, he checked the magazine and cocked the pistol, 'If anything goes down', he said, 'Stay outta me way'. Well, that's the brief done. He then placed the weapon under his left thigh with the pistol grip pointing to his right-hand side.

We stuck to the main roads as we drove towards Palace Barracks in Hollywood. I tried to get views down the side roads as we went along, trying to see the 'real' Belfast. But, to my disappointment the city looked much the same as any other city in England. That was until we came to an Army checkpoint. Two Land-Rover Snatches parked at angles across the main road to filter the traffic into singe file, two soldiers protruded from the top of each Snatch, weapons trained on the flanking arcs of the checkpoint, more troops stood in the road checking the cars as they went through. Slug waited patiently in the line of cars. We were five cars away from the check-point as we slowly passed two more solders buried in the hedges next to the road. 'Cut-offs', Slug muttered to me.

Eventually, we drove into the checkpoint for our turn. The handle of Slug's pistol was still protruding from under his thigh, and I had visions of the soldiers letting rip at us when they saw it.

Slug wound down his window next to the checkpoint commander.

'Al-reeet Tommo', he said with a grin.
'Alright Slug', replied Tommo in a Cornish accent.

Tommo and Slug chatted casually as they went through the motions of a genuine vehicle check. Two more soldiers made a show of opening the boot and checking the underside of the car before Tommo eventually waved us through.

Slug drove us out the check-point, I clocked more cut-offs on the far side of the checkpoint as we passed them and headed on towards Hollywood.

'They're from C Company' Slug said, 'Do you know what Company you're going to?'.
'No' I replied.
'That's ok, I'll dump you at the guard room until we find out what to do with you'.
In the guard-room I was met by an angry looking RP (Regimental Provost) leaning against the desk. He was a Lance Corporal.

'You with the Light Infantry?', he said as he looked at my civvies.
'Yeah', I nodded.
'Yes - Fucking - Corporal', he retorted with a sneer, '
'Yes Corporal', I replied.
'Go wait in the back with the QRF lads', he snapped.
As I walked through to the back room I could hear the RP espousing his opinions on gob-shite new recruits:
'Wouldn't have happened back in my day...'

I dumped my kit in a corner. The large room was lined with bunk-beds along the walls, some soldiers lay on the beds, some reading, some sleeping, all fully dressed - boots an' all. Three lads sat at a small table to one side playing cards. I took a seat with some lads watching an old TV set. More moulded plastic chairs. One of the guys looked over at me, clocking my civvies - 'Have you just come from the depot?'

'Yeah' I answered, 'Finished last Friday'.

'What Rifle Company are you going to?' he asked.

'Dunno yet' I answered.

The conversation was cut short as Slug walked back in. 'Get yer stuff, Roberts', he said. 'Yer going to B Company, Serjeant Willet's Platoon'. Mock laughter rang out around the room, 'Serjeant Willet, you're fucked, ha-ha', 'Was nice knowing ya!' shouted one lad morosely.

Slug dropped me off at B Company offices, I stood outside on the pavement while he went in and told them I was here. Slug came out a minute later, and with a 'See ya later' jumped back in the Sierra and drove off.

'ROBERTS!', came a bark from inside the office. I walked in and stood to attention. Serjeant Willet sat behind a desk at the far wall, a dog-eared sofa to one side of the room, on it sat three of the platoon's members drinking tea from chipped cups.

'Stand easy', he said.

The next few minutes were spent in silence as he read through some files on his desk, mine I assumed. Eventually, he looked up at me...

'You got good reports from depot, but this is Battalion, and we rotate back onto OPs on Monday so you'd better switch on fast'. He continued, 'First we need to get you down to Bally-Kilner for NIRTT'. I must have had a confused look on my face, 'Northern Ireland Reinforcement Training Team', he said with the tone of talking go a child. He glanced back down at my files.

'You from Sheffield?'

'Yes Serjeant' I said.

With that, one of the lads piped up from the sofa, 'What team do you support?'

'United', I replied casually.

Serjeant Willet's eye-brows narrowed just as I pinged the small Sheffield Wednesday flag hanging to the side of his desk. Fuck.

'Get - the fuck - out of my office' he said with calm disdain.

I hurriedly left the office and stood on the pavements with my bags. I could hear them laughing inside. For nearly an hour I stood there. Eventually, he came out with a grin and took me to my room in the barracks. I walked in to find three lads on one of the beds watching some weird euro-porn on a battered old TV with a top-loader video recorder. I found the obvious empty bed-space in the other corner and began to unpack my kit whilst listening to Germans with mullet hair-cuts and dodgy moustaches gang-banging some fat Kraut chick.

If not immediately welcoming, the lads in my room turned out to be top blokes with loads of experience that they were happy to share before I went down to the NIRTT course. I learnt loads form Serjeant Willet too. He turned out to be one of the top Serjeants in the battalion, with loads of knowledge and experience.

People may often think that going straight from training to OPs can be seen as some sort of baptism of fire. No - the real baptism of fire, the real learning curve, is going from a training-platoon of 30 boys to a fighting-battalion of 600 men.

I spent the next few weeks learning a totally new system of soldiering, a system that was a lot slower and more deliberate to the conventional soldiering we'd been taught in training. We used teams and multiples (a multiple is made up of three teams of four men) instead of sections and platoons. We practiced urban patrols, rural patrols, searches, VCPs, public order, stops, cordons, Rules of Engagement, judgment shoots. Interacting with the public, working alongside the RUC, and a whole host of non-soldering related skills such as log-books, and how to stand in a sanger (an elevated observation platform or tower) staring into the dark for hours on end. We practiced a lot of 'Sanger' shoots, and I learned how my POA (Point of Aim) would be affected firing from an elevated position. OPs in Belfast was not much of a crack, and was an anti-climax. At the time, the powers that be were very sensitive to the way the Army was perceived in Northern Ireland, and as such we were forced to adopt a softly-softly approach.

Eventually we were sent back to the mainland, to be based at a place called Bulford in the heart of Salisbury plain. But we were back to Northern Ireland within a few months. This time it would be different, this time we were going to South Armagh. We flew from England to South Armagh in a Chinook helicopter and landed at our base in Bessbrook Mill. The battalion was then split up and sent to various outposts. I was chosen to be attached to the Recce (Reconnaissance) Patrols platoon, which was great because those guys didn't have to stag-on at the Mill.

South Armagh is known as Bandit Country to all who've been there, and 'enjoys' an infamous status in the history of the troubles. The IRA 'Cells' in South Armagh were some of the busiest, most daring, and ruthless in the province. And even amongst the IRA itself, South Armagh members were respected and feared. Indeed, many of the South Armagh leaders exercised great influence on IRA and Sinn Fein doctrine and policy. And, as South Armagh shares a border with the Republic of Ireland, the South Armagh IRA were some of the biggest money-makers for the cause, utilising large smuggling operations from South to North.

Everyone in Recce Platoon was senior, and in some cases old (one of the corporals had joined the battalion before I was born). All of them had multiple Northern Ireland deployments under their belts and the platoon exuded an easy-going confidence. There was very little bullshit from my team commander Mally, and my multiple commander Garcie. There was a senior Lance-jack in my team called Frankie. Frankie was one of the most knowledgeable and best soldiers I'd come across since joining the battalion. I would often pack my OPs kit at the same time as him, copying what he did - as he packed an item, I packed the same item, imitating his organisation and set-up. Looking back, he must have found this annoying, if not a bit pathetic. He knew an unbelievable amount about the IRA, he'd been here loads and basically knew who all the IRA were by name and job-tile. 'If we know who they are, why don't they get lifted?' I asked him one night. 'They have to be "caught" doing something' was his answer. 'This is still the UK, and we're still governed by the rule of law'. Strangely, in years to come I'd overtake Frankie in the ranks. Something which I couldn't understand - not that I got promoted, but that he was overlooked when so many lesser guys (and in many cases, dickheads) were promoted first. The Army works in mysterious ways.

The pace of operations was faster in South Armagh than in Belfast and we spent our days and nights zipping all over the county in helicopters doing VCPs, spotting for other units, covering other units, and gathering intelligence. We called these Eagle OPs. We'd touch down in fields at lightning speed, jump out and dash for cover, we'd fit our ECM and radio antennas and emerge through the hedgerows to stop unsuspecting vehicles and conduct some snap searches. Often, we wouldn't even touch down, the helicopter gunner would throw out the ab-sail ropes and we'd 'fast-rope' down into the fields below. The gunners would have us three on a rope at one time as we slid down to the grass.

One time, near a place called Whitecross, I was on the rope and the helo moved in the winds as I was about half-way down. I slid down much faster than I planned and totally missed the field, landing on the middle of a country lane in a heap just as a car came screeching toward me. The driver skidded to a stop a few inches from my legs. I thought I was a goner, I was shaking as I stood up in front of the bonnet and locked eyes with an equally-shocked lady gripping the steering wheel. Needless to say, she was given a pass. As I waved her through I tried to force a smile at her, which was not reciprocated. I took up my position on the small grass bank at the side of the road, still shaking. Frankie came and sat next to me and handed me his coffee flask. I unscrewed the lid and took a swig of the hot liquid, and fuck-me it was hot. I pulled a face and looked at Frankie 'What's this?' I asked him, he grinned 'It's called Gunfire, half black coffee, half rum'. I grinned back and took another couple of swigs. I felt better after that.

~

Next up came Kosovo. The initial invasion had already ended by the time we'd gotten there, and like our previous deployments the companies were split up and sent to different places. The AOR (Area of Responsibility) for us was a place just outside Pristina called Kosovo-Polje, or Fogje-Polje if you're a Serb. There was a lot of Northern Ireland-style patrolling, just without the helos, vehicles, or any kind of support, infrastructure, or resources really. We based ourselves in old factories, disused schools, or any other shell of a building that was large enough for a company of Combat Infantrymen.

We went out in four-man teams to patrol and learn the AOR. We'd gather our intelligence and centralise all the information we'd found out with patrol reports that went to the company 2i/c (Second in Command) officer. I was still a Rifleman, a Private, but for the first time I was given some responsibility of command. I led some of the four-man teams on patrols around Kosovo-Polje, calling in my report lines, mapping out our route, and controlling the formation of the team. There were usually other teams on the ground with us at any one time, and we were rarely out of range of another team who could provide mutual support.

Our tasks gradually became more focused, and as information was analysed and transferred to intelligence, we started to receive more specific missions. The intel. officers gave us specific houses and buildings to raid and search, the most we found were weapons caches that were mainly rifles, pistols and machine guns, some old, some new, we confiscated loads and they were taken away to be destroyed.

Kosovo-Polje has a complex of flats that are mainly the inhabitants of the ethnic Serbs who live in the area. I sat in an improvised briefing room as we were given formal orders to raid and search multiple flats in the blocks. I was given my own team to command, so listened intently as the company commander issued orders for which block and specific flat my team would be hitting.

That night I sat in the back of a Saxon armoured vehicle. We were in full combat-fighting order - webbing, day sacks, body-armor, Kevlar-helmets, faces blacked out with cam-cream, and holding our weapons. It was pitch black, we'd been here ages.

Eventually, the radio crackles into life and we're given the 'go'. I lead my team at a swift pace through the complex of flats and we go firm (halted) next to some walls in a communal area. I look around, I can see all the other call-signs dashing about in the shadows, in and out of alleyways, up flights of concrete stairs, all looking for their respective targets. My target is at ground level, bonus. I check the map and point to a blue door across the open courtyard, the other three lads nod their acknowledgment.

We run over and take up positions along the brick wall adjacent to the door. I bang on the door with my fist, nothing, I bang again. Eventually, the door cracks open about a centimetre. I barge in, my team follows. There's a living room that looks like some kind of cheap seventies porn set. We search the occupants of the room, all middle-aged men, one guy who looks like a cheap copy of a seventies Mafioso - moustache, gold chains, and leather jacket. He's relieved of a small handgun, I don't recognise the model. It's no big deal, most people have guns in this part of the world. The lads quickly go through the flat and began to search the side rooms.

That's when shit got weird. I was left alone for a few minutes in the main room, and looking around the room, in the corner I clocked a small circular platform with a silver pole mounted in the middle that went up to the ceiling. The cogs were turning. Eventually the lads came back with the all clear. The last lad, Dava, came back with a young girl in tow. She was about my age, 21. She walked in, casually sat down, and lit a cigarette.

I'd tried to keep the atmosphere civil with the occupants of the flat, and they didn't seem too put out by our little visit. Eventually in broken English and sign language, I tried to explain that we were going, and thanked the main guy. He nodded and held out his hand for us to shake, ok. He then started talking to us in fast Serbian, he was smiling, but I didn't understand a word. Unexpectedly, he turned and spoke to the other occupants of the room. Some shit Eastern European pop music came on and the girl instantly stood up, dropped her dress to the floor and began dancing around the pole in her underwear. He turned back to us grinning, and using hand signs, he offered us shots, I declined, I was unsure what to do, we just looked at each other. The company commander didn't cover this eventuality in the 'actions-on' phase of his orders. We were just stood there in full fighting gear complete with blacked out faces - fucking bizarre. The girl was straight faced, not happy, but not sad. I made a mental to put this shit in our de-brief, then we bugged-out.

Kosovo was also the first time I'd seen a multinational force. All the NATO countries were there, and of course, the Russians. I was on a foot-patrol, we had a corporal with us this time, Tatty, and I took my place at the back of the four-man team. We patrolled for about an hour, exploring the back streets, taking up fire positions while Tatty did map-checks. As we headed down one particular road, I clocked what I thought was a school building ahead. The Russian flag was flying over the roof. As our team commander passed the front of the building I heard a commotion and shouting from up ahead. As I closed in I could see there was a Russian officer on the front steps of the school shouting Russian shit and obscenities toward us Brits. Getting closer I could see he was obviously drunk as fuck, he had a bottle of vodka in one hand and a pistol in the other, some other junior officers were trying to hold him back and calm him down, but they were tip-toeing around him - shit-scared. Tatty pushed on, not rising to the volley of abuse, we didn't understand him anyway. Being at the back of the patrol, I came level with the Russian officer last, he looked at me, and looking back at him I said - 'Hey, where's the fucking Kursk?'. He went mad shouting, as his officers grabbed his arms and held him back. I knew he only needed to understand one word to get my insult - 'Kursk'. The Kursk was a Russian submarine that had sank recently. It was global news and of huge embarrassment to the Russians, especially since they didn't have the means to rescue it. Many other countries *did* have the means, and the UK sent some specialist salvage ships to help, but the Russians were too proud - or ignorant - to accept. I walked on, grinning to myself.

The NATO troops were friendly and accommodating. We spent some time with the Italian Carbonari. They had a good set up with an excellent dining hall, and their food was great. The Scandinavians were great too, they had bars in their camps, and many of their soldiers played rock music (as in - they played the music themselves live on stage) in the evenings. Basically everyone had better camps than us, and everyone had better vehicles than us. One American lad said to me 'Don't worry, if it rolls, its good'.

We went into the rural areas of Kosovo, into the countryside. Intel. had us searching certain houses in small villages in the middle of nowhere. One time we found some weird chemicals hidden in a farmhouse. We confiscated them and passed them up the chain, but we never got any feedback on if they were dodgy.

After one house search we mounted up in the back of our Saxon armoured-vehicle. A lad called Mark had been tasked with searching the upstairs of the house, he'd been through all the bedrooms and annexes. Once the back doors were closed he reached into his pocket - 'Lads, look what I found' he said with a mordant grin. He then proceeded to pull out a huge pair of women's knickers, and, holding them up to the light, he opened them out. They were fucking rancid, covered in shit, piss, and dried blood. They stank too, and we all covered our noses as the fits of laughter began to emanate through the vehicle. I pictured the fat housewife that had sat at her kitchen table while we went through her house. The vehicle commander, Poppy, who had his head stuck up the turret, shouted down at us 'What the fuck is up with you guys?'. We were gagging on the smell by now in between our fits of laughter. 'The worst thing is, they weren't in a laundry bag or the bins' he said. 'They were folded up neatly in a drawer, ready to be used again' We challenged Mark to outdo himself on the subsequent house searches. He accepted the challenge.

After a while we were given a female interpreter, so the grotty-knickers game had to come to an end. She explained about the Serbs before NATO had intervened. She explained about the mass executions, and the mass graves. She'd escaped to the hills with some other civilians and they spent months living off the land, eating leaves and grass to survive. She explained the Rape chambers, basements in various public buildings where non-Serb women were tied up and kept as sex things until they died either from the abuse or just plain starvation. Some of the women were chained up alone usually to pipes or radiators, many were chained to other women, often the other women would be a friend or family member. She told us that many of the women had to endure the rape attacks whilst chained to the dead bodies of their sisters' or even their mother's naked rotting corpses. I'd inferred a lot about how the Serbs treated women over the past few months, and I was glad Kosovo was on its first step to separating from them, if for no other reason than that. I cast my mind back to the girl in the flat dancing away on the pole. Should I have done more? Maybe I could have feigned wanting some alone time with her and then asked her if she wanted rescuing. Who knows?

We got back to the UK and had the usual post-operational drinking session. I was a reasonably fit soldier up until then, but during my time in Kosovo my body changed, I filled out, gained a bit of definition, and gained some weight, the good kind of weight. Suddenly, out of the blue, I was twice as fit. PT sessions that I found tough before now came to me easily.

I was duly selected for a promotion course. They beasted us, and I blitzed it. Me and my two mates were selected from the course to go up to the Recce (Patrols) Platoon - the top platoon in the battalion, the platoon I'd been attached to when we were in South Armagh. My two mates, Barney and Ex, were both from South Yorkshire also, so it was great that we would be going to the same platoon, and we could car-pool when we went home.

~

Next mission - Sierra Leone, Africa.

Sierra Leone is beautiful to look at, but it stinks of piss and shit. All the time. Everywhere. We conducted the usual OPs. Most of our security patrols were done in vehicles, this time we were given WMIKs (Weapons-Mounted Installation Kit) - which were basically cut down and stripped down LandRovers that were customised for mounted machine guns and ancillary ammo. We did patrols around the city areas, and patrols deep into the jungle using the off-road paths and tracks. We often escorted the IMATT (International Military Training and Advisory Team) who were from English-speaking counties such as Canada and Australia. Most of them were British officers and Serjeant-Majors. Their job was to advise and consult the newly formed SLA (Sierra Leone Army) in their war against internal rebel groups such as the RUF (Revolutionary United Front) or the infamous West-Side Boys. Because we were working in small teams, these IMATT guys were more approachable and after listening to their advisory briefs with the SLA, I'd sit and chat to them about battle and field tactics. They were more than happy to impart their knowledge in this informal setting, and most of them seemed to enjoy it.

Halfway through our deployment the newly promoted Lance-Corporals were pooled onto a training team to assimilate, teach, and train the new local recruits who wanted to change sides. We were basically divided into groups of threes or fours and given a company each to train. We all chipped in on some of the large-scale training lessons such as fire-power demonstrations or platoon attacks.

The new SLA recruits were basically just re-branded rebels and had no soldiering ability or ethos whatsoever. We schooled them in all sorts of lessons from parade-drill, to marksmanship, to field tactics. They were shit at everything. The UK government had given them all the British Armies old SLRs (Self-Loading Rifles), the old boys in our regiment loved it and treated them like long-lost friends. I thought it was great too, and it gave me a chance to get to know a new (or should I say old) weapon intimately as I would be expected to teach it.

The jungle was harsh, humid, and hot. Our combats were drenched and stuck to us all the time. The air was thin and dusty, and when we got to the training centre a few of us began to run and train every morning. We got fit. The West-African

attitude of doing everything in slow-motion was hard for us Brits to accept at first. Our thoughts were that this is your country, your climate, you should be used to it. But the African 'soldiers' were slow and unfit, and we Brits found the PT easy with them, when really it should have been the other way around.
We'd often stay out overnight with our designated company of trainees. One day, we were training troops in basic infantry skills - shooting, ambushing.

We've been marching the troops all day through the green hills – me, another NCO called Jay and an SLA instructor. We started off at the back of the line of soldiers, but the SLA are slow and by late afternoon we'd overtaken them.

At the top of a hill Jay - another newly promoted Lance Corporal in our regiment, myself, and the SLA instructor, sit down, ready to count the men through. I pass around a water bottle - it's meltingly hot, so humid our DPMs are stuck to our backs. Jay turns on his crappy transistor radio, tunes it to BBC World Service. Our one connection with home. We fall silent, losing count of the passing soldiers, as the news sinks in. '... terrorist hijackings... two planes hit the Twin Towers... towers collapsed... plane flew into the Pentagon... passengers tried to resume control... plane crashed into field in Pennsylvania... suicide missions... death toll not yet known, but expected to be several thousand...'

Back at base, we check the news.
8.46 a.m.: American Airlines Flight 11 flew into the North Tower of the World Trade Centre.
9.03 a.m.: United Airlines Flight 175 flew into the South Tower of the World Trade Centre.
9.37 a.m.: American Airlines Flight 77 flew into the Pentagon.
9:59 a.m.: The South Tower collapsed.
10.03 a.m.: United Airlines Flight 93 crashed into the ground in Pennsylvania.
10:28 a.m. The North Tower collapsed.

Descriptions so fucked-up it's hard to get your head round them. Massive plumes of smoke pumping from the top of towers, jet-black against the blue sky. People injured, dying. Sirens. Screaming. The fucking inane comments of the shocked American news reporters as they comment on events unfolding on their screen
'What's that we're looking at?'
'What was that? A plane? Another plane?'

'*A huge explosion raining debris on all of us. Oh. WE BETTER GET OUTTA THE WAY!*'
'*The whole building has collapsed? Really?*'
'*Oh crap.*'
'*They seem to have a problem with the North Tower. It's falling down.*'

This is 9/11. America under attack on a scale that blows the biggest terrorist attack on the country to date, the Oklahoma City bomb that killed 168, out of the window. A whole world of people has watched this unfold on their TV screens. We've fucking missed it while marching about the sweaty green hills of Sierra Leone.

Everyone in the battalion is talking about it. It's like passing a pile-up on the M1. Gory fascination. Obsession for details. Questions for the future.

'*What are the Twin Towers, anyway?*'
'*The World Trade Centre, you thick fuck.*'
'*Americans won't take it lying down. We'll see some action out of this.*'
'*Who's behind it?*
'*Fuck knows. The Americans' look for a way to take revenge*'.
'*Bush'll be popular now.*'
'*War? This is what this means*'.

~

In 2002 I was in Brecon, South Wales. I stood in a line of around 80 Lance Corporals, all from different regiments across the Infantry. Two staff instructors made their way down the line. When the first one reached me, I removed the screw lids from my water bottles and held them out for him to inspect. 'Okay', he nodded, 'Put 'em away'. I looked down the line, waiting for the next instructor, I saw some other soldiers doing push-ups before running off to the Jerry-cans to fill up their water bottles.

The second instructor came level with me. He handed me a set of weighing scales with a hook on the end. I quickly hooked them onto my Bergan and Webbing and lifted them off the ground. The instructor leaned in, 'Fifty-one pounds', he said, 'Slightly over but no worries'. I handed the scales back as he moved on to the next guy. I quickly chugged half a bottle of water down my neck in the hopes of making my kit lighter, and maybe a boost from the extra hydration. I put my Webbing on over my shoulders and threaded my role-pin belt around my waist. I then hauled my Bergan onto my back, and with my Rifle in one hand made my way over to the ranks of the other waiting troops. I stood there, slightly stooped due to the weight on me, for what seemed like an age waiting for the staff to finish their checks. A few of the lads around me chatted nervously while waiting. Eventually, everyone was stood in a long snake, three ranks wide. The PTI set off at a blistering pace as we all jostled for position trying to keep up…

An hour and forty minutes later there were only 10 of us left with the front group, we crossed the finish line and were immediately directed to one side of an open-ended farm complex. Our kit was weighed, and we were told to get ourselves administered. I dropped my Bergan, the relief on my shoulders was great, and I felt that I could've floated away. I quickly took of my shirt and put on a dry base-layer. After a quick brew-up with the guy next to me we watched over the next twenty minutes or so as soldiers crossed the finish line. At the two-hour mark the PTI staff began sending guys to the other side of the complex, away from us, I assumed these were the guys that had failed the course (on the first day), and I didn't much envy them going back to their regiments so soon with a CFT (Combat Fitness Test) fail.

We spent the next four months in the field. The Brecon school of Infantry training is the pinnacle of current warfare tactics. This was SCBC - the Section Commanders Battle Course. We were learning to command sections and platoons ready for our operational roles. Our days and nights were spent on the practical application of tactics, Section attacks up to Company level, defence, fighting patrols, recognisance, ambushes, ranges, and a whole plethora of modern infantry strategies. This was all done with minimum sleep and minimum food, the calories we burnt through during that time were exponential, and I was the fittest I'd ever been in my life.

After the course I was supposed to return directly back to our Battalion in Cyrus. We were posted there soon after leaving Sierra Leone. However, I chanced a sly week off before returning, no one noticed and nothing was said. Bonus. When I got back I was summoned to the Company Serjeant Major's office - CSM Stanley, where he was sitting behind his desk. Captain Smith, my platoon commander, was stood beside him. Both were straight-faced.

'Why are you incorrectly dressed?', asked the CSM, I looked down at myself wondering what indiscretion I had committed with my uniform.

The CSM laughed, Captain Smith cracked a smile, 'Here, get yourself sorted out' the CSM said whilst throwing a Corporal's rank slide at me. 'Well done, you're a Full-Screw now'.

'And keep on top of all that shit you've learnt, 'cos we're expecting to get our desert kit issued soon'.

III.XIV

Sure enough, George W. Bush is soon on TV issuing Saddam with an ultimatum: leave the country with his sons within forty-eight hours or face a devastating attack by the US-led forces. Later, I find myself commanding a cut down Land Rover-weapons platform guiding my driver toward Basra, a corporal and team commander in the Reconnaissance Platoon.

Are we here because of 9/11? Well, the American troops we meet out here certainly think so. I'm not that I'm bothered why we're here. I've been ready to go for years. People say, 'Why would you want to go to war?' It's like being picked to play for England then getting stuck on the bench. Don't want to fire blanks on Salisbury plain all my life.

Iraq isn't quite what I expect. Yeah, it's dry and dusty and hot and there are blokes wearing Arab headdresses. But it's not as primitive as I'd pictured.

We drive on free-flowing tarmac highways. Yes, full of potholes, but passable. There's a functioning society here. There are some homeless, displaced, floating about. But there are also people grafting for a living. People getting up and going to work - doctors, lawyers, shopkeepers. Some of them even speak good English. As my platoon and I work through neighbourhoods, house to house, hunting for weapons and bad guys, I expect to be met with aggression, distrust, suspicion by the residents. There's a lot of that, but it's isolated resistance that the British soldiers take care of quickly. I'm surprised to find that many locals we meet aren't overtly hostile. In fact, some are friendly.

One thanks me for the invasion, grinning, delighted. I think he'd shake my hand if I didn't have two hands on my rifle.
'Don't thank me, mate. Thank Bush and Blair,' is my response.

One afternoon we're in Basra, clearing a shithole housing estate. It's claustrophobic, ugly concrete buildings rammed in close together, but not close enough to block out the rays of the sun, which is beating down hot enough to melt a soldier in full CEFO: belt kit, day pack, body armour, Para helmet, weapon. The stifling heat is doing nothing to help me swallow back the stench of raw sewage that's thick in the air. I'm covered in sweat, dust and crap from the day's work…

We are the point fire team. I'm covering a corner, in a firing position, waiting for the next section to come up and take the lead; we need the respite and a replen from the rear. SA80 up, kneeling, I scan around for threats.

Movement to my left. I hear the latch of a door as someone unbolts the lock. I switch my safety catch to the 'fire' position as I twist around, weapon targeted at the door two metres away that has cracked open. Inquisitive black eyes peek out at me. The door opens wider.

I grip the rifle. Aim between the eyes, spread around the street, I know my team will be clocking this and ready to cover me. The door opens more. I place my finger on the trigger.

It's a just a girl. Early teens. Long, dark hair. Some kind of kaftan dress, blue. She's smiling at me. Grinning. Totally unfazed by the rifle pointing at her face.

I let out a breath of relief. For god's sake, I was going to kill you… A giggle from behind, then other beaming, curious faces appear in the crack. All girls. Younger than her. She takes my measure, then closes the door.

I wait. Sweat runs down my neck from my sodden hair. The door opens again, wider now, and she steps out, relaxed. The other girls assemble in the doorway, whispering in Arabic and gesturing at me. She's walking towards me, holding out a glass of what I assume is water.

Hard to tell, given that it's less that clear. 'Hot,' she says in English, pointing at the sun. 'Drink.' I don't know what's in the water to turn it off colour. But given the stink in the air, I've a fair idea. Hearts and minds, I think. We're here to liberate these people. And man do they need it.

Her face is open, delighted that she's able to give me something. I smile, nod my thanks and lift the glass to my mouth. Lips firmly clamped together, I hold my breath and pretend to sip it. Once, twice. A snigger from across the street.

'You want some, mate?' I call to my mukker.

'Nah, you're all right, mate,' he laughs.

'Shukran,' I tell the girl as I hand back the still-full glass.

She smiles and prances back into her house, closing the door behind her.

It's a surreal experience. I'm here to save her, but she's prepared to risk herself to come out here and show me a little human kindness. Stupid? Unaware of the danger she put herself in? Perhaps. Or maybe she actually just gave a fuck about another human being.

President Bush on-board the USS Abraham Lincoln aircraft carrier gives a speech in which he announces the end of major combat operations in the Iraq War. Behind him, the warship's banner states 'Mission Accomplished'. Somewhat premature, given the shit-storm that is to come. And the fact that Saddam's still out there, free.

The lads and I study the 'Most-wanted Iraqis' playing cards we've been issued. The aces and kings are reserved for the real baddies – Hussein is the Ace of Spades; Chemical Ali is the King of Spades; Saddam's son Qusay is the Ace of Clubs; his other son, Uday, is the Ace of Hearts. Based on intel we carry out operations around Basra, kicking in doors and storming specific houses looking for them, looking for him. I always put myself on point when hitting these houses, there was no way anyone in the platoon was going to get Saddam but me. I enjoyed raiding these houses, it was real OPs; before 9/11 these jobs would have been the domain of Delta Force or the SAS. After one house an old guy told me in decent English that Saddam had been in Basra that week but he didn't know where. I asked where he learned to speak English so well; he said London, and then proceeded to pull out and show me his UK passport - we passed him back through the lines for the RMPs to get a proper de-brief. Unfortunately, we didn't come across Saddam or any of his top hench-men. Shame, would have got some kudos for capturing or killing any of them. Best we achieve with the pack is a run of card games.

Passes the time when you're not busy rooting about in corners of dark, dingy Iraqi houses looking for Saddam Abd al-Majid al-Tikriti Hussein.

III.XV

A firefight is one thing; a pre-emptive kill is something else. Our platoon is running a vehicle checkpoint when we receive a message over the net that a convoy of vehicles carrying armed men is approaching Red 9, a big crossroads nearby. We mount up and head out to investigate. Upon arrival at Red 9 I see several vehicles heading southeast on the Red route, all containing civilian-dressed men, most armed with pistols or AKs.

We follow the vehicles as they head South-East on the Red route. The rear civilian vehicle - a white pickup truck carrying a gaggle of Iraqis - must be fifteen passengers, falls back behind the other vehicles. We've arranged for other call signs to block the other vehicles further up; we have these guys so we intercept the vehicle.

Our commander, a Captain, stops the pickup truck and debuses with the call sign to investigate. He orders the civilians to get out of their vehicle, but four ignore him. A crowd gathers around the vehicles, civilians from the streets around. It's a wide dual-carriageway, nice bit of greenery in the central reservation, and the crowds are some way off, so I don't feel too hemmed in. Still, beneath the open curiosity in the local people's faces lurks hostility.

By now, I'm out of my WMIK (open Land Rover) watching the four men, who refuse to get down from the pick-up. They're all armed. I focus on one man who's sitting down with his rifle in an upright position, the butt on the floor and one hand on the barrel. I tighten my grip on my rifle.

Suddenly, in a fluid motion, he stands, brings his weapon to a horizontal position and tucks the butt under his armpit, with one hand on the pistol grip and one hand on the barrel. His rifle is aimed at one of the soldiers in my call sign.
I bring my rifle up, aim.

His index finger moves to the trigger. I shoot once, twice, in quick succession. Single shots, double-tap, an automatic decision. Time slows.

The Iraqi falls in the back of the pickup, tries to sit up, then falls back down.

The three guys either side of him flinch their bodies in shock. A few centimetres off target and I'd have floored them too. Are they next? They're no doubt wondering. I remain in a standing fire position, weapon aimed - I'm ready to kill every last one of them.

Exclamations and gestures from the onlookers. The lads from my call sign spread out, pushing people back.

Then slow-motion dissipates and real time returns.
Our Captain is looking around his teams.
One of the Iraqi men in the back of the truck cries in English, 'Look! They kill this man!' Outraged, he's appointed himself as spokesman.

Already members of my call sign are up in the back of the pickup, confiscating weapons. That's the best thing about Recce Platoon: we're the battalion's top platoon, who know how to use our brains, and we react professionally, knowing what to do without being told.

Our captain raises an eyebrow, and I see he doesn't know who's fired, I go to him, grab him by the arm and make sure he looks me in the eyes.
'That was me', I say in a clear and deliberate manner.
There's no time for explanations; they'll come later.
'Ok… first aid, Robbo,' he instructs.

Standard British Army procedure - neutralise the threat, then administer essential first aid as long as it is safe to do so. Were the tables turned, the enemy would have no such respect for us.

I go to the back of our wagon to get a med kit. By the time I climb up into the back of the pickup another soldier, is administering first aid and trying to keep the man conscious. There are two bullet wounds to the chest - I met my target with both shots - and an exit wound at the back that's sheeting blood. I shove a field dressing on the man's back, though I know there's little point.

The dying man says nothing but stares up at me with eyes that say, 'I'm a goner, aren't I?' The soldier and I move the Iraqi - and his rifle, so as not to leave it on the streets - to the back of our vehicle and drive him to the nearest British medical centre in Basra. There, we carry him inside. The medics dive straight in, cool and professional.

Why bother? You may be wondering. Standard operating procedure. We're in security mode since victory was declared. Outside, a colleague and I unload the Iraqi's weapons, which was racked and ready to fire.

A few minutes later a medic comes out. 'He's dead, lads, and you need to get the hell out of the building. Grenades on his body. We're evacuating. Go.'

Once the grenades are made safe by some Engineers, we collect the body bag, load it into the truck and drive it to the nearest Iraqi hospital. Can't say I'm particularly bothered about driving with a corpse in my vehicle. But if it was up to me I'd have left him where he dropped.

Back at base, news has spread. I'm the first of my unit to kill an enemy in this way - during 'peacetime', without returning fire. A few look at me with what might by envy; most say, 'Good job, mate.'

I get wind of the odd muttering questioning the context of the shoot, usually by people who weren't there. But my mates - and those who were there - defend me.

I don't feel sad about the killing, and I don't feel for the man I shot. To me, at that time, it was just something that happened. I don't feel the need to deal with it, or process it in any singular way. To me there was no moral dilemma, no moral conflict, no moral decision. Why? Because he was a clear and succinct threat, a threat that emanated risks, risks that could befall consequences, consequences of further deaths - death of a colleague, a mate, even the deaths of innocent onlookers (there were plenty of bystanders in the vicinity that could also have been hit). In the end the decision was made for me; the decision was made by the threat, a threat that he, the gunman, decided to pose.

What if the man I shot had been allowed to fire? He might have killed a lad in my team. What if that bullet went through my team mate, killed him and killed a civilian? What if he fired multiple bullets? What if he fired automatic bursts? What if he emptied the full magazine of 30 rounds on full automatic in 3.5 seconds? *What if he had second thoughts - what if he was about to lay down his weapon and submit to us?* The point is, the Rules of Engagement don't require us to read minds, nor do they require us to predict the future. They require us to interpret what is unfolding in front us in the existing situation, to consider the risks presented at that particular time - in the here and now.

Later, I'm interviewed by the Military Police. There'd be no sign of this during war-time, but as this is the post conflict phase the Army's playing it careful. I write up a statement, and answer their questions. I'm not concerned - the killing was lawful, within the Rules of Engagement. There's a wider context developing in Basra, coalition forces are being attacked more and more, militias, rebels, and insurgencies are becoming more organised and gaining in confidence. The British Army is thin on the ground, it's a busy time for the coalition as a whole. The RMPs must agree that I'm not at fault, because there's no further investigation for now. The Iraqi made his decision: his decision, his consequence - fuck him.

I'm content with my actions - and that night I sleep easily.

I did my job.

III.XVI

Back in June, six British soldiers, members of the Royal Military Police, were killed in Al Majar al-Kabir. It's initially reported in the press as 'unprovoked murder'; later, a British Major-General revises the cause to 'a misunderstanding'. Locals were pissed off by British Army searches conducted in the area to confiscate weapons. British units had been working to find heavy weapons like rocket-propelled grenade launchers, anti-aircraft guns, mortars and other heavy weapons (not AKs; so many people have them it's unrealistic to expect the locals to give them up and be weaponless). British leaders met local community leaders and made a deal: the Iraqis would hand over the weapons if the British got the hell out of their town and stop searching homes.

But the next day, a foot patrol deployed. The locals assumed the soldiers were there to search for weapons. There are mixed reports about what happened next, but a street battle broke out. Thousands of local people came out to attack the soldiers, who later moved out via a Chinook lift.

Unbeknownst to them, six RMPs were still a mile away in the local police station that day on a totally separate mission, training Iraqi officers. The mob turned. The RMPs were stuck.

According to media reports, the firefight in the police station lasted ninety minutes before the RMPs (who are not trained or equipped Infantrymen), outnumbered many hundreds to one, ran out of ammo. Isolated and alone, with no radio to call for backup, they made a last stand, but to no avail.

The local people were unrepentant, and promised more bloodshed. In Basra, according to the The Telegraph, soldiers 'abandoned their berets, the symbol of a relaxed approach to patrolling, and donned helmets instead'.

The Guardian asks, 'How were six men allowed to die when hundreds of heavily-armed reinforcements were just a mile or so away?' I wonder the same thing myself.

Weeks later, in the hot summer, I pull over a civilian while manning a checkpoint outside Basra.

Open desert. Very isolated. The Army is stretched, many small units are working in far too much isolation, our two-multiple platoon is on our own in the middle of no-where most of the time. There's no infrastructures in place in Iraq yet, no phone signals. Our longest-range communication is a radio called the PRC320, designed back in the '70s.

We're conducting car checks, and we get a guy who looks shifty as hell. Scowling. Trying not to make eye contact.

I nod to Brad, the lad I'm working with, and he helps me pull the bloke from the vehicle to the side of the road.

'Sit there,' I tell him, shoving him down onto the dusty ground a few metres from his car. 'Stay still. Understand?'

The guy gives no sign of understanding, just mutters something moodily in Arabic.

My oppo, Brad, searches the man while I keep my weapon trained on him.

'Fuck me!' I hear from Brad.
'What is it?' I shout.

Brad pulls something from the Iraqis pocket, he shows me what he's found. A handgun, a Browning HP pistol. A British Army issue weapon.

Given that the deaths of the six RMPs were the heaviest losses sustained by British forces since the end of the war, the British Army has been wanting to hunt down the killers with a passion. Their weapons are missing, taken from their dead bodies. Now we have a civilian who has a Browning.

He might have been one of the guys there that day. He might've killed one, more. He might've helped, or stood back and done nothing while they were killed. Or he might quite simply have bought the gun in a cafe that morning.
I look at the Iraqi man.

He looks back at me with a sneer.

'Give him it back,' I say slowly to Brad.

Brad eyeballs me. He knows what I'm thinking - if the Iraqi's holding the weapon, I can kill him. I can get away with it. If he's holding a weapon, aiming it at me. It's lawful, within the Rules of Engagement. And he's carrying a fucking Browning; he's complicit in the deaths of six British men, six RMPs.

There's a moment when the world stills. The path ahead splits into two. A choice. This time there is a moral decision to be made.

'Forget it,' says Brad, making my mind up for me. 'It's not worth it.'
I'm seething at Brad. But... fuck! He's right; this piece-of-shit Iraqi isn't worth shooting. Not like this. But I wish I had, and it's hard to swallow.

~

Around this time we start getting briefed in O Groups about the disbanding of 'Saddam's Army'. It's a US strategy, backed by Britain, which means de-ba'thification - the police and the armed forces are to be disbanded, and in their place the Coalition plan to build up their own police and Army.

Recipe for chaos, in my book. Soon enough we'll have a disbanded security force personnel pissed off and running about the country with weapons. But for now, we're just about surviving in our soft-skin open-topped vehicles. So when we receive orders one day to escort a couple of chaps, there's no hard-core security - just a WMIK front and two at the back and the SUV that we're escorting in the middle.

'Who are these guys?' I ask our Colour-Serjeant, Jack.
'Private security.'
'Who do they work for?'
'Some company.'
'What, like security guards or bodyguards?'
'No mate, contractors.'
The contractors we're to escort interest me. I'm like a little kid, full of questions:

What do they do? For who? How? When? How much do they make?

I volunteer myself to ride in with the two guys. I'm curious. And besides, they've got air-con, win-win. They're nice blokes – mature, in their 50s, confident, and open to answering my questions. One is British, the other South African. Both are ex-Special Forces. They've recently arrived in the country and are doing recces preparing for the arrival of their client, who's working for a company contracted to build up the infrastructure. They explain the basics of the private contracting industry: you're a contractor who gets paid to protect.

It's interesting stuff. A whole new world opening up. It hasn't occurred to me before there's any choice other than what I do now.

Then the South African guy asks, 'You got a bird back home?'
'Yeah,' I reply.
Nikki. I met her just before we moved out to Iraq; we had a couple of dates. We've been writing letters every week full of random stuff like 'What's your favourite pizza?' in an effort to get to know each other.

The South African throws me a sat phone. I'm impressed; I've not seen one of these out in the field being chucked about without a second thought to the costs of calling home.

'Call her,' he says. 'Go on.'
Cool, I think as I dial her number. No free phone calls in the Army. These guys have freedom.

It's nothing really, just a casual crossing of paths, but it plants the seed of an idea in my head. I decide that when I get home I'll do some research on privately-hired contactors.

~

At Basra air-station, we're waiting for the RAF to take us back to Cyprus. We're done here. The lads have made a table and chairs out of their Bergans and are playing cards next to the runway.

113

I walk away from them, and find the toilets - real toilets, like in a real airport. Not the shovel recces (a shit in the field), improvised holes, and the makeshift porta-loos we'd been using whilst out here, that usually came accompanied by the sound of some squaddie grunting away next to you. I don't need to use them but I go in anyway and just sit in a cubicle alone. Its silent. I realise this is the first time in over six months that I'm alone, I literally haven't been by myself since we got here. I've always needed the occasional bit of alone time, and sitting there in the silence was great.

After about ten minutes I wandered back to the lads and took a seat. I felt recharged by that tiny amount of cognitive distance. And at that time, in those circumstances, it was like I'd just been on a two-week holiday.

I leave Iraq ready for a beer. Such a fucking dry country. As the plane takes off on the dusty runway, I know I'll be back some day - but in what capacity?

III.XVII

A couple of weeks later, I was given an unusual task by the Company and Platoon commanders. Iraq was in full counter-insurgency mode now, as the insurrection was gaining momentum throughout the country - and Cyprus was the obvious last stop before flying into Basra airport for most personnel coming from the UK.

As a weapons instructor from the Recce Platoon, and clearly being quite current on Iraq, I was told that these two guys were turning up in the morning and that I'd be taking them through some weapons drills with our rifles and pistols as they were heading to Iraq soon. I did wonder why two guys about to go operational would need weapons training so late before their deployment, I resolved to ask them when I met them.

The next morning, I met these two guys at our gates, escorting them through our camp I took them to a classroom I had prepared with our weapons. Both guys turned up in civvies, and both were in their late 30s or early 40s. They were friendly and as we walked we chatted. Inevitably, I asked them what they were doing in Iraq, and to my surprise both were quite open about what they did - although they left out who they actually did it for. Turns out they were Intelligence operatives, and as such had rarely touched conventional weaponry over the last few years.

We spent a good few hours getting up to speed on the SA80 A2 assault rifle and Browning pistol drills, and they both took to it quickly. I'd also prepped the classroom with a GPMG, a Minimi, and an L96 Sniper-Rifle just to show them, as a bit of variety and interest. They got hands-on and thanked me for the extra effort I'd made. Before we finished they decided it was their turn to pick my brain. Knowing I'd just got back from Iraq, they began asking me loads of questions about my deployment. Everything from our intelligence structure, our support, to the types of ground missions we'd conducted. As they'd been quite open with me I, in turn, responded likewise, and as these guys were Brits about to deploy I felt it was at least professional courtesy to assist them with as much information as I could give. Eventually, we got onto the subject of enemy contacts, and in particular the story of my pre-emptive kill. I relayed the story to them in detail whilst they nodded and listened. And this led us to discussing the ROE (Rules of Engagement) in relative element to Iraq. They both seemed very knowledgeable on the ROE and I inferred a lot of experience from Northern Ireland from their conversation. In the end, they thanked me for the weapons lesson, and on being so candid with illustrating the ROE though my own personal experience.

We shook hands and parted ways. Another chance meeting that reminded me of the two PMC contractors I'd met in Iraq. *The cogs were turning.* And as much as I loved soldiering, the prospect of waiting for the next war became a frustration for me. From then on, my mind was forging a different route to the one the Army would have me take. I knew my path lay in seeking out my next war for myself, rather than waiting for it to come to me. It weighed on me, and I felt that I needed to get back to the fighting. Was this some kind of a fucked-up reversal of a stress disorder - where mundanity caused me cognitive frustration, perhaps? Or perhaps I felt that I hadn't exhausted my full potential, or maybe I just hadn't proved myself to myself fully yet.

Nonetheless, by the end of 2003 Iraq was the most assessable war on the planet - and possibly in recent history, not just for the coalition armed forces, privately hired contractors, international mercenaries, Iraqi mercenaries, and TCN (Third Country National) guards but also for any budding jihadist from around the globe that fancied themselves as a terrorist, guerrilla, insurgent, or martyr.

Undeniably, the Iraq war had inadvertently offered Islamic-based terrorism easy access to British and American forces. Before, it would have taken long-winded planning, money, and foresight to attack the US or UK, such as those attacks seen on 9/11. Coalition forces in Iraq now offered a genuine and physical target for Al Qaeda proxies at a lower and broader level. This concept, of course, went both ways. Consider the Clinton administration's missile strikes on East Africa in 1998. Now US troops could take the fight to the heart of terrorism - through the Iraq occupation - with less reliance on intercontinental ballistics. People like me, and the all these civilian-clothes-wearing types I'd been meeting, were now the face of the war on terror.

In the end, all this deep thinking made me hungry. Fuck it, time for scoff. As I walked past the guard room on my way to the cook-house, I clocked the RP that had sneered and talked at me like shit on my first day in battalion. He was standing on the gate doing guard duty in the sun, he wasn't an RP anymore.

'Alright Robbo', he said smiling as I walked past.

'Alright' I replied impassively.

He was still a Lance Corporal, in just a few years I'd overtaken him in rank - I pondered if that would have engaged a change in his attitude toward 'gob-shite-recruits', probably not, thick cunt. Anyway, I bet those two PMCs I'd rode with in Iraq didn't have to put up with shit-bags like this guy. More pros than cons...

A few days later, one of the Colour Serjeants from Recce Platoon - Jack - gave me the week off, well not officially, but he said he'd cover for me while I disappeared. Nikki was in Cyprus; her parents are Cypriot and she was in Nicosia visiting family. I borrowed a mate's car, no insurance, no tax, no registration, no idea where I was going, and drove half way across the country - from Dhekelia to Nicosia - reading a small map in one hand whilst driving to see her. We met at a TGIs restaurant. She was stood in the car park looking great, small, thin, long dark hair, and bronzed skin, smiling as I pulled into the car park. As I walked over her cousin appeared by her side. He walked up to me, said hello, and shook my hand. I think he gave a little nod to Nikki before jumping in his car and driving off. Obviously, I'd passed some weird Greek test because Nikki saw out the rest of the day with me. I set myself up in a cheap hotel in the old part of the city. We spent the days walking in the sun, holding hands, eating outdoors, and took the occasional day trip to the beach. During the evenings we'd have a drink and go to some of the night-clubs around Nicosia. I spent loads of money that week, but it was worth every penny. Eventually, we started to spend our nights together too, wrapped around each other's wet bodies in the hot and humid Cypriot nights.

I was falling in love.

I got back to Alexandra barracks the next Saturday night. As I drove through the gates I could see Recce Platoon's offices' lights on. I parked up and walked over. Apparently the post-war decompression was in full swing. Some alco-shot concoction was handed to me and I was told to chug it. I did, it was awful. Then the drinking games began: pull-ups, press-ups, shuttle-sprints, all with shots in between, the winner would get a shot, and the loser would get a double shot. We went at it most of the night. Thank fuck for Sundays.

III.XVIII

Back in the UK, the more I find out about private military contractors in Iraq, the more it seems obvious that it's the best career choice.

In 2004 while training in Norway I read about an American PMC that got caught out in Iraq; it was 31st March. Fallujah. Iraqi insurgents, aided by the so-called Iraqi Civil Defence Corps, ambushed two SUVs and killed the four Blackwater contractors inside who were en route to pick up kitchen equipment. Locals dragged the bodies from the vehicles, beat them, hacked at them, burned them and then hanged them above a bridge over the Euphrates. The video images were broadcast worldwide.

Blackwater was slated by the media for sending the four-man team out alone into a known hot zone: undermanned (there would usually have been six); in soft-skin, not armoured, vehicles; lightly armed; with no maps; pushed to deploy before they were fully prepared. But that's not the complete picture, I think. The team that was taken out was call sign N-1. That same day a second team, B-2, was sent out in exactly the same conditions. Both had their orders. B-2, however, ignored the order to drive through Fallujah, drove around the city and returned to Baghdad safely that day. N-1 followed the order blindly and were massacred. The operators were responsible for their actions. Companies hire contractors to make sensible decisions on the ground. N-1 – all former Navy Seals – should have ditched the command to go through Fallujah. Contractors need to have a brain, need to think for themselves and not just do as they're told meekly when it's clear that on the ground the order is bullshit, otherwise what's the point of hiring men with top-notch military backgrounds? Don't just please a corporate boss; use the brain and military training you were hired for.

I've gone from knowing nothing about contractors to hearing about them all over the place. Soldiers are quitting the forces to go private. In mess halls, rumours fly about who's got an 'in' at a PMC and of course we talk about the perks.

In the Army, at corporal level I'm taking home about £1,600 per month. And the Army is cutting pensions all over the place. Rumour has it, private contracting can earn you $200,000 per year. Tax free, because you're working out of the country. I wouldn't even need a pension on that. After just one rotation as a contractor I'd have a deposit for a house. And I would have total security.

Then there's the freedom to consider. No more Army hierarchy. Yes, I'd have a team leader, and that team leader would have a boss. But the red tape and bureaucracy and politics would be behind me. Just do the job and make the money. Simples.

The rotation – usually two to three months on and then around one off – would mean I'd see more of home. Compare that to six-month stints in Iraq in the Army. Sure, when I was in country as a contractor I'd be grafting the whole time, but I'm not one to sit about anyway.

Best of all, I'd get to do what I do best. I'd miss the green kit, but with the number of blokes moving into private contracting, it was clear I'd still have the camaraderie of Army life. A no-brainer then, really.

The only potential down-side is the risk, but this doesn't faze me. When you're in the Army, you're willing to put your life on the line, I made a will at 18 years old. They can choose to send you anywhere that you may get whacked. A mate of mine Paul 'Taff' Thomas from Mortars Platoon. Serves in Kosovo, Northern Ireland and then Iraq, and he gets a second tour of Iraq almost straight away, attached to the Cheshire Regiment. Weeks later, he's killed in a huge ambush with rifles, machine guns and RPGs in Basra.

Private contracting would be no different to the Army in that sense. In fact, I'd have more ability to protect myself - to make my own calls. And I figure if I'm going to get wasted, it might as well be with some more zeros on the bank balance.

So I sign off, give my notice to the Army. I'm based in Edinburgh, and then I do a tour of South Armagh, Northern Ireland again - the platoon is spilt up and sent to various outposts. At the end of my tour I stop in at Bessbrook Mill and bump into a group of mates from my platoon. Over a beer we catch up. Shots follow beer, and it soon descends into one of those legendary shitfaced nights.

'Where you been, Robbo?'

III.XVIII

'Golf Two Zero, and then Crossmaglen.'
Jeers and jibes.
'Nah, it was all right.'
'What you doin' here?'
'On my way out.'
'To do what?'
'Private hire, Iraq.'
One of the lads whistles. 'Army won't like that.'

The Army hates losing good men to private companies. It's invested years of training in us. Money, time, energy. Nothing it can do about it, though.

'That's where the money is,' I tell them. 'Blokes are buying Porsches and Ducati's. Buying houses. Building extensions.'

We get another round in, despite the fact it's late and we're the one ones left in the NAAFI.

Slurring our words, we debate as well as a group of inebriated soldiers can manage. Is Robbo doing the right thing? Is Robbo a tool for leaving the Army? Is he going to miss the Army? How much money, exactly, can you make going doing that?

An MP comes over to tell us to break it up. We tell him, politely, to fuck off, and steam right on.

The final verdict is split. Lads like Barney, Buncy and Ex are up for private contracting. Black Scotty (Philip Scott), Browny (Lee Brownson) and Tom Gaden are sticking with the Army.

Though I don't know it that day, our paths are set. And for three of us, those paths will lead to a sad end.

III.XIX

Towards the end of your service, you get civvy courses paid for by the Army that will help you in your post-Army career. I opt for a month-long close protection course, run by some ex-Special Forces types, which touches on Iraq a lot. We're set up in a B&B in Hereford, which makes quite a change from Army quarters. The focus of the course is protocol. We're taken through drills for protecting clients: driving, medical training, risk assessment, venue assessment.

Much of it seems to involve wearing a suit and poncing about in posh places. A bunch of rough Army lads being knocked into shape to fit in with the hoity-toity. Don't say 'fuck', say 'oh dear'. Don't park by a puddle; important people mustn't get their shoes wet.

We go to a swanky restaurant and have a lesson in table etiquette. Fucking silverware all over the place. The next morning, the instructor gives a debrief – well, he has to earn his wage, so he's got to tick the box. His feedback for me is nothing useful like 'Gary, always walk on the left of the client because you're right-handed and that means you can grab the client and reach for your pistol with your shooting hand at the same time' or 'Make sure you position yourself so you can see all exits'. No, his debrief is this: 'Gary, you ate your dessert with a spoon. You should have used a fork for lemon torte.'

The expectation is that we'll go to work in London as high-level bodyguards. Yawn. I've seen that Kevin Costner film, it was shit. I don't want to be standing outside changing rooms in Harrods waiting for some millionaire's spoilt kids to try on designer fucking socks. Celebrities don't interest me either. And what's wrong with a fucking spoon for dessert?

Ninety percent of the guys on the course with me are also spooners who are planning to go into Iraq. We swap contacts and info on opportunities for private work.

I tell my family I'm going into private security. They haven't much clue what it means, but they can't argue with the benefits I list.

'Perhaps you'll do it for a short while, to build up some savings, and then retire and do something easier, safer?' a friend suggests.

Not likely, I think.

I ask Nikki, whether she minds. She says it's alright.

Good job, because I'm going anyway.

III.XX

I'm well out of my comfort zone. Job applications. Interviews. Suits. But I'm convinced it's worth it. To get into this trade.

I've filled out some paperwork. I've done some phone interviews. I've agreed to work for one company and am waiting impatiently for the uplift when Armorgroup calls and offers me an interview.

So while I'm still in the Army, with my official leaving date a couple of months away, I head down to London for an interview with a major private company. It's a glorious summer day. I roar down the M1 in the outside lane in my Lotus Elise.

In central London I park in an underground garage and join the throngs of workers on Buckingham Gate heading back to their offices after lunch. I'm uncomfortable in my black suit, white shirt, blue tie and smart black shoes that I've bought for the occasion. But I fit right in.

I have a flashback to the last time I was interviewed, when entering the Army. Then, I was a teenager, inexperienced, clueless, and cocksure. Probably slumped a bit in my seat. Now, I'm a professional. Or at least that's what I tell myself as I enter the swanky office building, get a security pass, travel up in the lift and sit in a soulless waiting room surrounded by other equally-uncomfortable-looking soldiers. (One of them, Chris, will later be on my team in Iraq.)

I'm not nervous. I wouldn't be here if I wasn't interesting to the company. I'm more curious as to how this will pan out. I've no idea where the contract is for; but I suspect – hope – it's Iraq.

It's a woman interviewing me, which throws me slightly. But it's soon clear that she's ex-military, and knows her stuff.

We sit in a meeting room with a view over London. I try not to watch black cabs and red buses meander about on the road below, but to focus on the questions.

We talk through my CV and my experiences in places like Northern Ireland, the former Yugoslavia, Africa, and Iraq.

'You got promoted pretty fast through the ranks,' she comments. Then: 'How long have you been out of the Army?'

'Errr… actually I'm still in' I reply, 'I'm available, but my official leave date is next week'.

She smiles. 'Good to know.'

She starts explaining the contract.

'The life insurance covers you for two hundred and fifty thou. We compensate for loss of limb as well, and give you a wage while you rehabilitate.'

I nod. Good news for Nikki.

'Have you got a will?'

'An Army one,' I admit. 'But I'll make a new one.'

She asks me whether I have any questions. I deliberately don't ask about money; I want to give the right impression. Besides, I know whatever they're paying will be a whole heap more than I'm used to. Instead, I focus on the job.

'What kind of contract would I get?'

'Can't say at this point. But you're pretty sharp and easy going, so I think a protective security detail - PSD - would suit you, working with our clients.'

Finally, she smiles, thanks me for my time, and promises to call me soon.

An hour after entering the building I'm back out in the sunshine, taking off my suit jacket and tie and undoing the top button on my shirt.

III.XXI

A couple of days later the lady from Armorgroup calls and offers me the job officially. PSD work in Iraq.

We talk money. I manage to keep the grin out of my voice.

She sends the paperwork and I have a medical. All straightforward. She sends me flight details. I'm to come to the head office to sign my contract, and then head to Heathrow.

I get to London without a hitch. I fly to Kuwait, then on to Baghdad. The light aircraft I'm on dives down steeply in its descent, in case of enemy fire.

I disembark onto the scorching tarmac. It's like stepping into a furnace. The airport is quiet – a few commercial planes, abandoned since 2003, are scattered about, covered in dust.

A team is waiting for me, to take me to the Green Zone.

'Gary Roberts?' The team leader strides over. 'Welcome to Armorgroup, mate.'

III.XXII

I arrive at my new home, a compound in the Green Zone. It's late, and I'm given the keys to my room and told to get my head down.

Outside my room, I quietly put the key in the lock and crack open the door. Its pitch black inside. Shit; I'm not going to be popular putting the light on and waking the other guys. Nothing for it: I fumble about until I find the light switch and flip it. Jesus H.

The room is big. Wood-panelled walls. Thick carpet. Double bed. Satellite TV. Fridge. Desk. En-suite shower. And there's no roommates. This is all mine.

The next morning, after a decent kip, I check out the rest of the place. It's a fucking oasis in the middle of a war zone. Palm trees, green grass, TV showing Premiership matches. Staff on hand to clean our rooms and do our laundry. And the food! Lobster. Caviar. Steak.

It's a long way from the Army Barracks I'm used to.

Billions of dollars are being thrown into Iraq at this time, and this is one of the big contracts – Armorgroup's flagship one. We're a small division of Armorgroup, set aside from the main company's base (AGI). Our job is to protect American engineers who are working to rebuild the Iraqi power system. The clients are living on the site – hence the luxury. The contract's so lucrative, AG can afford all the trimmings.

First job: get kitted out. In the storeroom the QM tells me help myself to body armour, a rifle and all the ammo I can carry. 'It's not like the Army here,' he explains. 'It's no issue if you "lose" a couple of rounds. If you need more ammo, just let me know.'

After years of British weapons, now I'm using an American one, an M4. Doesn't bother me as I've used them before. I'm not a weapons freak – as long as it does what it's supposed to, I'm happy.

Then it's on to training, a week of briefings and training exercises. The contract has a dedicated trainer, a Scottish ex-military chap. This is rare; it shows how lucrative the contract is. He takes my team – team leader Fraz, Aussie; Kiwi McGoo; and me – through the basics of the contract and how we're expected to operate.

'This is high-pro, not low-pro, work. You'll be in armoured Toyota Land Cruisers. Two vehicles. Two of you in the front vehicle, with up to two clients. Two of you in the back. Rear gunner.

'You drive fast, aggressively. You keep your distance from other vehicles – at least a hundred metres behind. You keep to the middle of the road, to avoid the roadside bombs. Fight through traffic. Drive on the opposite carriage when necessary to avoid static or slow-moving vehicles, or contacts.

'If you get into a contact, you drive through. *You drive through.* You don't stop and engage the enemy. Your priority is to get the clients out safely.

'If a vehicle is immobilised, you push it through. Bumper to bumper, shove it out of the kill zone. If you can't push it, you hook up or ditch it. You pull up alongside, cross-deck, and get the clients into the working vehicle. Cram everyone in, put fire down - and get outta there.'

We're told to watch the Americans. 'Don't get too close to a US call sign,' the trainer instructs. 'Stay back, stay away. They'll fucking shoot up anything moving, anything out of the ordinary.'

It's my first indication of how the American presence has changed in Iraq since I was here in 2003. Then, you would see an American truck on its own on the road, no armour, open-backed, with just one person driving. Now, that's unheard of. The Americans move in packs, are armoured and weaponed up to the hilt, and jittery as fuck. There are plenty of cases of Americans firing shots at PMC vehicles. They just haven't cottoned on to PMCs yet.

Every day we go to the centre of the Green Zone and train alongside a whole army of other PSDs in the shadow of the Arc of Triumph, the crossed swords. We hammer out drills – driving, shooting, and changing tyres. By the end of the week we've got a tyre change down to ninety seconds. I'm not learning new skills – I did all this stuff in the Army – but I'm applying them to new circumstances: new vehicles, new weapons, and new drills.

I enjoy it.

The other guys, on the whole, seem sound. Experienced, mature. Youngest of us is late-twenties, going up to Falklands vets aged fifty or so; most are in their thirties and forties. No homesick teenage gobshites to deal with here like you get in the Army.

Some of them are clearly just there for the money. Some, like me, have left the military planning to go private. Some are people who've been out of the game and then seen an opportunity to get back into exciting work.

There are a couple of new guys like me, but most of them have been out a few months. We're all former Infantrymen or Marines; a lot of us have been to Iraq before. Depends on the guy whether you encounter respect, friendliness or a competitive edge.

I'm in the office, asking where the gym is. Paul McGuigan, huge bloke, Scottish, ex-Royal Marine, overhears and offers to show me. He chucks an old *FHM* magazine to one side and I follow him outside. On the way we chat about this and that. He's easy going, welcoming.

We have a brew later on, and again over the next few years when our paths cross now and then. Until Paul is murdered by a colleague, that is.

III.XXIII

On the PSD contract I have enemy contacts. The first, which takes place on my first rotation on Route Predators, is small-arms fire that we drive straight through though the vehicles are riddled and need to disappear to the mechanic's shop.

Later, on Route Sonics, it's an IED, just a drive-through. The panelling on the front vehicle takes a hit, but the armour isn't compromised and we're all fine. Chris, the lad I met in London, is driving. During the third, a client gets a smack in the face.

Before a mission, we brief the engineers carefully on what to do if we get into a situation. 'If something goes down and we have to move,' I tell them, 'I'm going to grab you and I'm going to bundle you into the vehicle. Got it?' They nod; what else can they do?

We're at a power station in Baghdad when we come under fire – mortars. Instantly, I grab the back of my client's jacket and shove him with all my strength through the open door of the truck onto the back seat. He falls flat on his face – no time to get his hands up to brace his fall. Within seconds the second client follows suit, and then I'm in the vehicle and we're out of there.

Fraz turns to check on the clients in the back. 'You okay?' The clients nod unconvincingly. They're white-faced, shaken, but not injured beyond a grazed cheek. We're not going to apologise for manhandling them. It's our job.

The PSD work is a real eye-opener for me in professionalism. You have to really be a fuck-up to get kicked out of the Army, here its different. The first firing I see comes after someone's caught drinking. This is Armorgroup's most important contract, worth millions, and they can't afford mistakes. So it's a dry contract – no booze. It's not that they think we'll all be nightmares if we have a drink. But there's always one who takes it too far, who can't handle it, whose judgement goes out the window. And they can't afford to have any loose cannons.

I figured the guy caught on the booze would get a warning, but he's straight out of there. It's a shame, because he's a good bloke, can handle his drink, but I guess they can't fuck around. The next colleague to be given the boot, though, now that's far and away the right thing.

Fraz is ex-Army and ex-Police. As my team leader, he's seems a good bloke. On the ball. Professional in training and professional out on tasks. But then he screws it all up by getting involved with an Iraqi girl. Not just any Iraqi girl: one who works for our client.

Their relationship is no secret. It's common knowledge among the guys and the local Iraqis - Fraz even gets to know her brother. I don't think it's in our contract that we can't fraternise with locals, but it's common sense to me that you keep business and pleasure separate. And don't we piss off the locals enough without using their girls?

Fraz says he's had girlfriends back home, but nothing long-term. He once told me that the problem is they don't get the job that we do. I had to disagree as there are many guys that have to spend long amounts of time away from their families in order to give them a better life, in all sorts of industries.

One day me and Chris (the lad I met at the interview) were shooting on the range. Fraz stood behind us, and with his phone out recorded an answer-machine message - pretending to be in an enemy contact whilst answering the phone. Chris and I rolled our eyes at each other and just carried on firing. No wonder he couldn't keep a bird, pulling shit like that, pretending to be some big-time action hero. I thought - what if your mum or someone rang you up and heard that answer message? They'd be worried shitless.

One evening, bored of sitting in my room, I decide to drop in on the lads and see if they want to hang out. By this point, my team consists of Fraz, team leader; Chris, and Jon. I try Fraz first. Chris opens the door. Inside I see Fraz sitting on the bed, head in his hands, breathing hard. Jon is standing anxiously over him. Fraz looks up and sees me. His eyes are bloodshot.

'They shot her, Gary!' he says. 'They fucking shot her.' I piece together the story from Fraz and the other lads. That afternoon she had taken a taxi home from work, as was her habit. She'd been dropped off in the usual spot. There, a man, a local, was waiting for her. He'd put four pistol rounds into her chest.

'How did you find out?' I ask.
'Her brother rang me.'
'Is she alive?'
'Yes. She's in the hospital. It's bad. She's fucked.'
I leave Jon and Chris to it with Fraz. I'm not too interested in this shit.

An hour later I come back to check on him. I'm appalled at the state Fraz is in. One of the managers has been called and has had to confiscate Fraz's weapon (we keep them in our rooms ready to stand-to in case of camp attack) and a medic has had to administer a sedative to calm him down. Still, he's talking rubbish, looking at a map and working out a route for a rescue mission.

'You're in, aren't you, Gary?' It's a statement, not a question.
'In on what?' I say with a tone of acerbity.
'I know where the hospital is. I'm busting her out. Gonna bring her to a decent hospital in the Green Zone.'
'What's the point of that?' is my response. 'And anyway, how do you think you'll get her through the checkpoints? And what about the medical care she'll need during the transit? You're fucking crazy mate. You need to pull yourself together.'
I roll my eyes. Fuck this…

Chris agrees to sit with Fraz that night to make sure he doesn't leave the room. We catch eyes on my exit and shake our heads in unison. The next morning, we get word that our team is to report to the central Armorgroup office in the Green Zone. Fraz has calmed down now, but he's told he's not allowed his weapon back. We drive to the Green Zone. Chris, Jon and I sit in the snooker room drinking tea while Fraz is in with the bosses.

'What do you think?' I ask.
'He fucked up, a warning maybe.'

But Chris makes the correct prediction. Chris has switched on to the business side of the industry much quicker than me, and whist I still had my 'Army head' on he grasped the consequences of Fraz's actions. Chris explains that the boss's decisions have to be made in a commercial and business context, and not with a military mindset anymore.

Sure enough, Fraz comes back and tells us dejectedly that he's on the next plane out. Job and girlfriend gone in the blink of an eye. Mental note - listen to Chris.

As much as I see why Fraz fell apart and I'm sorry that his girl's injured, I don't think the bosses can allow losing control to the point you have your weapon taken from you and are given medication.

We're here to do a job. We're not here to be emotive. There's no room for a loose cannon on your team. People like that can get you killed.

A couple of years later, Chris will bump into Fraz at Amman Airport in Jordan. He'll be with a new team, a new company. Chris will say, 'All right?' Fraz will nod but then blank him. Well, he'll hardly want his new colleagues to know *that* about him, now, will he?

Author, Gary Roberts with M21 Assault Rifle and ACOG: Forward Operating Base - Scania

Sierra Leone, West Africa

Reconnaissance (Recce) - Platoon 2002 > In the mountains of Cyprus. Author on back row, second from the left. Brownie is back row - far right.

Author: Southern Iraqi oil fields

Recce Platoon, Iraq

The Iraq / Syria border

Our Iraqi PMC gunners

Basra, Iraq

The gun-truck hotel

Our Iraqi team-gunners before a mission >
True mercenaries

Our Iraqi gunners cover us while we deliver convoy

Our Iraqi PMC crew > Iraq / Jordan border

Our team checking equipment > Abu Ghraib

Author > Baghdad

PMC gun truck being towed after IED blast

III.XXIV

'PSD is where it's at. Not convoys. They're full of cowboys, the conditions are shit and it's much too dangerous. Convoys is a mug's game. You wanna stick with PSD.' That's the consensus among a lot of the PSDs – Fraz included. It's bollocks, if you ask me. PSD work so far is pretty boring. And as for the risk, well, an IED on PSD is the same as an IED on convoys.

The PSD contract is winding down, and we're all wondering what our next contract will be. Frankly, I couldn't give a fuck as long as I'm kept working. But some of the lads are clearly anxious about the potential downturn in lifestyle.
Until now, we've been pretty isolated on our contract. We know of convoys, but I for one haven't seen any convoys in action…until right at the end of the PSD work.

We're coming out of Baghdad on Route Tampa when we come across an Armorgroup call sign that's static. They've been in a contact. I drive up to the rear gun truck. Beneath his helmet I recognise a colleague – Jeff, a Scottish bloke. He's standing at the open door of the truck, talking on his radio. I pull up alongside him.

'What's up?' I ask.
'IED. Our vehicles got through, but one of the Iraqi convoy drivers is dead. Small-arms fire after the IED – he got hit.'
'Fuck. Need anything?'
'No, we got it.'
'We okay to push through?'
'Yeah, mate. Go for it.'

We weave through the stationary trucks. As we pass the truck that's been hit, I see the smattering of bullet holes and blood all over a headrest. Could have been a contractor rather than an Iraqi. Could have been Jeff. Could be me.

A year after arriving in Baghdad, the caviar contract, as we call it, comes to an end. I've got my next contract with AGI (Armorgroup Iraq).

'No doubt we'll be issued our rations when we get there,' the lads joke. We know we can't expect luxury in the next job. Doesn't bother me really. It's nice to have, but fancy accommodation and decent nosh isn't why I do the job. I could get all that doing close protection in the UK.

At the AGI villas I walk up to the ops room to meet one of the bosses, Bill Shaw. It's a bog-standard room with a couple of desks and computers and a big map of Iraq on the wall. Bill's sitting behind a desk in a corner. He's a nice chap – an RMP who climbed the ranks to major, a northern bloke like me. He comes across as easy going.

Four years from now, Bill will hit the headlines when he's arrested in Afghanistan on bribery charges and slung in prison. Got to be one of the least safe places on earth for any ex-military, private-contracting Brit. Surrounded by Taliban prisoners who've sworn to wage jihad against foreigners like Bill, he'll be placed in solitary confinement for his own safety, given that there's a sizeable bounty on his head. The charges are bullshit, and after a living hell he'll be freed. But are you ever free from a fucking horrific experience like that?

Right now, though, he's running the ops at Armorgroup, and by the looks of it he's doing a good job.

'Help yourself to a long [rifle] and a short [pistol], and take some ammo too,' he tells me, gesturing to a pile of kit on the floor by his desk. 'You'll be going to Abu Ghraib. On convoys.' At this I smile.

'Can't give you a full briefing now, I'm afraid. One of the call signs is in a contact. Mike here will show you to your transit accommodation. There'll be a call sign down tomorrow to pick you up.'

I sit on my bed, de-bomb the thirty 5.56x45-millimetre rounds from each of my magazines to ease the springs, and then re-bomb them with twenty-eight rounds each. I also strip and clean the M21 rifle and the Glock 17 pistol issued to me. They're clean, but bone dry. I oil them up and do a functions test. Then I go for a walk around to see who I know.

AGI HQ is based in Baghdad's Red Zone, a compound of six detached villas. The compound is a little street blocked off into a cul-de-sac by tall concrete T-walls. Iraqi guards man the gate at the open end of the street. Once, the villas were homes to wealthy people in Baghdad; now - no doubt having paid off the Iraqi owners handsomely in order to occupy the buildings – the company has turned the houses into a base for operations. The buildings have been adapted to house offices, storehouses, accommodation and even a gym in a cellar.

There's an armoury that holds an impressive stash of weapons, mostly AK variants – some falling to bits, some in good nick. They have an armourer employed to fix the weapons. We don't have easy access – we need the QM's okay and then get let in through an armoured door – but they're pretty generous with giving out weapons and ammo. Another tick in the box for private contracting.

The mechanic's shop is a regular port of call, because of course we drive the vehicles hard, and they're often shot and blown to pieces. If you've got a decent vehicle, you dread it ending up in the shop. Then you're bound to get a shitty replacement. It's a tight cul-de-sac, and you need to be a decent driver to manoeuvre a gun truck around to get it in and out of the shop.

The ops room is the hub of operations. It's a large room, high-tech, windowless. Here, the watch-keeper sits at a desk before a wall of flat screen monitors. One in the corner shows BBC News, but the focus is on maps of Iraq showing coloured dots moving about – the GPS tracking of each call sign's transponder.

When a call sign hits their transponder, the dot starts bleeping to alert the watch-keeper. We're meant to always hit our transponder when in a contact - to provide a tracking point in case a truck goes missing; and so, if necessary, the company can alert another call sign or the Military to come and help. Some of the guys don't bother hitting the transponder button unless it's a really heavy contact. But I hit it for everything. I figure in doing so I'm justifying the job, and that it allows the company to get realistic stats it can give to the LMCC (Logistical Management Convoy Centre) that monitors the situation in Iraq for both military and PMC convoys. Upstairs is the managers' room – five (or so, depending on how many contracts we have at the time) project managers sitting with laptops at desks. The managers – ex-Serjeant Majors, most of them – aren't just desk jockeys, like NHS managers who have no medical training. These guys did tours of Northern Ireland in the seventies, eighties and nineties and are used to managing dozens of soldiers at a time. Most coming into the company do time on the ground and on the roads, so we have to respect for them for that.

Plus, outside the Army you lose the hierarchy - so they're bosses in corporate terms, but it's pretty friendly and we don't feel they're seriously senior. For example, in my battalion there was a bloke called Daz Sweatman who was a Serjeant Major while I was a corporal. Because of the hierarchy and the generation gap, we weren't mates, and I called him 'sir'. But when we cross paths both working for Armorgroup, it's a different story. We sit together at meal times and chat about people we both know. Turns out he's a top bloke. There's a sense of pulling together in this non-military setting. Each job is just a job, and the manager is pretty much on the same wage as us on the ground.

I get pissed off, though, when it's ex 'special' types who are automatically stuck in management posts. Yeah, I know they've got good experience – but doesn't mean if you sit them in front of a computer they can run a business, typing with one finger. In this world of private contracting, it doesn't matter if you're an ex-ninja. If you're a manager, you should manage well.

Some PSD guys live on site, along with the bosses. The rest of us live a thirty-minute drive away up Route Irish in Abu Ghraib, to the north-west of the city. Not the most salubrious of places to live in. Famous for two things: the Abu Ghraib Infant Formula Plant and the prison. The coalition was long-convinced that the factory that claimed to produce powdered milk for babies was a biological weapons production facility, and so they bombed the shit out of it during the Gulf War. Some CNN cameras filmed the destruction. Never found anything there but milk, though. As for the prison, in Saddam's day it was a favoured spot for torturing and executing political opponents (he released them all onto the streets upon imminent invasion). Then the US Army took it over, and some soldiers had a whale of a time abusing and torturing prisoners. Beatings. Strappado hanging. Rape. Sodomy. The media got wind of it. Big scandal.

We're based in Abu Ghraib Warehouse (AGW), from where the convoys set out. It's leased by the logistics company we're working for, and is a big compound with warehouses full of boxes, a truck-yard packed with lorries, a couple of offices for logistical managers and our accommodation. We get the top floor; the LNs (Iraqis) live below us.

It's no luxury hotel, but it does. Mine is a stark, bare box of a room. At least it has a decent single bed; the LNs on the floor below are crammed into bunk beds. Because I share the room I use the cheap wardrobes to separate the room into two halves so I get a little privacy. My roommate changes regularly, depending on who's on leave, who's out on a mission, who's quit.

Yes there are quitters. It's easy enough to get out. You just cite the danger or the workload or the conditions. If it's nothing personal, you see out your rotation first. Some give up and go home. One guy I know gave it up to work as a park ranger back in Yorkshire. Others move to other companies. It's pretty fluid, and one thing you don't want is a whinger on your team. Get on with it or fuck off. There's a TV room, but I don't use it much. The gym is the hub for us ex-pats. There's a culture of weight-training and fitness. It's where we catch up as we do our sets. We talk about the contract, sport, lads' shit. Not our personal lives much. Training keeps the adrenaline up; good for missions. Some take it seriously, though, and there are some big bastards there you wouldn't want to antagonize.

The AGW gym is nothing to write home about – just functional weights. Nothing like what you find in the American FOBs. They've got state-of-the-art equipment; some bases even have full basketball courts, running tracks with bleachers and football fields like a college campus back home. Other than the gym, the range is a place you bump into the lads and catch up. It's nothing like what you get in the Army, just a mound of soil and sand with a backstop rock and a wooden target – a stick with a panel on it; target's as low-key as a sheet of A4 paper with a dot drawn on it.

There's good-natured rivalry over our shooting skills, money changing hands between nationalities. The South Africans I meet, in particular, are good shots. We take the piss: 'Well you guys have gotta be good shots. Back home, if you don't kill what you shoot, you don't eat that day right?'

You rock up and do your thing with the Glock and the rifle. Endless supply of ammo. Snap shooting. Automatic and single shots. There are no fusty Army-style rules here, just common sense.

The cookhouse is the other place we come together – well, the ex-pats; the LNs don't come in here. It's run by an Indian catering company. They cook what they think Westerners want to eat – American-style grilled cheese sandwiches, burgers. It's all right. Big contrast to a meal out at TGI Friday's back home. At least there's fruit and veg – there's only so much meat and cheese and bread the body can handle.

Most of the guys supplement what they get at AGW in any case with food and drink they've bought offsite at FOB shops. Protein shakes are particularly popular. Not booze, though. It's banned at AGW – though we can get our hands on it if we want. In fact, in Camp Victory, an American base, there's an off-licence run by Iraqis. Despite the fact that American soldiers aren't allowed to drink. Go figure.

III.XXV

The next morning I'm heading out for Abu Ghraib.
'You new in country?' asks the guy driving me.
Cheeky cunt, I think – I'll fucking interview *you*, mate.
'No.'
'Contacts?'
It's a loaded question.
'A few. Plenty out here in my Army days too.'
He nods. I've passed the test.

To be fair, I'm the same. Never assume someone who's ex-military has seen action. Plenty big up being in Iraq, but in reality they're some fat cunt who was on some safe base doing traffic duty or sitting in a storeroom drinking coffee and stacking blankets. It's usually the people who shout the loudest who've got the least to shout about.

Day one on the new contract gives me a feel of what's to come. After all these quiet months, I get whacked on my first mission.

I'm attached to a team led by Kiwi Steve. We pick up our gun trucks and head to where the cargo trucks are waiting. They've been packed by the logistics company. I don't ask what we're transporting; it makes no difference to me.

The team leader briefs the LN truck drivers through an interpreter: ninety kilometres per hour, follow us, heads down, don't shit yourself and fuck off if something goes down.

Most of the LNs in our security teams speak some broken English; for those who don't there's a translator – nothing formal, just a bloke who speaks better English than the rest. The LNs should know it all anyway. They've come through more contacts than we have. But you've got to keep drilling it into them because they can be lazy and their reactions sometimes are beyond stupid.

It's new for me to be working with LNs. On PSD, we were all ex-pats. At this point, I'm pretty mistrustful of them, though later I'll come to respect them.

Well, some of them, sort of.

Steve goes in the front vehicle; I'm in the second with a driver and two top-cover gunners. I prefer being in the front vehicle, with a clear view of the road ahead and an eye on the map – geeky, I know, but I love maps – but I'm happy commanding the second truck that's leading the ten convoy trucks behind.
We're on the chicken run, heading north through al Mashada, near to where I recently came across Jeff's convoy with its dead LN driver, when the IED goes off. Right by my truck door.

The first I know about it is an almighty bang, and then in a split-second there's smoke and dust everywhere – it's even coming through the vents in the vehicle. 'Contact right! IED!' I say into the radio. My voice sounds muffled; the explosion has deafened my right ear.

I look at my driver. The truck is rocking from side to side, and he's fighting the wheel, trying to counteract the drag. The tyres must be knackered.

'Drive!' I order. Okay, not overly helpful, but he knows what I mean: 'I don't give a fuck, mate, how much of a struggle it is, keep hold of that wheel, keep your foot on the accelerator and get us the fuck away from here.'

By now we're clearing the smoke. Steve comes on the radio: 'Gary? You alright?'
'Steve, we have to stop and sort the wheels,' I say.
'Okay, but keep going for as long as you can.'
It's some feat of driving that the LN gets us a few hundred metres from the explosion site before conceding defeat and stopping.

We get out. I scan the surroundings carefully. Tree lines. Fields. The odd house. No one in sight. Still, I keep my rifle up, ready, as I inspect the damage. It's beyond a tyre change; the wheels are buckled and mangled. We'll need to replace all four wheels in the middle of a hot zone.

On board my truck are two spare wheels. Steve tells the other members of the team to bring a wheel over too. They do so, rolling their wheels up the length of the convoy.

Half a minute into the wheel change I'm looking at Steve, leaning against his truck ahead, when out of nowhere I see him tense, raise his rifle and fire a long burst on automatic.

I step to the back of the truck and kneel down, to use it as cover, crouch and peer out in the direction Steve's firing. I see them: guys moving up a tree line. Now they're returning fire.

I raise my rifle and fire half a magazine, one shot at a time – my British Army training, intent on making each round count and so saving ammo, clicks in automatically. With my ACOG zeroed optical sight, I focus on the centre of the body mass, the sternum area, for maximum lethal effect
.

The air around me erupts with noise as firing pins start hitting percussion caps and the LNs and ex-pats lay down a wall of fire at the enemy, PKMs, AKs, RPKs, and M21s all firing in discord. I'm the only one firing on single shot.

I'm acutely aware of the loud crack of air displacement as enemy rounds go slightly high and over our heads. They're flapping. Good.

The first man goes down, and then the next. I track my crosshairs ahead of them, let the target come to my point of aim. I've always been an ambush method kind of shooter - aim where the targets are about to be. It's accurate, I can maintain a stable firing position without having to twist my torso as I track them. I rake another guy with rapid single shots.

Soon, there are men lying dead, maybe half a dozen, probably more - some my kills, some others'. No Hollywood death dances here, just a quiet, sad crumpling to the ground. Their light-blue Iraqi Police shirts make the exit wounds easy to spot: dark-red holes and ripped clothing on their backs. I know from my Basra experience that the entry wounds on their fronts are just dots, invisible at this distance, and that our high-velocity rounds have mutilated their insides, ripping their bodies open upon exit.

I change my magazine for a full one, reload, and rack the first round. My mouth is dry with the taste of cordite from the spent bullet cases.

I break and shout to the LNs, 'Get the fuck on with it – get those fucking wheels changed now!'

It's a redundant instruction. They're working at lightning speed, especially the guys on the insurgents' side of the truck who have their backs to the tree line from where the small-arms fire is coming. No doubt they'd like to just get out, get to safety, and ditch the vehicle. But it's more than our jobs are worth. These armoured trucks are expensive, and the company wants them back. In fact, they're known for radioing a call sign that's hit their transponder to notify the ops room of a contact just to check that the vehicles (not the team) are okay. So come back a vehicle down and you'd better be able to justify it.

Ten minutes after the explosion, we get the hell out of there. I crack open a large bottle of water and throw half of it down my neck, then hand it to my driver, who does the same.

On the way back to Abu Ghraib my vehicle dies a slow death. A bullet has got into the engine and knackered it. I sit in the useless vehicle with my driver and gunners as another gun truck tows us back.

'So, your first convoy, Gary. What d'ya think, bro'? Too hot to handle?' Kiwi Steve asks on the radio as we drive back to the Abu Ghraib compound.

'Nah,' I reply. 'I don't give a fuck.'

Back in my room that night, my ear, the one that was nearest the explosion, is ringing. Can't hear a fucking thing through it. Have to turn my head to the good ear to listen. I shove my finger in it and it comes out encrusted with dried blood. Shrug my shoulders. Go to bed.

Well, what else am I to do? I'm hardly going to go bleating to a manager asking for medical support. That would mean gathering men up for a mission to drive me to a medical centre on a US base. Like I'll risk a team of men for a dodgy ear. I can just imagine the doctors' faces at the medical centre, used to dealing with gruesome, pulverised-flesh-and-bones injuries, the kind that mean amputation and plastic surgery and sending men home in bits or in body bags, when confronted with me and my gungy ear…

PART IV

"Certainly, there is no hunting like the hunting of man, and those who have hunted armed men long enough and liked it, never really care for anything else thereafter."

Ernest Hemingway

IV.XXVI

A week after the man with no legs, no arms, and no face, I'm on the way back to Baghdad from a mission to Fallujah. Marc, team leader, is in the second vehicle, with Greg upfront; Mick and I are bringing up the rear of the convoy. Our regular four-man team. The team members change a lot now; since the company changed to six-vehicle manoeuvres up north, the teams have been more fluid.

We're heading towards Baghdad along Route Mobile - a route that bisects Ramadi and Fallujah. It's hot as fuck here, so there's a big American presence. Lots of static call signs. Up on a bridge ahead we see an American tank, an Abrahams. Greg passes under, and then it's Marc's turn.

The explosion is so big it reverberates through my truck, eleven vehicles back in the convoy.

Greg, in the first vehicle, is on the radio at once. 'Marc, you okay? Marc, you okay?' not quite a contact report but I'll take it as one.
He's got zero visibility as he speeds through the smoke caused by the IED.
There's no reply.

'Marc, radio-check?'
In front the lorries are spreading out across the highway as the Iraqi drivers try to look at what's happened.

'Push through,' I tell my driver. He blares the horn and weaves around the lorries, up to the front. Just as I set eyes on the lead vehicle, battered but still barrelling along, Marc comes on the radio.

'I'm okay. Radio's fucked. I'm using the personal handheld. Got no breaks. Can't control the truck. Someone needs to get in front and slow us down.'

At my instruction my driver puts his foot down and we overtake Marc's truck. It's a mess – holes in the sides, wheels buckled. We pull in front and match the speed until a jolt tells me we're bumper to bumper.

'Brake,' I tell the driver. '*Slowly*, now.'

Under my guidance, he brakes carefully, trying to come to a slow and controlled halt. Essential, or the dim-witted Iraqi drivers behind will plough into the back of us and each other in a massive pile-up. Gradually, we move away from the pre-laid ambush, the kill zone.

Once we're stopped, a good mile beyond the IED site, I get out. Greg and Mick close the road front and rear to give us space to work – parking horizontally across the carriageway to block off the traffic at the front, the LNs in the buckets training their weapons on the civilian traffic. Marc is out of the wrecked vehicle.

'Y'alright?' I ask.
'Yep.'
'What was it?'
'Plastic sack beside the road. Too late to miss it once I saw it.'
'Cunts. Some balls they've got, placing one right under an American tank.'
We set to work organising the LNs to change the wheels on the knackered vehicle so we can tow it back to Abu Ghraib.
'You, get the jack.'
'You, get the wheel spanner.'
What is it with insurgents and wheel changes?
Then the shooting starts.
'Contact right, small arms!' I shout.

I get down in an irrigation ditch at the side of the road and start shooting from the kneeling position. Marc's hard at it from behind his engine block. The LNs have debussed and brought the machine guns with them, and they're firing them out now to the tree line where the insurgents are hiding.

The enemy fire slows then ceases.

A couple of cars appear in my peripheral vision. Civilian vehicles. Impatient with waiting at our roadblock, they're trying to box round by driving across the farmland between the trees and the road, right between us and the enemy. Fucking incredulous.

Firing again. Our side. I swing round to see one of the LNs – a heavy guy called Saif, new to the job – has got jittery and is shooting desperately.

I'm up on my feet, looking out at the civilian cars. One is shot up and is rolling to a stop. I'm too far away to see clearly, but I think I see the silhouette of the driver. No movement. Dead, no doubt. It's his own fucking fault for not staying back. Price he pays for hurrying to do whatever he was doing that afternoon.
'Hold fire! Fucking stop!'

I rush to the LN. He's shaking, sweating. I take his AK and put the safety catch on.

'Calm down, mate.'

'Americans coming to help? Americans coming to help?' he pleads, wild-eyed.

'No, mate,' I say.

He's clearly in shock, so I sit him in the vehicle and give him a bottle of water to drink.

With new wheels in place, we quickly hook Marc's vehicle up to mine. I volunteer to drive back so Marc can still command from the good gun truck. Both Marc's driver and mine look pretty shaken so they go in the towed one.

We head off. I don't look back at the car that contains the dead man our trigger-happy gunner has taken down. Fuck him.

IV.XXVII

Are most of us are in it for the money? Would we do the job if we could earn the same working in McDonald's? Or in the Army, for that matter. We're paid in US dollars, and there's a culture of keeping an eye on the currency exchange, watching Sky News. We cheer at a weak pound. Some contractors set up dollar accounts abroad; it's all about getting the most out of the pay. We don't pay tax; in the UK, the law says it's tax-free income if you're out of the country for at least ninety days a year.

What it adds up to is a tidy wage packet: I'm earning more than a Colonel in the Army. Some of the blokes get carried away. Spunk it all on the roulette at Las Vegas or houses fit for footballers. Worse are the stories you hear about gold-diggers who empty contractors' accounts while they're in Iraq, having a merry old time with their girlfriends and glamming up themselves, their families, their houses, their poodles, while their men are out of the way. Cheating too, while they can.

There's not much point taking the risks to make the money if you don't make the money work for you. I put a load of it into long-term investments. Properties. Sheffield's full of students and the rental market is strong. Beyond that, I have the odd treat now and again.

I have a Pretty Woman moment in a car showroom in Sheffield. I strut in wearing jeans and a t-shirt, confident, ready to buy a car. I've never bought a brand-new one before, but I've got the cash and figure, why not? A bloke in an expensive suit – starchy shirt, fat cufflinks, pointy shoes, the works – edges over to me.

'Um. Can I help you, sir?'

He looks like the word 'sir' sticks in his throat. I look around. I have an idea of what I want. All these sports cars are looking fucking great to me, though. There are no price tags. How are you meant to know what they cost? I point to one. Black. Low to the ground.

'That one. I'd like a test drive.'

He looks like he wants to say something, but I hold eye contact, daring him, and he backs away.

'Yes. Good choice. I'll get the keys.'

Ten minutes later I'm gunning it through Sheffield city centre. Being a total cock about it. I practise some racing starts, rev it up to four-thousand rpm and drop the clutch so aggressively the old girl in the next car stalls at the lights while I wheel-screech away.

Back at the showroom, the salesman looks relieved to see me. Like I'm going to nick it. It's kind of obvious amid the Ford Fiestas and Citroën Picassos in the city. Plus, it'll be GPS tracked.

'I'll take it,' I tell him.

He looks delighted. 'When would you like it? I believe we can order it in for next month...'

'No, I'll have it by the weekend.'

He blusters and dithers for a while, but finally, realising I'm serious, decides that's possible. We sit in his little box of an office at the back of the showroom while he types my details diligently into his computer.

'Job?'
'Security.'
He blinks. Scrolls through the list of job sectors on his screen for the closest match.
'Security guard? Will that do?'
'Go on then.'
'Super. Now, do you want finance, a loan?'

He looks carefully at me. I think he expects me to be stitching him up.
'No, just stick it on the visa.'

The moment the authorisation notice flicks up on his computer screen he visibly relaxes. Now I am a valued customer and he wants to shake my hand.

When I pick the car up, I take it for a long drive out into the Peak District. It's a beautiful day, and as I roar around the windy roads, the views are spectacular, a patchwork of tall trees and green hills and rocky crags and dry-stone walls. I drive down to Ladybower, where 617 Squadron trained in their specially adapted Lancaster bombers for the Dambuster raid on the Ruhr dams in May 1943. It's a good day to be in England.

Still, two days later I've swapped my sports car for a gun truck, oak trees for palm trees, and English sunshine for a desert sandstorm.

IV.XXVIII

Greg and Marc are on leave, so I'm with Mick and a couple of other guys – Bob, and another Mark. This time, I'm in the lead car, scanning ahead for threats. We're heading to an FOB east of Baghdad for a drop-off. None of us have been out there before and neither has anyone else we can find; it's in the middle of nowhere judging by the falcon-view (the electronic mapping on our laptops), so we've no recce of the route, just map recces; we're going in blind.

The first contact is small-arms fire on Route Irish, leading away from Baghdad Airport, just before the flyovers heading towards Green Zone. Route Irish is a favourite spot for insurgents. With its fences, blast walls and Jersey barriers, even if the military stop and counterattack, it's hard to get at them. Plus, there are plenty of escape routes out for them, with dense housing estates either in or around the area.

We're passing a huge building. Well, if you can call it that – it's abandoned, a skeleton really. No proper walls or windows. I've passed it a hundred times and never had anything from there. Today, though, insurgents have had bright idea of using it as a prime position for firing down on us.

There are a couple of them laying down heavy automatic fire. Their range is out and they miss us, bar the odd bullet hole in the vehicles. Shooting down (or up) is different to shooting level. It requires practice, and you have to adjust the weapon for the angle and range. Take any Iraqi on weapons training and he'll tell you he's a weapons expert. Ask him to show you how to adjust an AK sight and he won't have a clue.

We're not fazed by the attack. It's nothing we can't handle. And we've decent LNs on this mission – war-experienced. They rat-tat-tat right back and we roll under a flyover. There's lots of civilian traffic all bunched up. We're pretty safe here; the bridge affords a little protection. But the gunners have got all riled up in the contact and are now controlling traffic aggressively. It makes for an easier passage, though, for the drivers and commanders. As each vehicle leaves the contact zone, the radio crackles with a 'Clear' and Mick acknowledges with a double tap on his radio presell, and we roll on.

We hit Route Predators in south Baghdad and then Route Predators hits us. The IED goes off right by Mark's vehicle – the third gun truck, bringing up the rear of the convoy. Must have been small, as I hadn't seen it when scanning the road from up front, and it did minimal damage to Mark's windows. Bad guy watching us out there, nearby. Remote detonation.

Mark comes on the radio. 'Contact right. IED.'

I expect small-arms fire to follow the explosion, the usual format for a contact. I tell the driver to increase the speed.

'Easy, easy, mate,' I tell him as he instinctively stamps on the accelerator.

Calmly, slowly. A lot of guys put the pedal to the floor when in a contact, but you've got to keep control of the Iraqi drivers. As much as I'm watching the contact situation and thinking operationally, I have to keep one eye on the driver to make sure he doesn't do anything stupid. If he puts his foot down and lands me in a ditch, I'm dead.

Mick radios Mark. 'You all right?'
'Yes. It's made a fuckin' mess of my window and door, though.'
'Vehicle okay?'
'Yes. Push on.'

We map-read our way out of east Baghdad and head for Route Detroit where we can pick up speed. It's a road we've never been down before; we usually go to the main camps, and no one's done any drop-offs at that end of the country yet. It's a really long road, with rural land around – green fields (sallow green, not the rich green of the hills around Yorkshire). The road's in a shit state – a single carriageway like a country lane. No wonder it's quiet here in the back of beyond. I'd be happier in Baghdad quite frankly. We're a single convoy on an empty road in the middle of nowhere – an easy target. I'm ready for it. But the rest of the journey is uneventful, and we arrive at the FOB intact.

We inspect the vehicles. Some damage from bullets. But it's Mark's window that's the shock. The IED's created a neat circle of damage right by Mark's head. The window's cracked and splintered, but the armoured glass means it's still solid.

Any compromise in that glass and it would have been Mark's head taking the force of the blast.

'Fuck,' we chorus. Nothing else to say. We're not going to stand about and get melodramatic and girly with 'Oh my God, you could have died!' shit. Inside, we head to the intelligence cell. You never know what kind of reception you'll get from the Americans. Some don't like us, and won't go out of their way to help. Most of them, though, are decent enough. They're interested in private contractors; you can see the cogs turning in their heads. The most common question I get is, 'How much money are you on?' The expression on their faces when I tell them is priceless. In this int-cell we're greeted by a friendly officer who offers us a coffee.

'Cheers, mate.'
'How d'ya come in?'
'Route Detroit.'
'Jeez, maann, you came up that road?' He looks at us like we've just told him we've gang-banged his mum.
'We got lucky.'
'Doesn't surprise me, Coalition traffic is so sparse that way. It's so hot even our guys don't use that road.'

Bit late for the heads-up, I think. We'd taken Detroit to avoid Route Dover – we'd been avoiding it as far as possible since Steve Gilchrist was killed by the EFP. The officer takes us through the map of the area. 'Steer well clear of this road. Avoid that one. Go round so you miss that. I wouldn't go on that one without Apaches and tanks for cover...'

Clued up, we thank the guy and head to our accommodation for the night. I've got my usual kit with me – gym kit, sleeping bag, wash stuff, book (it's Johnny Nelson's autobiography this month) – so I'm set for an overnighter. We ex-pats get a decent kip in the base; the LNs, meanwhile, make do sleeping in the cabs of the trucks. The Americans don't want Iraqis in the camps.

I get their unease. We trust the LNs, but only to a point. That's why every morning we confiscate their mobile phones, so they can't tip anyone off about the convoy's movements.

161

I bring them takeaways I've had plated up in the DFAC. No pork. The LNs turn up at the start of every convoy with a carrier bag of food, but I figure a hot meal trumps a pack-up. Plus, they sometimes bring me a falafel or two.

'Got you salads, fat boys,' I tell them as I hand out the containers. 'Putting you on a diet.'

The Iraqis laugh. Arabs like to carry some weight. Wear it with pride. Shows they've got enough money to eat well.

'Be kitted up and ready to go at five. I'll be there at five thirty, and we roll at six,' I say. 'Don't be shagging each other past ten. Get your heads down and get a good sleep.'

They smile at me and chorus, 'Yes, Mr Gary.'

I like a bit of banter. Builds rapport. And respect. A lot of contractors throw their weight about and treat LNs like shit, shouting at them, slapping them, and swearing at them in an aggressive way. Not the way to get the best out of people. I do swear, mind. But it's not as an insult. Its part of the language on the job – of the Army, and of private contracting. It's a common language. Crosses the divide of boss/employee, and of nationalities too. Within a few months an LN is dropping 'fucking' in casually mid-sentence. Sometimes I hear it amid a torrent of Arabic. That makes me laugh. It sounds crass to outsiders, though. I recall Nikki's shocked expression one time I was home on leave and answered the phone to a contractor mate. I slipped at once into the parlance – fuck, fuck, and fuck. Must have sounded harsh. Now, I do my best to tone it down back in Sheffield.

The next morning we're heading back to Baghdad, having used the officer's guidance to pick what's hopefully a safer route.

We're driving through a little village, ugly concrete buildings to each side of the road. Through the murky rain I see a checkpoint coming up – typical jersey barriers, T-walls, two guards and an improvised hut they spend all day sleeping in.

'Mick, slow, slow. Checkpoint ahead,' I radio.

I notice a group of kids standing back from the checkpoint. They turn and run towards some houses. Then the guards at the checkpoint – Iraqi Police – leg it too. Bastards, I think.

'Guys, stand by,' I radio. 'We're gonna get it.'
Instantly, we're under fire – heavy small arms from the left.
'Push through,' Mick commands.

We do so, the LNs in the bucket putting down a wall of fire.
As we speed through the village I see, through the grey rain, muzzle flashes in the window of a house. It's a ruin, a big open space inside, and the blokes in there are fucking pounding us. Concrete's getting spat up randomly from the blast walls beside us.

A few miles down the road, we're ambushed again.
And then a few miles on, we're ambushed *again*.
And then a few miles on, we're ambushed **again**.

We keep rolling on while the LNs burn through magazines and link. We're back in Baghdad, nearly at the base, when we meet the final ambush for the day. We're on a flyover going over a housing estate when I hear the rat-tat-tat of PKM machine-gun fire. I look to the left. Fucking idiot insurgents right near us are firing from low ground up at us and we're on a bridge with a concrete wall – like they've got a chance of getting a decent hit. Our top gunners are in the perfect tactical position to gun them down.

As we pull through I nudge the driver and say, 'Check the gunners.' He knows what I mean: check they're okay and they got the bastards.

'Got them, Mr Gary,' the driver reports back.

I'm sceptical. Iraqi gunners are like schoolboys. Ask one how many enemy he got and he'll reply, 'I got fifty.' Yeah right – in a contact that lasted two minutes; they've only got fifty-round belts and it takes them an age to change them! Ask him how many women he has and he'll tell you, 'Six wives, no problem.'

163

I laugh at the response, and my driver laughs back.

Back at AGW, we debus.

The LNs are joking and smiling, relieved to be back. All they care about is getting their money, staying alive, and eating nonstop. They don't think big picture. They don't care who lives and dies beyond their immediate relatives and friends. 'Seven heavy contacts,' says Mick.

He doesn't have to say any more. I know what he means: What the fuck?
Still, the point is that we've rolled through all seven. It's not that the insurgents aren't trying hard to take us out; it's that in some areas they're opportunists, not planners. When their mate on a checkpoint calls to say white-eyes are en-route, they haven't long to set up. And they're shambolic, lacking the military training of our guys. They shoot first, think later. I mean, they're shooting at armoured vehicles with two gunners in the bucket, which should be easy for them, but they often make it hard on themselves with poor timing and planning.

'If it were me,' I say to Mick, 'I'd do it properly. Take out the front and rear trucks so its boxed in, then shoot up the convoys, commanders first.'

He agrees; any one of us guys could do a better job than the insurgents. For starters, I wouldn't miss when I shot at them. I wouldn't spray and pray. And I wouldn't position myself alongside a flyover firing up. Yeah, we'd do it better. Good job we're on this side, then.

The next day, another Armorgroup call sign is sent to the same FOB. They get in a hell of a contact, and end up with vehicles immobilised. Forced to abandon their vehicles, they storm a nearby building, defending it from the rooftop. The American Quick Reaction Force – Apaches and tanks – is called in to help them in the ensuing firefight and they all survive to tell the story.

Perhaps the bad guys aren't to be dismissed so lightly after all...

IV.XXIX

I'm on Route Mobile with a mixed team, heading back to AGW. No convoy, just four gun trucks. I'm team leader, in the second vehicle. The guy at the front comes on the radio. 'Stop, stop. Something in road.'

We all come to a stop.

'Don't know what it is,' he tells us. 'Looks off.'
'Turn around and cut across to the other carriageway,' I instruct.

There are gaps in the central reservation behind us we can use to cross over. Iraqi roads. Doesn't matter which side you drive on. Imagine doing that on the M1. He turns, and passes me. As my vehicle turns, I scan the road for the object that's worried him.

An animal of some sort. I take my optical sight off the weapon bracket for a better look. Through the times-four magnification I see it: a dog. In the middle of the road. Brown, non-descript. But its limbs are bent at weird angles. It looks unnatural.

Iraqis don't keep dogs as pets. They think they're unclean. But there are many wild dogs around. Then, in a moment, the dog is no longer there. Because some fucking insurgent spying on us from the scrubland around has hit a button and blown it up. A sharp, short bang. Smoke. And then a black, star-shaped scorch mark on the tarmac where Rover once lay.

'Fucking IED,' I radio. 'Can anyone see the trigger point?'
I'd like to find the cunt who's used a fucking dead dog to try to kill us.
I slow my driver down to scan around, but there's no sign of a bad guy.
Back in AGW, we discuss the idiocy of Iraqi insurgents.
'A fucking dog. Like we're just going to assume that's roadkill and drive right over it.'
'You'd at least put it in a neutral position on the side of the road. Stuck out like a sore thumb in the middle.'
'You'd at least fucking angle its limbs right. No wonder its legs were stuck up like

165

that. Fucking nothing left inside it but explosives.'
'Fucking Iraqis.'
'Need to go back to fucking bomb school.'
'Probably flunked it.'
'Bomb school? Like you can fail it! Like they say, "Nah, you aren't cut out to be an insurgent."'

It's a fair point. Armed forces and private contractors - there's a baseline. Even the shittest are reasonably trained at what they do. Not so the insurgents. Some of them probably get no training beyond which way to point an AK.

Put that way, doesn't seem like a fair fight. But then, who's playing fair?

Author, Gary Roberts > Al Muthana, Baghdad

Enemy contact using roadside IED > Al Baji

Roadside IED & small arms attack > Al Mosul

Roadside IED > Route Tampa, Northern Iraq

Convoy truck roadside IED > Baji bypass

US Army Hummer burning > North of Tikrit

Roadside IED (PSD) Chris is driving, I am rear gunner > Route Sonics, Baghdad

One of our sister teams burns out an unsalvageable gun truck after an enemy contact

PMC convoy waits while US Army conduct a controlled explosion > East of Baghdad

Our gunners 'pop' smoke during an insurgent ambush > Baghdad

Our gunners get busy on Route Tampa

US Army cass-evac a PMC > South of Mosul

Our PMC leaving Baghdad

With Alawi > FOB Scania, Route Tampa

With John > FOB Scania, Route Tampa

PSD team (Fraz is second from right) > Baghdad

IV.XXX

Switch on the news in the Western world and you'll hear all about insurgents in Baghdad, Mosul, Fallujah – everyone knows these places are war zones. But you won't hear about a tiny little rural village called Al Mashada. And yet that's where we routinely come into contact with the enemy.

We often pass through, and driving through the village without getting shot at is a rare occurrence. What sticks in the throat is that most of the gunfire comes from the police station or a tree line right next to the station.

One day one of the lads shoots up some insurgents and goes over to check they're dead. He shows me pictures he's taken on his mobile phone. Dead men lying like ragdolls in the dust, police badges pulled out from under their clothes and visible for the camera.

Your average insurgent isn't some crazy, fanatical gang member. He's just a normal bloke. And he may well work in the Iraqi Army or the police force. They've got balls, you've got to give them that. They'll often lay IEDs and shoot at us right by American call signs. It's a middle finger up to the Americans. And it creates confusion – us shooting, them shooting, Americans shooting.

The only people we can trust out here are our own guys and the Americans. Doesn't mean we always want to do things the American way, though.

Near Mashada I'm in the rear vehicle of a convoy when Marc radios to say there's a static American call sign ahead. We halt, and wait.

We're used to the Americans closing roads. It's usually because they've found an IED and the engineers are blowing it up. Sometimes, if you're some distance from a FOB or an alternate route, you're waiting for hours for the bomb disposal guys to arrive. You've no choice but to wait. It's not like you can go off-road with the convoy and box round. But the waiting around is tense, and you feel like a sitting duck.

If we see something that's off ourselves, we're not always so patient. Once I was out on a mission to Fallujah when Marc in the front gun truck saw something dodgy in the road ahead – an old artillery or mortar shell. He called us to a halt; IED alert. We wait, scanning around, while he surveyed the object through his optical sight. Finally, he got out of his vehicle and put two rounds into it to blow it off the road. We waited. Nothing. We drove past. Back at base in time for tea. No way would that have happened if we'd radioed the ops room, who'd have notified the EOD (Explosive Ordinance Disposal team) to come out.

Now, stuck behind the US call sign, I spot in the wing mirror two Hummers approaching from behind. Iraqi Army. They should keep their distance but they don't – they sandwich us in.

I hear gunfire. There's one hell of a firefight going on behind us somewhere. Marc comes on the radio. It's another Armorgroup call sign behind us being ambushed.

I can't turn around and drive back; the bastards behind are blocking the road. So I jump out of the vehicle with a SAW Machine gun, tell the LN gunners to come with me and sprint down the road towards the fight. As I pass the Iraqi Army, I eyeball them. They're on their mobiles – no doubt to their comrades who are shooting the shit out of my colleagues. They do nothing; they just calmly watch us we run past.

After a couple of hundred metres the shooting stops and Scouse Lee's convoy comes into view – they've rolled through the ambush. He slows to a halt when he sees me.

'Jesus – look at you. Ready for war.'

I suppose I must look a sight, standing with my light machine gun in the middle of the road, sweating and furious.

'I'll fucking kill them,' I say, grinning.

I could. Could do an about turn, stride back to the Iraqi Hummers and take the crooked officers out, one by one. It's what they'd do, if they had the chance. It's no more than they deserve.

But the Rules of Force aren't hot on revenge killings. And we're stuck here until the Americans clear the road ahead. Could be an hour or more still until we're clear. I don't want to create a mess then have the Americans stick their noses in. Say, 'What the fuck's this?'

You don't know quite what you'll get with an American. They're confused about why they're here. Some say world protection. Some, war on Saddam. Some, revenge for 9/11. Some, Christians against Muslims. And some, reconstructing Iraq.

So you get gung-ho soldiers. And you get do-gooding ones who are obsessed with following rules.

I return to my vehicle, past the Iraqis I'm just itching to hammer, and wait until I can move my convoy the hell away from the traitors at my back.

IV.XXXI

One of the best things about being a contractor is the time off. I've four weeks off, back in the UK, and Nikki's in the mood to get away. So, on a whim, I book us a cruise around the Greek islands.

Three weeks of sitting about on the deck of a swanky cruise liner, sunning myself. Bit pointless, really, soaking up the sun. I get enough of it in Iraq, and have permanently tanned skin. I'm hardly going to get back to Iraq and have all the lads crowd round going, 'Oo, check you and your tan. Been anywhere nice?' To be honest, a holiday for me is just being home. Going for an hour's run around the city streets. Mountain biking in the Peaks. Watching a match on a decent-sized telly. Listening to TalkSPORT. Being on a cruise, well, it's travelling. Being abroad. Exotic food and sights hold no attraction for me; see enough of them through work.

But for Nikki, stuck in Sheffield all the time and alone a lot while I'm away, it's a break. She needs it. She's got a bun in the oven.

Now that's a whole new territory for me. I picture a little boy – taking him to Bramall Lane, kicking a ball around with him in the park. Will he be interested in what I do? Will we buy him toy soldiers and a tank and a gun?

I'd be proud enough for him to follow in my footsteps. Armed forces first. Then, if he wanted, going private. There are fathers and sons out in Iraq on the circuit. Still, I'd only encourage it if he wanted it. It would be up to him.

We tour the waters around the islands – hundreds of them – and I have to agree with Nikki: they're not bad on the eye. All turquoise waters and cypress trees and ancient buildings. We disembark in Greece. Go to the Acropolis in Athens. All that history. It survived so many wars. Was once a military garrison, in fact. The Parthenon temple, built 447–438 BC, was torn up by Venetian artillery fire in 1687. Ottomans were using it as a gunpowder store. Now there's respect for historical monuments for you. Wherever you go, there's history of conflict.

I try to be Sheffield Gary. Not scanning the surroundings for threats. Not peppering conversation with the F word. I work my way through a stack of books. There's some coming through now written by various contractors in Iraq from various countries. I read them to see whether they're true to life; whether they've blagged; whether I recognise anyone in the stories – contracting's a small world.

After a week, I'm counting the days till I'll be back in Iraq. I'm ready. When I sit my legs jiggle, itching to be on the move.

On the last night, we share a table in the restaurant with another couple. Civil servant and a teacher. Nice. Tweed. Shockable. He asks me what I do and I tell him. The PG-version.

'Oh my!' The teacher has her hand to her mouth like I've told her I'm a guard at Broadmoor. 'Is it dangerous?'

I look at Nikki sitting next to me.

'Nah,' I say. 'Not at all.'

IV.XXXII

Paul McGuigan, that bloke who showed me the gym way back when I was new to PSDing? He's dead, along with another Armorgroup colleague, Darren Hoare.

Paul, thirty-seven, a former Royal Marine from the Scottish Borders, was shot twice in the chest and through the mouth. He never got to meet his daughter. Hoare, also thirty-seven, an ex-airman, was shot through the temple at close range. He left three kids.

The man with the gun? An Armorgroup contractor. Danny Fitzsimons. A mate calls me. 'Paul McGuigan's dead. And another guy, Darren Hoare.'

'Fuck. How?' I'm thinking contact. EFP.
'Shot.'
'Fucking insurgents.'
'No, mate. A contractor.'
'You what?'
'That Danny Fitzsimons from UQ.'
'Who?'

I have to think for a moment, then it clicks. I met him a few times. Way back. He was working with a team of guys I know, and one evening we found ourselves in the same room, sitting about, chatting. Danny was next to me. We were comparing notes on chicks back home. He showed me a photo of a girl on his phone, told me he met her on the internet.

'Alright, mate,' I said sceptically. She looked like a Barbie doll.

It was a passing encounter; there's no common ground to be mates. We exchanged the odd courtesy now and then when our paths crossed, dining halls and gyms, but I didn't think much of him, and I certainly didn't see a glimmer of what he'd become.

As Danny later tells it, Paul and Darren burst into his room and gave him a good kicking, then Paul threatened to kill him. Danny claims he shot the two men in self-defence.

It's a story that doesn't add up. As Paul's fiancée put it in an interview with the Daily Mail:

Paul had two gunshot wounds to his chest that were not fired at close range, and weren't the fatal shots. As Paul fell to his knees, a gun was put in his mouth and fired, severing his spinal cord and killing him. Darren Hoare was shot in his temple at close range. I would describe this as an execution.

Neither of the dead men's bodies bore signs of a fight. The situation is a fucking mess.

The media is all over the story. Want to know how this could have happened. How he had such easy access to a weapon (I keep my weapons with me in an old wardrobe, next to my boots). How someone capable of this was hired.

Armorgroup are under the media microscope. Some of the documents Danny presented in the recruitment process were supposedly forged. He'd been fired from two other security companies. He was a full of shit. Shocking to the world, perhaps. Not to those in the industry.

His family's distraught, understandably. They tell any journalist who'll listen Danny has post-traumatic stress disorder. We hear all about his 'long history of disturbed behaviour', as the BBC term it. And the horrible things he saw in Kosovo. It's the MOD's fault, they say. Should be better diagnosis and support for PTSD. Such a victim.

I'm not saying he didn't see some shit that's hard to process. But that's being a soldier. We've all been through it. And PTSD doesn't make you murder colleagues.

He's the first Westerner to stand trial in Iraq. Every update on the trial, posted and reposted on social media by various mates, is riddled with comments, pretty much all saying the same thing: Hang the fucker. I say let him rot in an Iraqi jail. The BBC reports that Danny's defiant in the face of the death penalty, saying, 'I'll die proud and I'll die strong. Only God can judge me at that point.'

In the end, he's convicted but gets twenty years. Should have been twenty for each of the men he killed at least, I think. His Iraqi lawyer says, 'A year in prison in Iraq is nine months and this means that twenty years in prison will, in fact, be fifteen years.' But who knows if he'll see fifteen years through in an Iraqi jail, surrounded by the kinds of blokes we've been fighting for years.

And he won't be left in peace to serve out his time, out of the media's gaze. In October 2012, a BBC documentary will reveal that G4S (who bought out Armorgroup) were warned about him. G4S evidently did not act on the tip-offs. Paul's mother will tell BBC News Online (1 October 2012): *'I want them to be charged with corporate manslaughter and be held accountable for what they did.'*

Danny's parents will agree: *'The people who we feel are responsible, who we hold responsible for putting that gun in Danny's hand, are without a shadow of a doubt G4S.'*

No doubt G4S has to accept some culpability. But in my mind, there's one person responsible for the murders, and that's the guy who chose to pull the trigger.

IV.XXXIII

On missions, a team is on its own. It's just you and the other ex-pats. Can't rely on the drivers. They're liable to drive too fast or too slow, or turn so hard the cargo hits the road (happened to us when we were transporting concrete T-walls. We had to abandon one in the road).

Can't rely on the gunners. They don't always know when or in which direction to shoot without clear instructions. And even then, they fucking do their own thing.

Can't rely on outside support. The American call sign coming up? Blocking your comms. The Armorgroup call sign coming up? Its gunners are liable to fire at you…

I'm in a thrown-together team, second to the rear of a convoy, in my favourite of Iraqi shitholes: Al Mushada. The first I know of a problem is a gunner in the bucket behind firing a warning shot.

Team leader Kiwi Tim comes on the net. 'Small arms. Keep going.'

Ahead, I see the police station coming up. Police will either be the shooters, or conveniently invisible.

'Which side, Tim, which side?' I ask.

I tell the driver to speed up in Arabic.

'Someone give us a side?'

It's not Tim's fault I haven't much idea what's going on. The radio's humming and screeching. Means Americans are in the area. They use electromagnetic jamming devices. Not helpful to us.

The police station is coming up. Surrounded by T-walls, paid for by American taxpayers, used as cover to shoot at American-hired contractors and American

Soldiers.

Without normal radio contact, we're out of sync.

'Was that a contact, matey?' asks the Scottish bloke behind.
'Mark, Gary, radio check.'
'I'm all right,' he comes back.
'Left or right?'
'Right side.'
Just as he says it, we get contact from the left side.

'Contact left,' I radio. The driver relays it to the gunners.

'Fire, left,' I tell the driver for the gunners' benefit. Yeah, you'd think it was obvious. But with Iraqis, assume nothing.

'Hey, easy!' I tell the driver. We're going around a bend and he's got his foot down, getting too close to the vehicle in front. Got to keep spaced out. Four small targets are better than one big one.

Ahead, I see the cause of the radio jam – an American call sign.
'American!' announces my driver. Warning the gunners to watch it.
'Keep going, keep going. We're all right, the rear,' says the man behind me on the radio. 'Watch out for green.' The Americans, he means.

Best not to shoot at the Americans, if you can help it. Again, you'd think that was obvious. Not for Iraqis...

On another mission we're in Dujail. It's a bog-standard Iraqi town. Square buildings. Palm trees. Pot-holed roads. Telegraph poles with wires hanging slack between like washing lines. You'd think it was nothing special. But say the name Dujail to any Iraqi and they'll have heard of it for one thing: a massacre.

It was in 1982. Saddam was pretty fucked off with some the residents – Shiites – who'd ambushed his motorcade during a visit to the area and done their darnedest to assassinate him. Killing those who'd attacked him wasn't enough. Eight hundred-odd people were rounded up and detained – women, children and men. Some were tortured. Some exiled. Some sent to detention centres. One hundred and six people were executed, including ten children. It was the Dujail Massacre that formed the basis for the primary charges that saw Hussein hanged.

You've got to hand it to the people of the town, they had some balls. How different it might have been if they'd succeeded in killing the dictator! But as it is, fast-forward to 2007 and they're hiding in tree lines beside the road once more. Only this time, they're shooting at *us*.

Our convoy is on the left side of the road, crossing back over to the right. Mick is at the front with a lad called Tom, and an American military convoy is coming the other way, towards us. My driver for the mission is a guy we've nicknamed Talib. No prizes for guessing who Talib looks like.

I think I hear gunfire. Mick hears it too. 'Is that gunfire, Gary?' he radios. I'm halfway through saying 'Don't know' when he adds, 'Contact right.'

Mick gives a target indication: 'Tree line. Two hundred metres. Right. To our rear right now.'

I instruct Talib to pull out to look down the line of the convoy. It's slowed; there's a bottleneck ahead. Another Armorgroup call sign is coming up after the Americans.

'Still hear 'em firing from there,' says Mick.
Talib says in Arabic. 'Put the machine guns right.'
'Fire, get firing,' I say because it's gone quiet above.
'Fucking hell, you dickhead!'

Tom in front has just seen the other Armorgroup call sign coming up alongside. They've been in contact and their gunners are powering through rounds. They only just stop in time before the overlap, before shooting at their own.

Then some fuckwit gunner on the truck in front of me decides to fire in the complete opposite direction to the insurgents' fire. Towards the Americans. 'Fucking hell! Stop!' I shout.
'No, American! Don't shoot at them!' relays Talib in Arabic.

Someone else radios, 'Still taking small arms from front.'
Then: 'Fucking hell. Fucking AG call sign nearly arced us up.'

The Armorgroup call sign is crossing over, trying to box past the slow-moving American convoy in front.

'Move right, move right,' I say in Arabic.
The Armorgroup call sign comes up our left side. My idiot driver starts waving cheerily at his mate in the opposing gun truck.
'All right, go go. Hey, drive,' I tell him.

'Point the PKCs at the fucking Ali Babas,' he tells the gunners.
'They fucking know.' I've told them a hundred times.
We pass a sign: Checkpoint 300 metres. It's a PVC – permanent vehicle checkpoint. Jersey barrier, blast walls, watch towers. Deserted.

The driver's trying to get on my good side now after pissing me off with his mid-contact waving moment. He points to the gunners on the truck in front. 'No good, no good. Americans,' he says.

We're still getting small-arms fire from the right.
'Still in contact right side here,' I radio.
'Quite heavy, weren't it, then?' says Mick.
'Don't know where it's coming from, mate. Can't see a firing point.'
Talib gives a wanker sign. Makes me laugh.

'Fucking Ali Baba,' he says to me.

Fucking Ali Baba, indeed.

IV.XXXIV

We're on our way up to Mosul on Route Santa Fe. Mick, team leader, is in the front. I'm in one of the rear vehicles.

We're not meant to be on Santa Fe – it's been designated a black route because of the amount of shit Armorgroup call signs have come into on the highway. But we've decided it's the lesser of evils in the routes available to us that day. And when Mick asks what I think, I back him up – sure, let's go on Santa Fe.

It's not long before we're under fire. Around this area insurgents often target the lorries rather than the security vehicles. Perhaps they're pissed at their fellow countrymen for working with us.

One of the lorries takes a beating from an IED, and the driver stops. At Mick's instruction, the convoy presses on out of the kill zone. I stay back with the lorry. I pull in behind him and get out.

The lorry's fucked – it's jack-knifed on itself, the middle part is a contorted mass of metal and the wheels are blown. I open the door to the cab, grab the driver – who's in shock and praying – and drag him back to my vehicle. He slumps in the back seat spouting gratitude on a loop: '*Shukran*, Allah. Thank you, Mr., Thank you. *Shukran*. Thank you, Allah.'

'Yes, yes. Now shut the fuck up and stay here.'

I radio Mick and explain the lorry's going nowhere. He agrees we should abandon it.

Before moving on to catch up with the convoy, I stick a frag grenade in the cab. It's not a huge explosion, but a decent-sized bang that blows out what's remaining of the windows. Fire will take hold and engulf the lorry soon enough. We're not meant to have grenades, but we all do. And we don't want to leave the lorry; easy pickings for the insurgents, and the ideal place to hide an IED.

Losing the cargo doesn't bother me. It's not like it's something really valuable, like weapons and ammo – then, we'd have a helicopter escort. I've no idea what's in this convoy; it's on the paperwork somewhere but I generally don't bother to look. Probably because doing so might put me in a bad mood. Once we drove to Mosul through two ambushes, and when we got there I saw them unload the Lorries. We'd put our necks on the line for just a few second-hand tyres.

I drive on now, and soon catch up to the rest of the Lorries. But they've stopped, and the drivers are disembarking, talking heatedly and gesturing down the road in the direction we've come.

Mick is out on the ground, shouting at them in his best scouse.
'What the fuck are you fucks doing! I didn't say you could stop.'

It becomes clear they're worried about their mate, the driver of the abandoned lorry. They think we've left him there, dead or dying.

'He's okay, you fucking shitbags! You, tell them...'
He gestures to the translator, who does his best to convey the meaning.
They're still flapping about.

Fuccccckkkkkk, working with LNs is like working with children. Inability to process basic information. Complete disinterest for plans. It's a wonder we ever pull an LN convoy together, what with their blatant disregard for order. Each morning at base we bring them together for a briefing. Usually, you do a register, turn around to get something, and when you look back round five of them have wondered off. Totally unprofessional.

I haul the driver (there's too many of them to learn their names) out of the back of my truck so they can see him. He's like a conquering hero – 'I'm all right! I made it!' – and all the drivers are laughing and clapping and cheering, '*Shukran, Allah!*'

'Right! Back to it!'
Eventually, the drivers do as they're told and climb back up into the cabs of their Lorries, and we're on our way.
'Fucking Iraqis,' I mutter as we drive out. My driver smiles but says nothing.
We pass through the Villas on the way back and Micks told to report to the boss.

The ops room know we've had a contact – we hit the transponder – and Mick has called in that we're a vehicle down.

Mick goes in first. He comes out looking shell-shocked.

'I've been sacked.'

I go straight in to see the boss.

'Have you just sacked Mick because we lost a truck during a contact? What else are we meant to do? If the lorry's screwed, we have to get out of there. If you're not going to back us up...'

'Gary mate. It's not cause you left the lorry. Mick's been dismissed for going against orders and taking the convoy on a black route. He's got to be held accountable. I've got to go to the client now and tell them we've lost the goods in a contact *on a road we shouldn't have been on.*'

'But we all agreed the route! I backed him up.'
'He's the TL. He gets paid more for a reason.'

I get it. He's meant to do as he's told. But if nothing had happened, it would have been a verbal warning, that's it. They're just covering their backs, showing the client someone's paid a price. It's not proportionate – it's a fucking lorry. And it's not consistent – I've known guys do far worse and be kept on. And as for following orders, that's bullshit. What about that Blackwater team who did as they were told? They ended up dead – and their parallel team, the ones who disobeyed orders, lived and got the job done. The job requires judgment, not blind following of orders.

I'm pissed on Mick's behalf. He's good at the job, a good team leader. They could have just given him a warning, or demoted him, or moved him to another contract. In the military, he'd have had a serious verbal debrief and that would have been it. But this isn't the military, this is the corporate world – and there are no second chances if the boss isn't in the mood to grant them.

A few weeks later, another team member, Lee, will also get the boot when the truck that's towing the truck he's in, which is knackered, hits a civilian. Lee isn't driving, but he's given the blame.

So Mick is on a plane home. Back to Britain, and then back to Iraq working for another private security firm. The magic of the private contractors' network: meet a Brit out here and you can bet you know the same people. It's a tight network, and if you have a good rep then you'll get helped out.

A few weeks later, when he's back in Baghdad, we meet for a brew. He shows up wearing his new sand-coloured flight suit.

'Fucking nearly didn't make it out, laa,' he tells me.
'How's that?'
'Security at Baghdad International. Forgot I had a few fuckin' frag and smoke grenades in the bottom of my bag, didn't I?'
'Fuck! You stupid cunt!'
'I know.'
'What did they do?'
'Ah, they were okay, I guess. Hard-arse questions. Backed off when I explained I'm PSD. Took 'em off me, though.'
'Well, what did you fucking expect? To get on a plane with them?'
'Ha. Guess not.'
I rib him a bit more, then tell him, 'Sorry you got screwed over.'
He grins at me. 'S'okay, laa. New contract's better paid.'

I'm careful to confirm route changes with the ops room from then on. But I don't worry about them sacking me. If they do, I'll just give Mick a bell and hook up with his new company.

IV.XXXV

Because we're contracted by the US government, they provide support. When we stop-off at a US base, we're fuelled up – fuel and provisions – 'candy' and 'soda', as they call them. While we may not be welcomed with open arms as fellow Americans would be, the military personnel accept our presence. We're part of their team, in a way.

When we're on a mission, it's good to know there's a fallback – that if we're beyond the realms of self-help, there are some big guns to call in. Casevac if someone's hurt badly. Tanks to the rescue if we're out of our depth in a firefight. Bomb disposal experts to diffuse a potential IED.

It's not like the British Army will help us out. Though we're all on the same side, we're not welcome to use their resources. They're separate, with their own stuff going on in the south.

One day we're on a mission when we get stopped behind a British Army roadblock. The Royal Engineers are there, diffusing a roadside bomb. I watch, interested, from my vehicle as they take an age – fucking over an hour – to clear the scene. Robot moving with painstaking care. Then a forensic scan to collect evidence.

Not like the Americans. In, out. Job done. I'm not sure whether to be impressed or infuriated by the care they take. Still, I suppose sometimes the Americans could learn a thing or two from the Brits, and vice versa. We're on Route Tampa heading north, escorting a convoy of lorries. Me, Marc, Greg and Jamie.

Today, the cargo is high-value, sensitive and volatile: ammo. An Apache helicopter has appeared and is pacing us, our eyes in the sky. They're tuned in to our radio frequency and giving us chat on what's up ahead.

We're coming into the town of Sammara. Instead of driving through the city, we take the bypass that connects to Route Tampa. There's a bridge across the river – around 500 metres wide – with a checkpoint at either end, which snarls up the traffic. We're doing our best to fight through cars, but it's slow going.

The chopper pilot comes on the radio to say he's going ahead to check out the situation at the other side of the bridge. He speeds off, a black spot against the blue sky.

Then boom: gunfire.
'Contact right! Small arms!'

We're straight down to business, gunners firing back at the insurgents. There are civilian cars all around. This is a recipe for disaster.

Bloody helicopter's AWOL. Out of radio range, the pilot's completely missed the fact we're under fire.

I fish a smoke grenade out of the cup holder, crack open my door and put a couple of bursts of automatic fire towards the enemy, I then roll it hard onto the ground away from our convoy in the direction of the contact. Bright red phosphorous, to signify danger, billows up into the air. That'll get his attention, I think. Nope.

Slowly, with the help of our gunners shrieking at them and waving their weapons, the civvies pull aside and we push on, cross the bridge and get out of the firing line. Then the Apache is back in range.

'Road ahead is clear...' the pilot tells us.
Yeah, thanks for that.

It's not the only experience I have with American pilots. Once, while escorting a convoy carrying fucking nothing of value – we're on our way back to AGW, our convoy is empty, having been dropped off – a helicopter escort gets itself confused as we overtake another, slow-moving convoy. It's meant to shadow that convoy, which must have something worth big bucks or that's majorly explosive on it. Instead, it slots in with us. Escorts us right across the country, the American pilot chatting away on the radio. We don't bother telling him he's fucked up. Don't look a gift horse in the mouth, as they say.

Perhaps it's unfair, though, to suggest there's a link between the two. It's not because they're American. Just in their own world. And sometimes they do take care of business.

I'm at a drop-off waiting for the convoy to unload when I hear the roar of a helicopter in the distance. We look up to see a group of three Apaches gunning it through the sky. It's a fucking impressive sight as they reach their target, in a housing estate, and take it in turns to hammer it, circling like giant robotic black birds of prey. Marc and I stand and watch. We get out our map and compasses and work out some back bearings to the Apaches' targets as best we can, to figure out where they're hammering. Haifa Street, central Baghdad.

'Good day to be a pilot,' he comments.
'Yeah. Someone's having a shit day over there, though.'

On one contract I come in and out of Baghdad on military flights, and I'm airlifted from the base into the Green Zone. Iraq from the air. It's nothing like those 'Earth from the Air' pictures you see from that aerial photographer guy, Yann Arthus-Bertrand. Still, the city looks better from above than down in the thick of it.

I take footage on my camera, alternating between pointing it out of my window and out over the gunner in front's weapon. I look down and try to identify roads. Amid the square lines of buildings that look like Tetris blocks the round roofs of mosques stand out. I see the Crossed Swords, Parade Square, the Monument to the Unknown soldiers (it's a weird-looking thing. Like a flying saucer crash-landed in Baghdad). The Tigris River. The zoo – yes, they have a zoo, though most of the animals died during the invasion.

From the air, it looks to be an innocuous place. Toyland, with miniature palm trees and tiny cars. But look around enough and you'll spot a puff of smoke billowing up from amid the buildings or a flash of orange and grey.

IV.XXXVI

Contact after contact, we drive through. That's the protocol. That's the job. But it sticks in your throat.

Marc and Greg and I come to an unspoken agreement: sometimes, when we can get away with it, we'll stop and take them on. When we've no convoy, just the gun trucks, the rules of the game change.

We're on a four-vehicle mission when the front vehicle is IED'd. We're in the wilderness, desert either side, just a row of huts – basic, no glass in the windows, even – a couple of metres away that must be the firing point.

Marc radios, 'I'm pulling left.'
Greg and I know this means he's going to stop and get out.
Marc gets out of the truck, leans around the bonnet and fires at where he believes the trigger point is.
Greg pulls over in front of Marc. Gets out of the truck, leans around the bonnet and shoots.

Basic principle of any infantryman: no movement without covering fire. I go round the safe side of Marc and Greg, and drive a bit further, up out of the contact but still within weapons range. I get out of the truck, lean around the bonnet and shoot. My gunners follow my lead and unleash their belt-fed weapons on the huts. We're providing a point of fire – giving Marc and Greg covering fire from a different angle.

Marc gives the order to break, and he and Greg peel off in turn with the knowledge that the covering fire from my gun truck will keep any insurgents' heads down while they extract towards me.

It's not the first or the last time we leave the relative safety of the armoured vehicles to retaliate.

We're on Route Predators heading west, back to Abu Ghraib, having made a drop-off. I'm in the last vehicle as second-in-command. To the right side of the large dual carriageway huge T-walls separate dense housing estates from the road. On the left side of the road there are no walls, just open ground interrupted by sporadic housing and the odd mosque.

Gunfire.

'Contact rear. Contact rear. Small arms,' I radio.

Seconds later: 'Contact left. Contact left. Small arms,' from Marc, at the front of the convoy.

We're getting pelted with bullets. The convoy halts, and the gunners get busy.

A movement in the corner of my eye catches my attention. One of the trucks in the stationary convoy is moving. It's turning around. One, two, three more follow suit. Then the bobtail in front of me roars into a messy three-point turn and guns it past me. The fuckwit Iraqi drivers are running scared.

'Fucking hell. Where they going?'

Jamie, the lad in charge of the other gun truck at the back, decides to give chase and round up the escapee drivers.

I get out of my vehicle amid bullets striking the road around me and the gun trucks and assess the scene. Up the line of trucks I see Marc out of his vehicle, shooting repeatedly at a target. Fucking insurgents are firing using mounds of dirt and scrap metal as cover, but they're firing over the top of the cover, therefore sky-lining and silhouetting themselves against the bland backdrop of sand, sky, and the odd sand-coloured building. Clearly, no one's told them you should always fire around cover.

Marc nails them, no problem.

Beyond Marc I can just make out Greg in the distance (unlike PSD we can often find ourselves hundreds of metres away from the nearest operator due to the size and length of a convoy). He's standing in the middle of the road with a Dragonov long-range rifle on his shoulder and is putting rounds down towards the enemy. I look in the direction of the other fire. The mosque. The insurgents are shooting from a mosque.

I clock a shooter beside the mosque, set him in my sights and fire rapid single shots. I keep missing. Fuck. He's up and running now. Away. Gun down, left on the ground in his firing position.

I switch to automatic and fire two bursts up his back.

He crumples to the ground and lies still. Dead. Maybe he knew about our Rules of Engagement, maybe he thought I wouldn't kill him without his AK, or that I wouldn't shoot him with his back to me. *He thought fucking wrong.*

I fire some more bursts into the windows of the mosque. I can't see the insurgents, but I know they're in there. I just want to keep their heads down.

Break. I drop to one knee behind the engine block of my gun truck for cover, magazine off – it's not totally empty but while I have the chance I'd rather have a full one on. I throw it in the foot well of the truck. Fresh mag on, chamber the top round, close the pouch, good to go…

I get back in the vehicle, tell the driver to turn around and head back up the way in support of Jamie. Amid the rattle of gunfire, a tinny, cheesy tune rings out. It's the ops room on the phone. Marc's hit the transponder to communicate that we're in a contact. He's not answering, so they've tried me.

'Wait out, wait out, mate,' I say. 'I'll call you back.'

On the way back down the road we're hit again: small-arms fire from buildings on the right side. I call the usual: 'Contact, right. Small arms.'

We press on down the road, slaloming around debris in the carriageway. Crushed orange cones. Fucking dick Iraqi drivers panicking and facing in all directions.

I'm chasing Jamie – who's chasing the drivers. Got to stay in range to bridge radio comms back to Marc.

My driver's shouting excitedly into his radio, connected to the gunners. They're jittery. Keep firing warning shots at civilians.

I get out of the vehicle and shout at them. 'Fucking stop! Calm down! Watch your fire!'

Finally, Jamie gets the trucks back on course – it's like herding headless chickens – and we pull the convoy back together.

Back at the AGW base, we ask what will happen to the LN drivers who went AWOL. Nothing much, it seems. A slap on the wrist. Mick got fired for disobeying black roads and choosing his own route. These guys keep their jobs despite disobeying orders and showing cowardice. The clients expect consummate professionalism from us contractors, but when it comes to the LNs, they accept what they get.

One of the lads asks me whether we made any kills.

'One for sure,' I reply, and tell him the story of the gunman by the mosque. 'Yeah, but you can't confirm that as yours,' he says. 'The LNs were firing also.' Not fucking likely, I think. That was precision.

I say nothing more. No need to press the point. Or point out that I'll lose no sleep over this kill - nor any other I've made or will make in the future.

I wonder if he died instantly, or if he had time to think as lay there on the dusty ground dying alone. I wonder if he had time to ponder the decisions he made that brought him to that point in his life. Or did he just experience an excruciatingly slow and agonising death? *Either way I don't give a fuck.* My mind on a hot shower followed by some hot food.

I lay on my bed that night with a book struggling to keep my eyes open, my little plastic Nokia lights up as it vibrates itself across my bedside table, a text from Nikki - *'Happy birthday hun xx'*.

I smile.

IV.XXXVII

It's Marc, back on my early days on convoys, who gave me the idea to mount a camera on the front of my vehicle. He did it with a handheld camera during one of our early contacts, with a vague idea that he could monetise footage of contacts, and when he showed me some of the footage, I could see the attraction. In a contact, in the moment, time moves so fast, and you're busy focusing on the threat, the road ahead and the LNs – making the driver drive and the gunners shoot. Often, you're straight from one drama into the next, and there's no time to process and make sense of it all. The footage provides another point of view. It's surreal watching it back - and pretty eye-opening. I decided Marc was onto something, and I got myself rigged up with a camera too – just a middle of the range thing. Expendable.

Each day I set the camera to record. If something interesting happens, I edit the footage. If it's been a dull day, I wipe the memory and start afresh the next day. I record it all. IEDs. Small-arms fire. A US Army Hummer burning at the side of the road. Our vehicles nudging civilian cars out of the way. Road rage from operators. Military helicopter escorts. The Americans blowing up an IED at the roadside. Rolling contacts while approaching Bradley APCs and Abrahams tanks. Me on target practice. A toilet break at Scania.

Put together with photos I take on missions, it adds up to a picture of a country and a time. Massive carriageways where driving is a free-for-all. Surprisingly green settings, given that when you think Iraq, you think desert. Red bursts of fire from muzzles concealed in buildings, ditches, tree lines. Bangs and flashes of explosives. A soundtrack of ex-pats sharing information while, simultaneously, Iraqis converse in Arabic.

An IED in Al Mashada puts an end to that initiative. The explosion is huge, deafening. It takes a lot to pierce the armoured metal panelling of the vehicle, more still to shatter the windscreen. But apparently whatever crap connects the windscreen to the metal frame is the weak link, because in the second after the boom and the smoke, I'm flinging my arms up to protect my face as the windscreen falls in on me.

Thankfully, the dashboard takes the brunt of the weight. That and my camera; smashed to bits.

The truck is fine. Just missing a windscreen. Once we've hauled the huge plate of glass out of the way, I put on the goggles attached to my helmet for the first time ever and tell my driver to start her up.

'But Mr Gary,' he says, gazing at my eyewear, 'I have no goggles!'
'And? What the fuck you want me to do about it?'

We head back to base, inhaling great quantities of dust and grime, the driver squinting moodily all the way.

IV.XXXVIII

I move to a new team, team 7-4, and I take over as team leader. It doesn't mean much. In convoys we're all about the team. It's not rank-and-file like in the Army, with a focus on hierarchy and 'leaders' throwing their weight about. Any one of us could be team leader, and often enough we are – stepping up when a bloke is off. You could easily find yourself in a team made up of team leaders.

It's a jump from my last team, where Greg, Marc, Mick and I had got to the point we were so in synch we used to joke we were telepathic. Instead of calling 'Red car, static, right, push round' I'd got to a point where I'd just radio 'Static, right' and they'd all know the deal.

Still, the first mission isn't my regular 7-4 team, just a set of guys thrown together for manning reasons. We're a mismatch of TLs, 2ICs and operators – Lofty and two lads who've just left Afghanistan, two jocks, Ferg and Baz. They've seen some action, but nothing like the shit they'll be confronted with here.

On our first mission together, we have a contact. We're in Mosul on a back route into FOB Diamondback. It's a narrow, winding road with a rock face towering above to the left and a cliff dropping down to the right – hairy driving all right. The Lorries have to take it slowly, so up the back, we're pretty much static.

Boom.
Black smoke up ahead.
Lofty comes on the radio: 'Contact. IED.'
And now gunfire, coming from above, from the cliff top.
'Fuck.'

I'm straight out of the vehicle and crouched behind the truck, aiming up at the edge of the cliff. No point sitting in a stationary vehicle hoping the LN gunners will sort it out.

The insurgents are barely visible as they try not to expose themselves, just their AK barrels and a flash of shemagh giving away their positions. I start firing.

I hear shots ringing out along the convoy; the other guys in the team are out too. My gunners in the bucket are struggling to get their machine guns, mounted on stands, to crane back at the required angle. One of them rips his gun off the stand and fires a volley of rounds up. Bullets are hitting the road all around.

Finally, the convoy gets moving, and a space opens up between the gun trucks and the Lorries. I get back in the vehicle.
'Push through,' I instruct on the radio.

Around the corner, Lofty comes on the net. 'Welcome to Iraq, boys.'
A few weeks later we're doing a drop-off in Iskanderia, a city in central Iraq. It's an uneventful journey, and there's an air of calm at the US FOB there.
I get chatting to the soldiers in charge of receiving the cargo.

'It's a nice setup here. Sweet. Easy,' he tells me.
'Oh yeah? How come?'

He pauses for a moment, gives me a piercing look and then says, 'Pays them off, doesn't he?'

I'm lost. 'Who?'
'The Colonel. The boss. He pays the locals not to hit us up.'
'Jeez. How much?'
'Seventy K a month, so I hear it.'
'Fuck me.'
'Yup.'
'Well, that's one way to put 'em down, I guess,' I say.
'Problem is,' continues the solider, 'we're pulling out soon enough.'
'Your unit?'
'Yeah.'
'So what's the next unit going to do?'
'No idea. But if they don't fancy stumping up the seventy K, they're going to have a whole load of immensely pissed locals on their hands.'

Jesus, I think. Fucking lazy cunt commanding officer. What does he think he's doing? He's fuelling the insurgents, making them stronger, wealthier, and better armed. He's giving them a helping hand so they can beat the shit out of the rest of us.

He might as well be up on the cliff with those Iraqi fuckers for all the good he's doing out there.

I wonder how many of his men know about this. Keep schtum. Work for a lazy traitor for shit pay. Makes me glad I have the freedom, as a private contractor, to choose who I work for. And no way would I work for someone paying off insurgents.

IV.XXXIX

Sixteenth of September 2007. Private security operators working for Blackwater shoot dead seventeen Iraqis in Nisour Square, Baghdad. The media sits up and takes notice. Private forces will never be the same again. It's not the first incident between Blackwater contractors and Iraqis since the 2004 killings of the Blackwater team in Fallujah.

In February 2005, four Blackwater contractors who were escorting a US State Department convoy shot up a car. Seventy rounds. They claimed the driver made them jittery; didn't stop when instructed. They got in some grief for providing false statements.

Christmas Eve 2005, so claims the Iraqi government, a drunk Blackwater employee shot dead the Iraqi vice-president's bodyguard. No charges were brought, however.

For their part, insurgents are out for blood: in January 2007, they shot down a Blackwater helicopter, killing the five contractors on board.

Now, in July 2007, the Blackwater PSDs were clearing a path for their clients, diplomats of the US State Department. According to the contractors, they came under fire and retaliated in self-defence. Conflicting reports indicate that they'd opened fire without provocation.

At the compound, it's the hot topic of conversation for the day.
'You see the news...?'
'Fucking mess.'
'As I heard it, they were definitely under fire.'
'Well, if they were, it's justified, isn't it?'
'Yeah, but seventeen? Sounds a lot.'
'Urban area. Big ambush.'
'Or the boys have got trigger-happy...'
'Must have been something in it, though. They can't have just started firing for no good reason.'
'There'll be an investigation. We'll get a clearer picture.'

'Wouldn't want to be one of those bastards right now.'

'Tell me about it. Fucking government'll be all over them.'

'Yeah. A load of dead Iraqis'll matter a damn sight more in their minds than the survival of the team and the diplomats.'

'It's just because there are so many. One or two dead and no one would complain.'

'Whatever – they've fucked it up for everyone.'

'How so?'

'Just you wait. They'll be all over us now.'

'All over Blackwater.'

'No, mate. This is too big. They're gonna start asking questions – who's policing the contractors. Before you know it we'll have rules and regs stuck down our throat. It'll be a fucking nightmare out here.'

The next day I'm at Camp Liberty doing a drop-off when I see a group of guys from Blackwater. Not those involved in the incident, but they look pretty sombre as they acknowledge us fellow soldiers with a nod. I see them get into their trucks outside and head out. The sides of their vehicles are freshly painted – the Blackwater logo has been thoroughly hidden.

In the following weeks, I keep an eye on news reports. We have internet access, and can watch BBC and American news channels. Sure enough, there's a media furore. Words like mercenary are being bandied about. Private Army. Accountability. Investigations are launched. The FBI concludes that fourteen of the deaths were unlawful.

It's the end of getting on with my job quietly. For the past couple of years, private contractors have been a mysterious breed. You meet a new bloke and he doesn't know what you are. So you explain, and you see the interest in his eyes.

Now, when I'm on the road and introduce myself to new people – guys at checkpoints, at bases where we do drop-offs – they nod with understanding. And their first question is always the same: 'Do you work for Blackwater?'

'No, I don't,' I say. Wouldn't care if I did, though, and would admit it happily. As long as they're paying me on time and the weapons are good to go, then I'm okay. I'm not bothered about the name on my pay cheques.

IV.XL

Abu Ghraib is closing, but there's a fairly new contract down south that's up scaling so most of us get moved down to Umm Qasr, a port. I know the area as I came through there with the Army in 2003. It's another convoy's contract. Team leader.

First job: introduce myself to my new 2IC. I get his room number from the ops manager and go knock on his door.

The bloke who answers is around fifty, muscular, lean and bald. He's wearing nothing but running shorts, so I get a full view of all his tattoos. And there are many. Paras. Falklands War. Skulls. 'Born to Kill' emblazoned on his forearm. I don't know whether to talk to him or read him.

'John Hunter? I'm Gary. You're with me tomorrow, mate.'
'Yeah, sound.' He grins.
I've clocked the accent. 'Whereabouts are you from?'
'Sheffield.'
'United or Wednesday?'
'United. You train as well, don't you?' He's eying up my shoulders and arms.
'Yeah.'
'Sweet. We'll get a good few sessions in at the FOB gyms.'
Yeah, I think.

The Umm Qsar contract is chaotic. Tiny compound. Shit accommodation. Electricity constantly cutting out. Unpleasant food, and not much of it. The Iraqis here haven't a fucking clue.

One of the TLs walks into the kitchen one day and finds a bloke cutting cheese with a knife dripping blood from the raw meat sliced up on the same chopping board. He does his best to explain basic food hygiene principles to the Iraqi. The guy just laughs and says, 'You crazy. Just use same knife.'

If the compound staff are ballbags, the LNs are fucking diabolical. Undisciplined. Lazy. Disrespectful. Ignorant. They don't wear uniforms. They don't turn up on time. Their focus in life is chain-smoking and talking shit amongst themselves, and - of course - eating.

On the first mission the vehicles are assembled and I call everyone together for a brief. As I'm talking my eye's caught by a flash of blue in the back of one of the gun trucks. I go over to investigate.

It's a fucking office chair. Torn up. Looks like it's been liberated from a skip. A chair in a gun bucket. That's how much effort an LN will put into being lazy.

'What the fucking FUCK is this?' I demand.
'Chair,' proclaims the Iraqi fuckwit gunner helpfully. 'Sit on.'
'You're not here to fucking sit down!' I roar at him. 'Lazy fucking cunt.'

He appears to cotton on that I'm not impressed, and climbs up into the back of the truck to demonstrate the tactical genius of his cruddy chair.

'See?' he says, swivelling it around 360 degrees. 'Moves.' He fakes a machine-gun noise and imitates having his gun up and moving around in a circle.

'The fucking gun's on a pivot. A stand!' I shout at him.

He looks blankly at me. Then: 'Look. Also moves.' And he demonstrates that the chair is on casters, and can slide wildly about the back of the truck. He appears to think this will impress me. Quite how he thinks he's going to manage sitting on this moving apparatus while in the back of a moving vehicle that's veering from side to side and bouncing over potholes – and that's without being under fire – I've no idea.

Who the fuck hired this LN? More to the point, how did his last TL let him get this cocksure? Clearly, just going through the motions to get his pay cheque (to my embarrassment I find out it was a former Rifleman who previously ran the team – he shall remain nameless).

I come down on him and the others like a ton of fucking bricks. No fucking flip-flops. No fucking smoking in the fucking vehicles. No fucking tardiness. No fucking Dr Dre driving: two fucking hands on the fucking steering wheel at eight and four. And no fucking chairs in the fucking gun buckets.

It doesn't make me their mate, sure enough. I don't care. That's not what I'm there for. And all Iraqis are standoffish at first, until they get to know you. Respect you. Bollocking over, I get into my vehicle.

Before we head out, I look up in the bucket. Check the LNs. They smile at me. One has no weapon.

'Where's your AK?' I demand.
'Mr Gary. I go to piss while you hand them out.' He says while imitating the hand action of pissing to get his point across.

Fucking imbecile bastard. Probably would have come along for the ride without even thinking to point out he was unarmed.

It's a bloody slog managing these men, but I figure its good experience. If I can command eighteen headless Iraqis, I can command any team.

Commanding them in Arabic helps. I've been working on learning it since I first came out in 2005 – I just point to things and ask LN drivers to translate. Now, I've a decent grip of Arabic, enough to instruct in the LNs' native tongue. And to bollock them, when necessary.

We're in Camp TQ, near Fallujah. We've overnighted, leaving the Lorries in the designated areas, the LNs bedding in their cabs for the night as is the norm. But the next morning, when we go to hook up with the LNs, there's one hell of a ruckus going on.

Another convoy is accusing our LNs (truck drivers, not the Armorgroup team guys) of stealing tyres off their lorries during the night. They're shouting at the drivers, our drivers are giving as good as they get.

I step in.

'You lot! Over there!' I bellow to my LNs, getting them to move back from the fray. 'You, come here and translate.'

207

The Military Police arrive and start throwing their weight about, suspecting everyone, listening to no one.

Pretty soon it becomes clear to me the AUL drivers – our convoy - have been up to no good. It's obvious from the chat between them, which I can understand while the Military Police can't. They've nicked the tyres, to resell, perhaps, or use on their personal vehicles.

I'm furious. I make them collect up the tyres and apologise to the guys on the other convoy.

It's not enough. We're thrown out of the camp.

'Sorry, Mr Gary,' they say to me sheepishly back at Umm Qsar.

They'd better hope Camp TQ doesn't hold a grudge next time we're that way.

IV.XLI

Christmas 2006 was overshadowed by the death of a colleague. Christmas 2007 is eerily similar.

We've had some days off. Not because the company thinks we should have a break for the holiday season; I think the truck company's having a break. I'm in my room when Jamie, a Brummie lad, ex-Rifleman, bursts in.

'Have you heard?'
'Heard what?'
'Richie Coel's died.'

I knew Richie for a long time. We were in the same battalion together whilst in the Army. A gentle giant with a great beaming smile. He's a great bloke. Was.

'How?' I ask simply.
'Don't know. They just found him like it. Dead in his room. They've locked up the room while they work out what to do. No protocol for this. Dead in your hut. Man. He's got a wife, hasn't he?'

I nod. 'And a little girl.'

Richie was well liked, well respected. To die alone, far from family; to have survived the Army, all the contacts here, and then go to sleep and not wake up... I think about the first time I saw Richie out here, working for Armorgroup. It was when I was going from PSD to convoys. 'Don't worry, mate,' he said. 'Convoys aren't that bad. If they were, I'd be out of here.' We were of a similar mind, me and him. He wasn't fazed by the hotter action on convoys. He was out there to do what he loved, and make the money.

I think about the time he strode into my room, beaming, with a bin liner slung over his shoulder, and asked what I was doing. He knew my team had been in a big enemy contact that day.

'Nowt,' I said.

He shut the door and dumped the contents of the bin liner onto the bed. Green cans. On the label: Farida Lager Beer. Established 1956. Genuine and Tasteful Beer.

'Dig in, mate!' he said happily, plonking himself down and pulling back a ring pull.

I thanked him and grabbed a can. Opened it. Tried not to react at the smell, like lighter fluid. Took a swig. Watery. Made me think of sweetcorn and marzipan and the water of the Tigris.

We had a good night, that night. Talking crap. Drinking crap. Others joined us, keen to be part of the buzz.

Now, the friendly guy with the beers is dead.

The lads sit in the common area outside our rooms – literally outside; it's fucking freezing – and remember our mate.

'He was a fucking awesome bloke,' says one of the lads.
'Remember that contact when he saved an LN? That "Dutch commando" bloke went to pieces. Trying to give first aid in shock. Fucking fiddling about taking his rig off. Richie stepped in and took over with the first aid. The bloke lived.'

'Remember the dodgy checkpoint? How did he get out of that?'
'He told me about it. Fucking corrupt Iraqis trying to kidnap the guys. He was at the back, did a U-turn and got help. British call sign behind, I think. He saved his team, the LNs – all of them.'

'Wasn't that the same area where the Crescent security team got lifted?'
'Yup.'
'Richie did well there. Our blokes would have been dead for sure.'
My phone beeps – a text message. It's from Coxy, a mate from the Army – Richie's best mate. He knows that Richie's dead, but that's about it. Richie's wife is in bits, he says, and is getting nothing out of Armorgroup. I tell him I'll keep him updated.

That evening, all the lads are preparing to accompany Richie to Basra. I go to Richie's room. He's in a body bag on the floor. The lads and I pick him up. He was a big guy, must have weighted seventeen stone, and I'm surprised at how easy we find it to lift him. He feels light.

We put him in the back of a truck, and head to Basra.

At the British base there, we carry him to the morgue.

A female soldier – very young – greets us. 'Put it in there,' she tells us, gesturing to an adjacent room.

We freeze, stare at her. She looks back, confused.

'Him. Not it,' says Jamie venomously.

She looks embarrassed, she apologises.

We leave Richie and trudge quietly off to the NAAFI. Drink tea. Eat bacon sandwiches. Think about how fucking unthinkable it is to die in your sleep aged twenty-eight.

IV.XLII

Richie was remembered for many things, not least the day he saved his colleagues from kidnapping.

It's the Crescent Security incident that has us all on alert for being snatched.

November, 2006. Baghdad. Five contractors from the Crescent Security Group, four Americans and an Austrian, are escorting a convoy near Safwan, in southeast Iraq on the border with Kuwait, when they're ambushed. Fake checkpoint. Iraqis in police uniforms. Well-armed. According to some sources, some of the Iraqis were former employees of Crescent Security. Pissed that they got ten per cent of the wages of the ex-pats.

In the aftermath, there's confusion. Reports that the Austrian guy was found dead and an American wounded. Officials have mixed up the kidnapping with another incident that day involving British contractors pulled over by Iraqi Police on the same road. As police checked paperwork, a car sped by and gunfire rang out. One Brit died and another was injured.

A video is released by the captors, dated and passed to The Associated Press. Each man appears alive and apparently uninjured.

'My name is John R. Young,' says the first. 'I'm forty-four years old. I'm from Kansas City, Missouri. The date is twenty-one December, two thousand and six. I'm well, my friends are well, we've been treated well.'

The next, Jon Cote, says, 'I'm being treated well. I can't be released until the prisoners from the American jails and the British jails are released.'

The Austrian, Bert Nussbaumer, says, 'I'm an Austrian citizen. I'm doing private security for Crescent Security in Iraq.

Josh Munns, of California, is next. 'I joined the Marine Corps in 2001, and I got out in 2005. After I got out of the Marine Corps, I went to work in the construction business, building swimming pools. After that, in July of 2006, I started working for Crescent Security out of Kuwait, and I don't know how long I've been here doing this, but today is December twenty-first, two thousand six.' They keep the emotional appeal to the end, with Paul Johnson Reuben saying, 'I just wanted to let my family know that I'm doing well.'

Patrick Reuben, Paul's brother, speaks out to the press about this brother, saying he was out there to make enough money to buy a house and a Hummer, then he was out of there. A Washington Post reporter says he spoke to Munns a few days before the abduction, and he'd say he was in Iraq doing private security because he loved the camaraderie and the adrenaline of combat.

It's all a muddle. Do the kidnappers – not visible in the video – want a ransom? Is it all about political pressure? Given the US and UK stance on not negotiating with terrorists, the men have little hope other than being rescued by Coalition forces.

The US military hunt for the men. They don't find them.

Sixteen months later, US officials in Baghdad are sent severed fingers. DNA tests are ordered. It's confirmed that these fingers belong to the missing men. Are they still alive?

Sadly, no. A few weeks later, the bodies of the contractors are found. They were executed.

I watch the video of them online again. They're serious, but not broken. They look like they're keeping it together. They look like they have hope, I think.

But it's not just the Crescent Security case that we follow. There are other cases; too many cases. And some are closer to home.

Take the case of Peter Moore, an IT consultant abducted in Baghdad along with four PSCs whose job it was to protect the consultant.

The story goes like this: Peter is working for an American company contracted to set up a data system at the Ministry of Finance. His protection team comprises Alan McMenemy, Jason Swindlehurst, Jason Creswell and Alec MacLachlan, all British ex-servicemen working for a security company called Garda World (which, it transpires, has no kidnapping insurance). They're abducted at gunpoint from Peter's place of work by men in Iraqi Police uniforms. The British government want to dismiss the captors as terrorists posing in uniforms; Peter is later adamant that the men revealed themselves to be legitimate members of Iraq security forces (shooting from police stations, anyone? The Iraqi forces are the traitors).

It's unclear exactly when the four PSCs are killed. Garda World's account differs to that of Peter. But what's fact is that they never make it home alive. As for Peter, he's eventually freed in exchange for the release of two Iraqi hostages, senior leaders of a Shia paramilitary group.

Later, in February 2012, he'll tell the Independent:

'I am sure that everyone involved in the rescue effort – the Foreign Office, the military – worked extremely hard and did their best. But something went very wrong and questions have to be asked. Four out five are dead, that's an 80 per cent failure rate in getting those kidnapped back alive, which is pretty poor by any standards. It would be good to know what lessons have been learned from this by the UK authorities, [for] if something like this happens again.'

With the British government's 'We do not give in to kidnap demands' policy, contractors like me in Iraq know that were we to be taken hostage, we'd have precious little chance of survival. Even if the government were prepared to push out the boat to save hostages, they're going to prioritise the likes of a civilian IT consultant over a PSC. Best we can do is pray we're never caught in that web; or if the worst happens, the Iraqi bastards who take us are stupid enough to leave a rifle within reach. That, and be prepared. So under my vehicle seat lies an unregistered AK, just in case I have to deal with some police or army officers trying to lift me and my team.

IV.XLIII

It would be a pretty shit job, hour after hour sitting in a gun truck, if you couldn't get on with the LNs in the vehicle. Good job, then, that I find I get on well with my translator and my driver at Umm Qsar. Saffa, the translator, is a young guy – one of the new generation of Iraqis who knows freedom: mobile phones, Adidas trainers, Man U. He's dreaming of breaking free, and I respect that.

Randomly, in a couple of years' time, after I've moved on from this contract, Saffa will pop up on social media. Nice big picture of him grinning at the camera. In the background, fountains, green grass, people in jeans and t-shirts, pigeons. And the unmistakable architecture of Sheffield Town Hall. What the fuck? I think. Good on him. He got out of there. Must have been listening when John and I talked about home. I'll take him for a beer one day. Get him pissed.

Alawai, my driver, is another LN that I come to like and respect. He's a cut above the others – butch, stocky, intelligent. And experienced. He used to be Saddam Hussein's bodyguard. It fascinates me: the switch from guarding Saddam, the most hated man in the West, to working for the Western forces. But while Alawai's happy enough to admit he was Saddam's right-hand man for a while in the nineties, when it comes to details, he's a closed book.

'Did you see him?' I ask when he first lets slip who his previous employer was. He looks at me like I'm soft in the head. 'Yes. Of course. I stand next to him every day.'
'What was he like?'
He shrugs.
'What did he do?'
He shrugs.
'Who else was he with?'
He shrugs.
'What was the pay like?'
He screws up his nose at that. 'Army pay.' He shakes his head.

I want to ask about his views on the regime. Whether he saw any action at Saddam's side. Whether he heard anything juicy. How he feels about swapping sides. Why he has. His wife and kids. But I don't. I do ask him one day what he thinks about Saddam's hanging. 'Yeah. Saddam's fucking gay,' is his reply. He's doing his best to speak the ex-pats' language. I don't think he has a clue what he's said.

Soon enough, Alawai's more than a driver. He adopts the role of head of the LNs. On a mission, he's right beside me. Watching out for me. Scouting the area. When it comes to security, he's switched on.

I introduce him to an American Marine one day as a former bodyguard to Saddam, and the guy asks if he can get a photo taken with Alawai (another desk soldier looking for war stories). He refuses. He won't have his picture out there. One day, I'm out with Alawai on a mission when we cross paths with one of my drivers from the Abu Ghraib days. Mustafa. Cool under pressure. Decent driver. Referred to the insurgents as Ali Babas. I introduce them.

'Alawai, this is Mustafa. Used to drive for me up in Abu Ghraib. Mustafa, this is Alawai, my driver now.'
The two Iraqis size each other up. They don't seem sure about each other, I guess because one's from Basra and the other, Baghdad.
Finally, Mustafa nods at Alawai and says to me, 'He good driver?'
'No,' I say. 'He's fucking shit.'
Alawai nods at Mustafa and says to me, 'He good driver?'
'No,' I say. 'He's fucking shit.'

It breaks the ice, and the two start jabbering in Arabic. I catch the words 'Britannia', 'drive' and, in English, 'shit'.

Back home on leave, I buy Alawai a Sheffield United baseball cap. He wears it with pride. It makes me smile – this serious, mature, experienced Iraqi man who's seen stuff I can only imagine driving me around in my footie team's cap. Between me, John and Alawai, the LNs start falling into line. Soon enough, this becomes one of the best teams on the contract. The LNs come to realise that we know our shit, and they develop pride in their work. Even to the point of pointing out the tactical mistakes of other teams in the camp during our morning admin – 'This gunner not look good, look.' They rib their brothers and cousins and friends on other teams about how shit theirs is and how good we are.

Alawai's support is pivotal to the LN's attitudes. This is a man who commands respect. If the Iraqis are being Iraqis (a disorganised gang fuck), just a word or a look from me to him and he'll grip them. Sometimes, though, it's me he reins in.

Fucking truck drivers leaving gaps in a convoy. It drives me insane. It's dangerous, lengthening the convoy. Make it too long and I could lose radio contact with the other vehicles. One day I lose it with a driver. I've told him to close up – pulling alongside, hand gestures and the gunners on top shouting across my message. He ignores me.

I order the convoy to stop. Hand Alawai my rifle. Jump out of the truck. Over to his vehicle. Fling open the door. Mount the step to the cab. Grab him by the front of his shirt and haul him out.

He stumbles, but before he can right himself I give him an open-handed whack around the face. Shout at him to stay fifty metres behind, keep the convoy together. 'That's enough,' says Alawai quietly.

I hadn't even notice him come up behind me. He hands me my rifle and I take it. Eyeball the driver, whose cheek has flared red. Dare him to cheek me. He climbs back in his cab, and stays the correct distance from the lorry in front for the rest of the mission.

Alawai is the ideal middleman. But he can't take away the LNs' jitters on a mission.

It's quieter now, in the south. Fewer contacts. But there's a busy EFP cell in the area, a threatening atmosphere all around. Militias are all over, and they don't take kindly to the Iraqis who work with us. When we've been north on a mission, there's a bridge we get to – Saf'wan – that seems to flick a switch in the LNs. They put on their sunglasses and cover their faces with their shemaghs.
I wonder what it's like for them. How they feel about the Coalition – the Americans, the Brits. Whether they wish we'd get the fuck out of their country. How far their sympathies extend to the insurgents. They'll happily shoot the bad guys up for us, but how much of that is for money, and how much because they believe it's right?

IV.XLIV

I'm sitting in traffic in Baghdad when I see him.

Allah.

It's two years since the EFP, since pulling Allah from the wrecked vehicle. He looks like shit. He's in a wheelchair, being pushed down the middle of the road by some guy. His white dishdasha covers his torso and arms, and is folded neatly where his legs should be. His legs have been amputated right at the top. He doesn't even have stumps.

Jesus. As if it isn't hard enough being an Iraqi in this country, now he's half an Iraqi. He can't even work now.

We're in a convoy, with four branded gun trucks. He's seen the Armorgroup logos, and he's looking up at the vehicles. What with his low height and the glare of the sun on the thick armoured windows, he can't see who's on board.

I reach into my pocket and pull out my wallet, count the cash. Eight hundred dollars. It's not much, but it's something – it's not like he can claim welfare benefits.

I'm reaching over to open the door to the truck when common sense kicks in. He's not talking to the gunners, not greeting them. Why not?

If I get out, I'm compromising his security. He can't defend himself now, disabled as he is. If he's seen taking a handout from a Westerner, private security, that might be the end for him.

I look down at him. I follow him in the truck mirror. He's looking away now, feigning disinterest. He knows there's nothing we can do to help him.

I wonder whether he'd be happy to see me. Whether he'd thank me for saving him. Or whether he wishes I'd shot him instead.

PART V

"You have enemies? Good. It means you've stood up for something at some point in our life..."

Winston Churchill

V.XLV

I'm on a run. Fallujah. The phone rings. It's Nikki.

'We had a little boy last night. You're a dad.'

The blokes congratulate me on the radio, and I text the ops manager to request the earliest flight home after the mission. I'll get a few days' 'compassionate' leave to meet my boy. It's a shame I missed the birth, but what can you do? If I'd taken leave on Nikki's due date and she'd delivered late, I wouldn't have been able to come home for weeks. This way, at least I see them both early on.

Fallujah is grey and cold today, rain begins to hit our windscreen, spitting at first, then getting steadily heavier. Talib flicks a switch and the rhythmic noise of the windscreen wipers becomes more and more hypnotic as my eyes flicker around the city.

I picture myself sat on the sofa back home cradling a little two-week old, whilst we watch TV. I'm explaining the offside rule to him, I think he gets it…

I'm snapped instantly out of my daydream as automatic gun-fire rakes down the side of the civilian Lorries we're escorting in front of us. The fire hits the load high up on the trailer and I know that won't give us any cause for concern. 'Contact right, Contact right, Small arms'. My driver steers our Gun-truck left, away from the contact, I reach over and pull the steering wheel gently back to the right. I'm guessing the Alibaba's are in the buildings beyond a hundred metres or so of waste-ground, and probably high up – that's where I'd be. I pull our Gun-truck over to the far right of the road and can here the crack of the enemy bullets going high over us.

The gunners in the back have got their act together now, they had probably switched off due to the rain, but now the sound of their PKM's fill our world as they incessantly burn through belts of ammo. I get on the radio, 'Keep rolling, keep rolling, all good'. I know the gunners are fine because they're still firing away. The convoy naturally slows as we go over some speed humps through a deserted military check point; there's a two second break in the fire as our guys pause while we bounce over them, then they're at it again. The convoy speeds up and soon all I can hear of the insurgents is the distant thump of their weapons – no crack – meaning we're now out of their kill zone. I reach over to my driver's chest rig and turn the volume down on his radio. In typical Iraqi fashion they're jabbering away at a million miles per hour on their net. Then, as if someone had flicked a switch, all the fire stops, friendly and enemy. The Gun-truck commanders check in one at a time over the radio, and then it's back to the rhythm of the windscreen wipers.

I tell the guys in the back through the driver to get some oil on the guns, they'll rust up in no time with this rain. I look over at my driver, 'Ok' I say, 'Ok' he replies, I use my hands to explain to him why I pulled us back to the right, he nods his head in acceptance. If the insurgents were elevated then going over to the left would have put us right in their fire; pulling us over to the right narrowed the range between them and us, and as a result the rounds went over us.

I pull my map onto my lap and figure out how far we've come, I'm glad to see we're only half-an-hour from the turn off to FOB TQ. My old Army mate Jay is there, the lad I worked with in Sierra Leone, he's working for an Iraqi PMC called Sabre and we're going to catch up over a brew…

Becoming a dad doesn't change anything. I do my job. I know the risks. I reason with myself they're low – on any one day, there are, say, two hundred call signs moving about Baghdad. One in two hundred, then. And if we're ambushed, I'm in one of fourteen vehicles and if we're hit, I'm one of four or five in the vehicle. The figures help.

But now there's a little bit more of me waiting in England, wanting me back home safely, and that matters. I'm not the swaggering, risk-taking young Army recruit I once was. I'm older, wiser. I'm not going to put myself in danger if I can help it. I'm going to have a brain, be careful.

I want my son to grow up to be proud of his dad. I want him to have a dad.

Two days of planes, trains, and taxis later, on a pleasant spring day I knock on the door of Nikki's parents' house – where she's been staying for help since giving birth. I see her approach through the frosted glass. She's holding something in her arms. Randomly, I think it's a loaf of bread.

The door swings open and there she is, tired-looking but smiling. I look down, and lay my eyes on 'the little man' for the first time. Tiny. Fragile. Looks like me.

The visit home is short, but I make time that week to fit in an important appointment. The tattooist makes a careful job of etching the word *Daniel* – my son's name – onto my back.

V.XLVI

We're on Route Predators again in early 2008 and find the convoy crammed onto one side of a dual carriageway because the other is heaving with thousands – thousands – of Iraqis. I'm rather annoyed. Before leaving we'd emailed the ops room to give our route, and they'd mentioned nothing about this massive event going on. They'd cancel a mission for a sandstorm, or while awaiting intelligence. Had they known about this, they'd have cancelled, I'm sure. Which means they didn't. Which doesn't exactly fill me full of confidence.

Good job Alawai knows his arse from his elbow.
'It's the Ashura,' he tells me. 'They are Shi'a Muslims.'
'What are they doing?' I ask.
'They remember Husayn ibn Ali, martyr of the Battle of Karbala.'
'When was that?'
'First century. They are making a pilgrimage to the shrine in Karbala. His tomb. It is a great day for them. They could not do this under Saddam.'

It's quite a sight. John, behind me in the convoy, gets his video camera out. There are so many people; you don't get this many at a United-Wednesday game. There can't be a house or a shop in the area with a person in it – they're all here, along with Iraqi soldiers and police running crowd and traffic control. Older men in their traditional outfits are mixed with young men wearing tracksuits and baseball caps. Some women and kids are with the men; it strikes me as unusual, and I realise then that it's rare to see families together on the streets. They're in drab clothes, most of them, and the day is grey and dreary, which makes the colourful flags they carry stand out. Huge red ones. White banners with Arabic on them. And lots of bright green Shi'ite flags.

I'm pretty relaxed, watching the people go by, until Alawai comments, 'In 2004, there were big attacks on the Ashura. Hundreds killed. Many more injured. Suicide bombers and mortars.'

'Right,' I say.
We push on out of there as best as we can.

V.XLVII

While I'm home on leave, getting to know my baby boy, I set aside an afternoon to travel to Wisbech to see a fellow contractor, Jon Neve. He's dying. Brain tumour. We worked together on the PSD contract. He'd moved onto another PSD contract while I went to convoys, and we'd kept in touch on email and texts. Nice bloke. Fit; into his weights. He's been ill for a good while, but he'd always told the lads he was okay, getting better. But recently a mate had seen him and reported back to me he's been putting a spin on it. He's no better; he's on his way out.

I drop him a line, tell him I've got some slack time and will take him for lunch. I pick him up from his parents' house, where he's staying now. His driving license has been revoked; he's pissed as hell about that. Hell, I would be too. Bad enough he's dying; now he's stuck getting lifts from people like a fucking fourteen-year-old.

His dad takes me aside. 'His short-term memory's shot. He'll be forgetful. Vague.' Perhaps it'll give him a chance to forget, for a short while at least, that he's ill, I think.

He looks terrible. He was always stocky, but now muscle's become puffiness. His hair is patchy, his eyes hollow, haunted. I hide my horror and my sympathy. No doubt he gets enough of that as it is.

He takes me to a country pub. Nice, quintessentially English. Olde worlde. Open fire. Old man in the corner reading the paper while his collie dozes under the table. It's a long way from the places we used to chat over a drink in Iraq.

Over a pint of beer and a plate of fish and chips, he tells me he's all right. Doesn't want to talk about the obvious, so we chat about Iraq and the lads we both know. 'Glad to be out of there,' he tells me. 'Was only in it for the money.'

I'm not convinced. I know if I were in his place, I'd choose Iraq over a slow death any day.

A couple of hours later I drop him home and we say our goodbyes. Casual,

225

normal - as we would if we were to meet up for a beer in a few months, or bump into each other on the circuit in Iraq.

As I drive home, I think that's it. I won't see him again.

This way, he says his goodbyes. But he knows it's coming, has known for ages. He's losing control of his life, is losing his independence – his memories – himself. I feel sorry for him. For his family. I wouldn't like to go out like that.

A while after I get an email from my mate saying Jon's passed away. I email a few other mates who knew him and share the news. Can't go to the funeral, though, as I'm in another country. Not sure I'd want to anyway. I said goodbye to the living Jon, not the dead Jon.

V.XLVIII

My team – Team 9-8 – are close-knit now. John H, Karl from Stoke – one of two brothers on the private contracting circuit – and a Fijian lad called Leds. I'm the TL.

Karl's driver, Fat-Ali, is our main punching bag. He's a fat bastard, won't stop eating. I think he's taken the job just so he can get access to all the food on US bases. He brings pastries from home, from shops, and begs us to get him more from the DFAC. He lines them up on the dashboard on a mission – fucking seven, eight sandwiches – and works his way through them, washing them down with cans of shitty Iraqi pop. Karl has to inhale the fumes from a hotchpotch of flavours. Not for long, though. Fat-Ali has finished them in twenty minutes and is moaning about being hungry.

John keeps the job interesting too.

One day, we've left FOB Scania and are heading southbound back to UQ. We're freewheeling – just the four gun trucks, no lorries. We come up behind an American call sign moving slowly. The Americans like to give you permission to pass. I don't see why we need their say-so. So we gun it and speed past without giving them a chance to block our way.

They don't like that one bit. The rear gunner is standing up in his turret and shouting at me as I pass. I smile back at him.

I radio to the back, tell John we've caused an upset. He empties his wallet – he's got three thousand dollars on him – and fans the notes out nicely. As his vehicle passes the rear gunner, he waves the money at him.

The gunner goes nuts, he's fucking fuming, waving his fists in the air like a mental gorilla!

We laugh and accelerate on.

V.XLIX

The contract in UQ – with American United Logistics – is starting to look uncertain. It's up for renewal soon, and the contractors are all talking about a rumour that the company's going to condense teams down to two men. It will save AUL money, but none of us guys are happy. Two ex-pats to manage eighteen Iraqis and protect ten lorries? Sounds like something out of a Wild West cowboy movie. It's asking for trouble.

A four-man team works. You get to a point where it's running like clockwork. I don't have to tell the lads what to do; they already know. We get to the drop-off and one will collect water, another will take charge of fuelling up, the third will get scoff, and I'll go in the office and sign in the convoy.

Four men means four people with the brains, the experience and the skill to keep everyone on the right lines. Four guys you can trust.

Two men? It would be a gang fuck during contacts. We work hard enough as it is – that's pushing it too far. I've never heard of two-man teams (at that point) on convoys in any PMC in Iraq. You'd think the company would realise there's a reason no other company is attempting this measure for cost-cutting. It's fucking suicide.

The bottom line is the client's problem, not ours. If they can't afford the security, they should get the fuck out of Iraq. But of course they can afford it. They just think this is regular business. It's not. It's the business of war.

One of the bosses must get wind of the rumblings of unrest, because he comes down from Baghdad and pulls us all together for a pep talk. Doesn't want to wake up tomorrow and find we've all quit for better contracts with competitors.

'I know you're unhappy.'
We stare blankly at him.
'Don't worry. We're going to stick to four-man teams.'
He pauses. Seems to expect us to be delighted.
'The accommodation's not ideal, I know. And the food. We're going to make

changes. This is going to get better. But we need to be clear: this is the corporate world. It's all about keeping the contract.'

Subtext: the pecking order is client, boss, operator. Shut up and do your job. The corporate world. Office politics. Bitching about the big bosses. It's not so different to any other job in that sense.

A big Maori Kiwi stands up while boss man is in mid-sentence and walks straight to the door. Obviously feeling patronised. He knows he can be with a new company within days.

This isn't the first time there's been tension between the bosses and the operators. I came off leave once to find they'd rejigged the teams, and made some 2ICs team leaders. Blokes didn't want the 'promotions'. There were ex-Serjeant Majors, who'd been in command for years. Now they just wanted to be operators and get on with their jobs. No fuss. Do the job, get the money.

The team leader is responsible for the convoy and has to put up with all the bureaucratic shit on the bases. It can take you a whole day, sometimes, to get the load signed for. To get ten Iraqi drivers through security into the base. And that can drive you mad.

A reservist who signed in my convoy one day said to me, 'We were expecting you two hours ago.'

Five fucking contacts we'd had on the way to the drop-off. I told her that. Told her to take my tardiness up with my boss if she had a problem.

No doubt when she's back from Iraq, she'll be telling people she's an Iraqi vet. Not a fucking clue what went on, though, outside the confines of her nice, safe office in her nice, safe camp that's a little slice of America in the desert.

I can see why some people don't want to be TL, then. Don't mind it myself. But I get why you want an easier life, and it's not like you get paid much more for TL anyway. Salaries are pretty much equal.

Management aren't impressed by the refusals to accept promotions. 'Show me where in my contract it says I have to do that, say the guys. This isn't the Army. We don't have to do as we're told, ask no questions. Freedom to choose.

I know it can be tough for the bosses, though. Organising the logistics. Stuck between the clients and the employees. Walking a tightrope. Struggling to please. But they have to treat us as employees, not underlings. And they have to listen to us.

And when it comes to the two-man team shit, it's their job to know what needs to be done. To advise – no, to tell – the client what's essential for security. If you're going to cut costs and compromise security in doing so, you might as well start sending out convoys with no protection for all the good we can do.

I don't give a shit about the crappy food and accommodation. I do, however, care about being able to do my job with reasonable, controlled risks.

We ex-pats have some power. We'd vote with our feet if we thought they were taking *unreasonable* risks with our lives. There's a limit as to how far we're prepared to push being expendable.

V.L

You get to know plenty of guys on the circuit, and it's not uncommon to cross paths with colleagues at airports on your way in and out of Iraq. You get a mix. Blokes happy to be heading home for some leave. Blokes happy to be coming back. Blokes who are unhappy either way.

I fly from Baghdad to Dubai. They're small planes. Fifteen- or thirty-seaters. Two propellers. Old – made 1948, one of them. Air pressure alarms always going off during the flight. One of my mates swore that during a dive down – done right before landing in Iraq to avoid rockets – rivets came loose on the wing. No stewardess. No safety demonstration. If you go down, you just kiss your arse goodbye.

If the plane's worrying, the pilot is worse. I once boarded to find the pilot stretched out across three seats having a kip. He woke up as the passengers got on and staggered to the cockpit, started flicking switches. I had a look through the door. Had a tiny GPS device suckered to the flight deck, the kind of thing you buy in Millets. Reassuring. Still, there's no choice but to get on with it. Close your mind and hope for the best.

In Dubai, I arrive at the small, shitty terminal used for flights to places like Iraq and Afghanistan, and take a taxi to the terminal for the Westerners' flights. What a fucking contrast. It's huge. Smart. The kind of place you can shop. I do. I pick up an Omega diving watch there one day when I'm with a fellow contractor who picks out a Breitling.

From Dubai, I usually fly to Manchester. As I get off the plane, I walk past a newsagent's and scan the headlines. Usually, it's some shit about Katie Price or the Royals. I grab a filter coffee at Starbucks and watch Sky News. If there's a story about Iraq, it's doom and gloom.

I think, *Can I just turn around and go back to the real world?*

Back home, I slot back into daily life. Shopping with the missus is somewhat surreal after weeks spent in a gun truck being shot at in the open spaces of Iraq.

231

The thing with being in Iraq is that you're with people who get you. Army mates, contractor mates, they know what you're about, what you've seen, how it all works. You can ring up a bloke from your platoon you haven't seen in a five, six, seven years and it'll be like nothing's changed. It's easy. In Sheffield, family and friends I've known all my life, they're separate from the life I have abroad.

My mate Steve, the lad I went to St. Mary's and Notre Dame school with, invites me to go see Sheffield United v Crystal Palace along with some of his mates that I don't know. These are blokes who've never been further than northern England and the odd package holiday to Magaluf.

'Gary's just back from Iraq,' he tells them as he introduces me. 'Killing Saddam's fans and all that.'

His mates look a bit taken aback. Then curiosity replaces uneasiness.

'You in the Army, then?'
'Was.'
'So why you out there now then?'
'I'm a private contractor.'
'What's than then?'
'It's hard to explain.'
'Try.'
'It's complicated. Protecting convoys, mostly.'
'Kill anyone?'

Lesson learned - next time, make something up.

V.LI

We stay in FOB Scania often. It's the first and last stop when going north and back. Scania's getting mortared a lot at this time. Every night we lie in our fold up beds with nothing to protect us but a flimsy tent and listen to the boom of mortars as the Americans retaliate. It doesn't stop us sleeping. We have to trust those out fighting to keep us safe.

Still, a mate, John Mac, loses half his hand there when a mortar lands on the toilet block whilst he's on the shitter.

He told me later he knew he shouldn't have gone on the mission. He'd put his back out in the gym the night before, was bent over at near ninety degrees going to his vehicle that morning. But he decided to tough it out. Figured that if anything happened on the way, adrenaline would kick in and get him through. He was acting TL, and he didn't want to make some other guy take his place. Told me, 'Because if something happened to them, I'd never have forgiven myself.'

The mission went fine. It was at the stop-over at Scania that it happened. Normally, at eight p.m. he'd have been in the gym, but he'd passed because of his back. As he put it to me, 'My arse was rotten. As you are aware, the food is awesome. I was farting like fuck and Lofty was like, "Ya smelly Scottish git, you need to go and pull your arse thru!" So not long after that I was like, fuck it, I'm knackered and I'm gonna go for a crap then shower and bed.'

If he'd picked the end toilet, the rocket would have killed him. It tore through the roof, two cubicles down. John was on his feet, opening the door to his cubicle, when it hit. He was thrown forward and ended up with a pipe stuck in his shoulder and shrapnel in his face and neck. He picked himself up, walked to the front gate and asked the American guard there to get him some fucking morphine.

He was cass-evaced to Baghdad and operated on to remove the pipe and shrapnel. Now, he's trying to wrangle a hand transplant as part of his settlement.

'Get that and I'll maybe see you lot again one day,' he says to me. 'But it would probably take a lot to get me back out there. Wouldn't mind having another bash. Fuck, I can still fire weapons, believe it or not.'

The strangest thing? It wasn't the first time John was blown up in a toilet. Happened in Baghdad too, before then. But I guess that toilet block was better built, reinforced concrete with steel bars running through, because he escaped unscathed.

Just goes to show: you can't even take a shit in peace in Iraq.

V.LII

Death doesn't scare me. Pain? That's something else.

If I were John Mac with bits of shrapnel in me and my fingers missing, I'd have wanted morphine right there with me.

We're at a camp called Bucca near Umm Qasr when John Hunter and I have the idea of getting hold of some medical supplies.

As well as the team first-aid kit, all operators keep a personal one – mine contains a tourniquet, a dressing, Israeli bandages, an assortment of dressings, and morphine. I keep it in a pouch on my rig, easy to grab. It's for me in the event of injury. Though I once shared it with Allah, the LN whose legs got blown off.

Morphine is like gold dust out here. It's a controlled drug, so it's not easy to get hold of, but all the contractors want a few vials ready, just in case. If you've been shot or had a limb blown off, if you're dying, you don't want to be screaming as you go. Numbed and floating, that's the way.

The medical centre in Bucca is inside the prison compound. We pass cage after cage of Iraqi prisoners in orange jumpsuits. All ages, young to old. They look okay; pissed but not maltreated. Some stare at us; some just get on with their conversations. We take some photos on the off chance that we catch something interesting, but really there's no news here – the most interesting element of the cells is the washing line hanging in each, on which old-man-style vests are drying.

At the medical centre, the American Army nurse is quite happy for us to help ourselves to out-of-date supplies. We're shown into a huge room. 'All of this stuff will be discarded,' says the nurse. Army red tape. If a plaster's past its use-by, it's ditched. The budget is so immense, the staff simply ask for more supplies whenever they want them.

John and I are like kids in a sweet shop. We fill every pocket with dressings and vials of morphine.

235

Then we go for a coffee and a Subway.

American bases in Iraq are homes from home. All those figures of people working in war zone? Plenty of them are on secure bases dishing out coffee or serving behind a till. Or up a tower with a gun. Or running a gate. Not running about getting shot at and jostling with IEDs. Nice and safe.

Back at Umm Qasr we dish out supplies to the other lads. They flock round us; the morphine black market.

John and I keep plenty for ourselves.

Priority one: stay alive.
Priority two: stay clear of nightmarish painful deaths.

V.LIII

A mate from the Army, Tom Gaden, hooks up with me online, and we realise that we're both in UQ, just over the fence from each other. He's in the Army still. 'Come over one night,' he says. 'We're due a catch-up.'

So John and I jump straight in the Gun truck and drive round to see him. The base is full of Infantrymen, Riflemen. They look so young. Seems so long ago I was one of them.

'Blimey, look at you!' are Tom's first words. I was a racing snake in the Army, into running. Now I'm into weightlifting as well, and have put on the muscle at the gym.

We sit in the cookhouse, having a cup of tea, catching up on what mutual friends are up to. Some are still in the Army. Some are contractors.

Soon we're in a huddle of blokes, all wanting to find out more about what we do.

'How much are you making?'
We tell them…
Stunned silence.
'Tax free.'
'Holy shit. Just while you're out here?'
'Nope. It's spread across. So I get paid when I'm back home too.'
'How often do you get home?'
'Eight weeks on, four weeks off.'
'Jesus H. We're here for over six months!'
And so the comparisons go on.
'What's with the stubble?' teases Tom, pointing to my chin.
'No rank breathing down my neck,' I point out.
'Where do I sign!' jokes one of the young lads.
'You need experience,' I say. 'Though if some company suddenly needs a load of guys, you might get lucky. Generally, it's about contacts. Who you know.'
'Remember Bessbrook Mill?' Tom asks me.

237

The night the lads from my platoon and I sat up till we were kicked out of the NAAFI, right before I left the Army. We talked then about private contracting. It was a strange new beast; mysterious. I remember Tom, Black Scotty and Browny and all the others were all for sticking with the Army. Now, there's a light of curiosity in Tom's eyes.

Later, when we're saying our goodbyes, he asks for my email, to keep in touch. The private security work is interesting him, I think.

Before I go he gives me a Rifles Corporal rank slide as a parting gift… 'Don't forget where you come from,' he says. *Subtext: one day he'll be hitting me up for help getting work.*

That's the last day I'll see Tom. He's killed in Helmand Province, Afghanistan, the following year, while on an escort patrol, along with two colleagues. The vehicle he's travelling in is blown up by an IED.

And what of Black Scotty and Browny?

Serjeant Philip Scott remained in the Army. While on a fighting patrol in Helmand Province, Afghanistan, on 5 November 2009, he was killed by an IED explosion. The last time I saw him he was a Lance Corporal and my 2IC.

Corporal Lee Brownson also remained in the Army. While patrolling in Helmand Province, Afghanistan, on 15 January 2010, he was killed by an IED explosion. Just a month before he'd saved two colleagues and put his life on the line to save another when a US helicopter mistakenly fired on their base in Sangin. He was posthumously awarded the Conspicuous Gallantry Cross for his bravery in the incident. That's how I remember him. A small lad, but hard as fuck. Once, out on exercise with him in the mountains of Cyprus, we were starting the long tab back to camp when he came up to me. Said casually, 'Fell over back there.' Then he showed me his hand – messed up, fingers broken at fucked-up angles and facing the wrong way. He was chilled, took it on the chin and carried on tabbing. Brave bloke.

Three mates. Three from my platoon. The three of the dozen who got wankered that night in Bessbrook Mill who chose to stay in the Army, not leave for private work. All killed in action. All by fucking IEDs.

How many IEDs have I seen blow up next to me, in front of me, beside me, behind me, under me? My ears are ringing from the constant peppering of gunfire and explosions.

Yet I'm here, alive, and they're not.

Because they stayed in the Army? Because they were in Afghanistan or Iraq? Because their luck ran out? I don't know.

V.LIV

I stick Sky News on before Daniel's up and I'm stuck with kids' TV. In Iraq, I'll pick up a newspaper one of the blokes has brought back from leave, see what its angle is. Check news websites, though the internet connection's too slow for streaming, so it's articles only. Watch American news channels in the US camps. Something like Fox – which is all they're allowed to watch. Subjective as hell. But the media portrayal of the situation in Iraq fucks me off.

It's all doom and gloom, sensationalised. There's a down slant in the insurgents' favour. They cover what they want to cover; ignore the rest.
'Another American soldier was killed in Baghdad...'
'A British soldier has been killed by a roadside bomb in Basra, taking the toll on British forces to...'

There's no mention of the many soldiers who survived the day a Coalition soldier lost his life. There's no mention of the fifty, or hundred insurgents taken out the same day a Coalition soldier lost his life.

It's like putting out a report in Britain saying '*Eight Thousand Dead in a Week: The Country Mourns*'. Fuck, you'd think, reading that. What the hell's happened? Well, nothing much... Grannies passing away in their wing-backed chairs. Sick people dying in hospitals. Drivers losing control and ploughing into central reservations, telegraph poles, pedestrians. Eight thousand, statistically, is a pretty average mortality rate for England and Wales. But how easily the media can twist that into drama. Which is annoying, but not disastrous if those reading the newspapers and news websites and watching the news reports have a brain and can think for themselves. But seriously, how many citizens are out there who just accept what they're told?

The media have a responsibility to present a balanced view. But they're highly selective in the incidents they report on. If it bleeds, it leads, as they say. But only when that blood is seeping out of a Coalition soldier – not an insurgent.

The result is eroding support for the Coalition and fuelling the insurgents. Every headline that puts down the Coalition is a victory for the insurgents. The terrorist mentality is simple, based on Chinese general Sun Tzu's philosophy: kill one, scare ten thousand. And fuck does the media help them with this. Shout about a suicide bombing that killed five people. Don't bother mentioning the successful completion of a massive infrastructure project that's got sewage off the streets. For the men who lose their lives, I find it disrespectful. They knew what they had signed up for. They were there to do a job, were willing to die for it if it came to it. To dramatize the death, to suggest that soldiers shouldn't have been there in the first place or were let down, it's taking away something from him. Tell us that fifty fucking bad guys were taken out in an operation. Then, at the end, thank the one soldier who gave his life for that victory to have taken place, and honour him.

Plus any guy who's down on the ground in Iraq can spot the mistakes. They get causes of death wrong. They misreport circumstances of deaths. They talk about British soldiers while beaming out images of American ones. They talk about Route Irish as being the worst road in the word, when it's not even close to some in Mosul and Fallujah. They bang on about Baghdad and Basra. They know nothing of Al Mushada, where not being attacked on a run-through is shocking. The problem is, the journalists, on the whole, hole up around the Green Zone. They don't see what's going on around the country as a whole. They talk about stuff they haven't seen. They talk about stuff they know nothing about – those providing the news have little or no experience in counter-insurgency and reconstruction. They might have a nice white certificate from some school of journalism, but what qualifies them to accurately analyse warfare?

It's nothing new, of course. In 1982 British radio services reported that Argentine bombs weren't fused properly, then we lost *HMS Coventry* and *HMS Ardent* sunk by correctly-fused bombs. I guess those 'journalists' didn't realise that Argentine intelligence might be listening also. Journalists fucking up is old news; still, it sticks in the throat.

Then there's their portrayal of guys like me, PMCs. Since Blackwater came on the radar they've tended to paint private contractors in a negative light. Like we're all insane, bloodthirsty cowboys with no idea of right and wrong. Gunslingers, mercenaries - they love those words. They seem unsure about us, about who we are. Don't know what neat little box to put us in. Infantrymen, Marines – that's easy. Doing their duty. Courageous. Honourable. But blokes who work for the

Coalition outside of the armed forces, who carry a rifle but don't wear a uniform, what to do with those?

You're unlikely to read a report on a contractor getting killed in Iraq, but if you do, the report is bound to make some comment on the number of contractors in the country, why they're there and whether they should be in the first place. Never mind that the contractor knew the risks, was happy enough to be there. Yeah, it's fucking sad he's died. Yeah, especially when he had a wife and a kid and was only a day off going home on leave. But that's life. That's the nature of the job. It's the money that makes them most on edge, I think. Armed forces equals basic pay. But contractors, it's becoming common knowledge we're on a decent whack. And that, for some reason, is something to be commented on. I think, sometimes, they assume we're like hired guns or something similar. They watch too much Hollywood bullshit; think it's a dirty business with Rambo wannabes running about with pockets stuffed full of bloodied money.

As for attacks on private contractors, they're par for the course. Over three hundred contacts in four years. But apparently, we're overpaid.

V.LV

I'm back in Sheffield, on leave, and friends are emailing me updates on the contract, which is up for renewal and will possibly go to another PMC.

It doesn't bother me. I'm due a bonus for accrued leave – five figures – which will see me through until the next job.

I've already sent my CV to another PMC. Most of the lads have – we saw which way the wind was blowing with the UQ contract, and covered our backs. You can take your chances and hope the new PSC takes on all the operators in place when they move in, so it's just a change of t-shirt logo. Or you can be proactive... A few days later I'm in London. In my suit. In an office block.

The interview lasts less than five minutes. The interviewer looks at my CV, tells me I'm exactly what they're looking for and hands me the contract to sign. Seventeen weeks with no break. Five figures.

I scrawl my name where she indicates. A couple of days later, I'm in a villa in the Red Zone of Baghdad with fifteen other blokes. A handful of South Africans. Some Brits. And an Aussie – Adam. Turns out Adam had met John from my team when he was in the Army. Stopped him at a checkpoint on Route Tampa. He'd quizzed John on private security. And now here we are, working together.

I do a couple of convoys, and then I start getting requests for PSD tasks. First up, I'm high-pro, escorting high-level US military officers – colonels and generals – from the Green Zone around Baghdad. They're military men, so theoretically they know the ropes. But for all I know they've been sitting behind a desk for twenty years, so I treat them as I would any other client.

Once the clients are in the back of the car, I turn and give them a briefing:

'Colonel Brown? I'm your team leader today.
'First, confirm your Blood group? Thanks.
'Have you told anyone of your movements today? No? Good.
'Your only job is to sit tight. If something goes down, you let me deal with it. If

243

we come into a contact, stay calm. The top gunners and I will be on top of it. If we get small-arms fire, we'll up our speed. If the vehicle becomes immobilised, I will move you to the other one. Don't resist; go with it.'

'If it all goes bad and I'm down, grab my weapon. The bag beside you contains spare magazines. Get on the radio to Adam in front. Or use this phone to call the Ops room.'

It's heavy stuff, but it doesn't faze them. They thank me for the brief. I hope they feel at ease with it, reassured by my thorough approach.

I hope they fucking do what I've told them if we're ambushed.

Author, Al Tikrit

Allah. Within a month of this photo he will be blown to pieces.

24 hours after the roadside EFP >
The other side of the truck was blown to bits.

Aussie Gaz with his Soviet RPK rifle > Iraq

Marc stands next to his gun truck after
his roadside IED > Abu Ghraib

Low Profile PSD vehicle OPs with Aussie Adam > Baghdad

Ex-pats, Northern Iraq

Vehicle drills with Chris > Baghdad

Hitching a ride with the US pilots (with Jon Neve) > Green Zone
Baghdad 2005

The PMC convoy's ex-pats (author 4th from
the left) > Abu Ghraib

Aboard one of the largest oil tankers in the world - Somali piracy waters. Author posing with members of an Indian crew after a piracy attack.

Sitrep

REPORTED ATTACK

01.06.2017: ██████ UTC: POSN: ████████N - ████████E, AROUND 103 NM EAST
OF ████████████:
SIX PERSONS ARMED WITH GUNS IN A SKIFF APPROACHED AND FIRED UPON A
TANKER UNDERWAY. ALARM RAISED. NON-ESSENTIAL CREW RETREATED TO THE
CITADEL. SPEED INCREASED. EVASIVE MANOEUVRES CONDUCTED AND ONBOARD
ARMED SECURITY TEAM FIRED ████████ SHOTS RESULTING IN THE SKIFFS
MOVING AWAY. A MOTHER VESSEL WAS SEEN IN THE VICINITY. VESSEL IS
SAFE.

Daz Sweatman

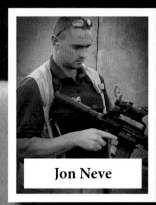

Jon Neve

Lee Brownson

Richie Coel

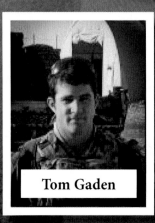

Tom Gaden

Phillip Scott

The background to this page is Tom Gaden's rank slide. He gave it to me the last time I saw him before he was killed.

V.LVI

After the military brass, I'm given new clients to protect: Japanese journalists for Channel NHK. The powers that be have decided that they'll travel low-pro – so no branding on the cars, and sitting in traffic rather than pushing through. The plan is to avoid attracting attention. Frankly, given that the cars are Mercedes and BMWs and your average Iraqi civilian drives a piece of shit, the idea that we'll blend in seems flawed to me. But I crack on and wear a big shirt over my body armour, and a shemagh on my head. It's not a great look with my North Face cargos.

The Japanese TV channel is paying my company five thousand dollars a day. But the journalists do very little. Every few days we pick them up from the Sheraton Hotel in Baghdad and take them for a meeting across town, usually in an FOB. Most of the journalists in town stay at the Sheraton, and they have security firms like mine protecting them. Except the BBC, which contracts its own operators. One day a BBC journalist approaches me in the reception area and asks if I'll speak on camera about my time in Iraq. I refuse. Don't want my face out there. The bloke will be lucky to find anyone happy to talk while we're still contracted by companies and in the thick of it.

As usual, I've briefed the journalists before we start the journey. As usual, they've answered 'Yes, yes, yes' to every point. They're very quiet men. Distant. Unemotional. I'm not sure how good their English is, how much they understand. I figure it doesn't matter in the end. If it all goes tits up, I'll cross-deck them with brute force.

We're on Route Oilers in Baghdad. It's an urban area – we drive past a church (yes, Christian), the university, shops and cafes. None of this existed when I first came to Iraq in 2003; now, these stand as testament to the journey the country has been on.

We're going over a bridge. There's a checkpoint up ahead. Blast walls funnel traffic into a single lane. A guard on one side of the road; two more on the other side. Usually, I'd be in the second vehicle, with Adam behind me, and heading the convoy would be a low-key vehicle, not armoured, with LNs scouting the area for threats. But this time I've taken the lead because the LN driver was incapable of following a new route I'd laid out for him. Reading a map. Fucking difficult, apparently.

I go through first. I slow, out of respect, but I don't stop. If I stopped for every fucking checkpoint it would take us an age to get anywhere. Plus I don't want to be static if I can help it. Sitting duck.

I go through fine. With my dark skin and the beard I've grown, I can pass as Iraqi - hopefully.

As I pass, the Iraqi soldier gives me the slightest of nods and I continue through. Adam's next, ten seconds behind me. They must add up his white skin, blond hair and blue eyes and think Westerner. I hear the cracks of gunfire behind.

'Contact rear! Small arms!'
The journalists were talking in the back; silence falls at once.

'Drive through,' I command on the radio. Soon we're out of range, away down the road.

'Adam, check-in?'
'We're okay. Checkpoint guards firing at us. Back windscreen's taken a pounding.'
I want to reply, 'Fucking bastards; and fucking low-pro – if we were high-pro, they wouldn't have dared.' But I don't; this is PSD, not convoys, and we have to be professional in front of clients.

I turn around to check on the journalists. They're frozen, white faced.
'Your first contact?' I ask.
They nod, as one.
'We're fine now' I smile, 'Don't worry.'

They don't look very reassured. I turn back around and grin to myself.

Well, there's a story for you, I think. Better than the stuff they'd usually be reporting, sitting comfortably in their plush hotel and talking about violence and an enemy they've never even met.

LMCC (Logistical Management Convoy Centre) in the Green Zone monitors convoys for both military and civilian contracts. I find out a mate of mine has wangled a cushy desk job there so I make some time for a catch-up and have a nosey. I take Adam with me.

There, the guys recognise a fellow stats-fan and they pull up all the data from all convoys since the transponders (panic buttons) were introduced. I sift through the computer files and tables and focus on the Abu Ghraib Armorgroup teams.

Average, average – Contacts per rotation: twenty. Eight months of work per year equates to eighty contacts per year. Four years on the contract means *three hundred and twenty contacts in total.* And that's a minimum figure, because I know plenty of operators didn't even bother hitting the transponder unless the situation was really fraught. Not to mention the teams that were well above the average.

Goes to show, any of my mates on that contract has a book in him.

V.LVII

2009...

The contract winds down. I'm already back in touch with the HR woman from Armourgroup, lining up more work.

I spend my third Christmas in a row in Iraq. The LNs bring me Christmas cards, which is touching. Muslims buying Christmas cards! As Christmases go, its shit – but I'm sure it will be my last in this country.

The work is changing, and the Status of Forces Agreement (SOFA) that's come into effect is fucking up how private contractors operate. Iraqis are running the show again, drunk on power, and making it up as they go along. We'll have rules upon rules to follow. We'll be accountable under Iraqi criminal law.

I'm not tiptoeing about Iraqis. They'll create a total headache for us all. Besides, there are enough shitholes around the world for me to work in.

Northern Baghdad, I'm on what we call Banana Bridge – so called because it's shaped like a banana – when checkpoint guards block us, gesturing at us to stop. We do, and my driver starts conversing with the guard in Arabic, shouting through the armoured glass. There's a lot of headshaking, and the guard keeps pointing at me. He looks pissed.

'What's going on, Saif?' I ask.
He turns to me. 'They think you Iraqi. I tell them no. You American.'

I raise up my rifle – M4, American – and show it the guard. He seems to click then. Backs off. Let's us through.

Once we're past the checkpoint I say to Saif, 'Why did you tell him I'm American?'
He smiles. 'American more dangerous.'

I find myself, somehow, a little offended. Then I remember Blackwater.
There's no big farewell when I leave. An ex-pat team takes me to the airport, and

I sit on a cold, hard plastic seat and wait for my flight. I stare up at the boards that announce flights. They're those old-fashioned flicker boards, frozen on a host of European cities – Paris, Milan, London. Have been since the start of the war. The airport's humming with a mix of contractors and Iraqis. Side by side, going about their business.

I look at the Westerners striding about. Getting on with it all. Joking with mates. Scratching their balls.

I look at the Iraqis bumbling about. No sense of urgency. Jabbering to each other in fast-paced Arabic. Scratching their beards.

Will I miss Iraq?

Seriously. Who misses Iraq?

V.LVIII

I step out of the plane onto the rickety steps and survey the scene. Tiny airport. Empty shells of a building. Snowy mountains in the distance whose tops are invisible in the misty low cloud.

I zip my North Face jacket up to my chin and climb down the rickety steps to the frosty runway. Fuck is it cold here. Iraq in winter wasn't exactly desert-hot, but this is really cold. It's a shock after the couple of weeks back in Sheffield, where it was typical northern England weather for March – drizzly, mostly, and fresh, but not Arctic. Even a few days of spring sunshine.

I follow the other passengers – locals – to the terminal, if you can call the tiny shack-like building that. I stand in line at customs behind a man holding a chicken. At the front of the line, the customs officer grabs my passport, checks the visa, stamps it and grunts then waves me through.

I grab my backpack from a pile in the middle of an open floor – luggage reclaim - and walk to arrivals, all of ten metres. I scan the crowd but see no one I know, so I head outside.

Thick snow blankets the ground. A big open circle surrounded by cars. In the middle is a flagpole on which a black, green and red flag flutters feebly in the breeze.

'Gary!'

I spot him, bald head standing out among the shemaghs, leaning casually against a G-500. I walk over, grinning, and we slap each other on the back.

'The dream team back in action,' says John Hunter. 'You're gonna like it here, mate. Don't be fooled by the snow. It's hot as hell.'

'Welcome to Afghanistan!'

AFTERWORD

The history of the soldiers for hire is a long one, if you are prepared to relate the profession to the related (but not revered) one of mercenary, which dates right back in the history of war. But the PMC is a relatively new entity (since the 1980s and the corporatisation of military 'services') and its evolution is changing warfare and reconstruction.

Between 2003, the invasion of Iraq, and 2012, more private security contractors worked in Iraq (for the US Department of Defence) than Coalition troops. There is no fixed total figure for contractors in the country, but in 2007 the Los Angeles Times reported that '*More than 180,000 civilians – including Americans, foreigners and Iraqis – are working in Iraq under US contracts, according to State and Defence department figures*'. According to the Iraq Coalition Casualty Count, during that year there were 468 foreign private contractor deaths, of which 225 were private military contractors. However, I suspect this figure is under-reported – attacks on PSDs are shouted about; attacks on convoys are par for the course.

Today, a lot of the circuit guys I come across could use a rotation or two on convoys, where it was hottest, to put things in perspective. If I come across a former operator who worked in Iraq during the time period covered in this book, I know I can be fairly confident he will have seen some. Because for those of us on convoys, we earned every one of our dollars.

Now, the number of contractors in the country has reduced as the country 'stabilises' and troops pull out. Many contractors have moved on to other work, such as 'teams on board' protection for ships against piracy around Somalia, and private military support in Afghanistan, Libya, Syria, Lebanon and so on.

But what of the contractors who still remain in Iraq, protecting diplomats, training the Iraqi Police and military force, and advising the government? The State Department is taking over contracting operations, and there is some concern that it lacks experience in such matters. The contractors in country will be managed by the US Embassy in Baghdad (the largest in the world), which will have around 1,700 diplomats and representatives of various agencies – protected by around 5,000 security contractors. The plan is to eventually bring in Iraqi locals and reduce contractor numbers. Still, as long as there are diplomats there, they'll need private security.

For private security contractors, then, the future looks bright. In the aftermath of 9/11, the private security industry bucked the trend and gained in strength against other industries whose stock fell. Outsourcing is a growing part of how business – and government – operates. And civilians are becoming more vocal about sending troops into dangerous places for political reasons they disagree with – so why not hire someone to do the dirty work you don't want your son/ daughter to do?

Yes, more regulation of private security contractors is on the cards, and it is likely that political stability will mean no large-scale need for the service. But as long as private contractors continue to operate, organisations will continue to hire us. Because we're readily available, we're cost-effective, we're experienced, and we're capable.

And, of course… we're expendable.

The backlash to the Iraq war has been wide and far-ranging and is continuing over a decade after the invasion. This backlash continues as many perceive the war to have been robbed of its legitimacy, due to non-existent WMDs, and supposed links to Al-Qaeda remaining unproven. The insurgency that ensued after the invasion robbed the invasion of its initial successes, as one US general stated – 'We won the war, but lost the peace'. Today it is reckoned that Tehran has more influence in Baghdad than America and Britain. The Sunni minority has been marginalised, enabling violent Salafists to sweep through Sunni areas whilst routing the Iraqi Army.

In 2016 a large scale investigation into the UK's governmental policy towards Iraq from 2001 to 2009 was published. The so-called Chilcot Inquiry covered the background to the decision to go to war, whether we were properly prepared and equipped, how the conflict was conducted, and what planning (or not) was in place for its aftermath, a period of time that saw intense sectarian violence, terrorism, crime, and conflict.

The Chilcot report reasoned that the UK chose to join the US's invasion of Iraq long before all peaceful solutions had been exhausted. This view point maybe true. However, the report's time span (expediently) only begins from 2001. The explanations for the US-led invasion of Iraq will always be contentious, open to debate and subjective to the perspective of various viewpoints. No one reason for the war should be viewed in isolation: the various elements outlined above are all inter-linked and mutually support each other and should be viewed in this perspective. The same can be said for the time periods involved - the build-up to the 2003 war must be seen from at least August 1990, and combined with these various reasons, one can identify why Iraq was invaded.

The Chilcot report also places much emphasis on weapons of mass destruction, and asserts a policy on the Iraq invasion was made on the basis of flawed intelligence analysis that was not challenged and should have been.

Supposedly there were no WMD in Iraq, but one can argue that it took the invasion to find that out. However, the discrediting of intelligence must not be used in the perception of hindsight. Hindsight must be used as a learning aid.

Not one agency - whether that be intelligence or weapons inspectors or any other - from any nation, said before the invasion that Iraq does not have WMD. The evidence was merely not there to categorically say it did. One problem is that intelligence is open to any interpretation - one person sees a mobile nerve agent production facility, the next sees an ice cream van. Either could be right, both could be wrong. Intelligence itself is a very inconsistent entity, if they under-report and something goes wrong they are to blame, but no one will berate them for over-reporting, especially if they get it right. Furthermore, the intelligence gatherer cannot be responsible for decision-makers reading intelligence with an insufficiently critical outlook, or interpreting their analysis to fit certain policies. One can see why WMD and intelligence was used to such a high degree in the pre-war build up. The reason did fit with the text of UN Resolution 687 and many others, and many were sure they existed in Iraq. The intelligence and the interpretations pointed in the direction of WMD on some level, after all why would Saddam go to such effort to deny the UN inspectors and diplomatic approaches, and why would Saddam bring war upon himself and his populace to protect nothing. The legal profession might refer to these actions as 'guilty demeanour'.

There was also very little time to prepare the British forces in readiness for the war. As the Chilcot report states:

'The risks were neither properly identified nor fully exposed to ministers, resulting in equipment shortfalls.'

However, the report does not make it clear which person or persons were responsible with in the MOD for identifying or articulating such shortfalls. And in this humble soldier's opinion, delays in providing adequately protected patrol vehicles should not have been tolerated (let alone the total lack of intelligence, reconnaissance equipment, and helicopters).

Yet, it is still the aftermath of the Iraq war that remains the sticking point in the legacy of the Iraq invasion. It seems the aftermath and consequences of the invasion were wholly underestimated and therefore inadequate.

Both the US and the UK governments failed to achieve their own stated objectives in Iraq. More than 200 Brits died as a result of the conflict. Iraqi people suffered greatly. By July 2009, at least 150,000 Iraqis had died, probably many more. More than one million were displaced.

It is also stated that Tony Blair greatly over-estimated his influence on US decision-making. Indeed, one must consider the position of the US after 9/11 and that the invasion of Iraq was a manifestation of expression within the context of the so-called 'War on Terror'.

And as for regime change, it is unlikely that even the opponents of the war were huge admirers of Saddam Hussain and his regime, few would deny that living under Saddam's rule was brutal, unjust and humiliating. Torture, killings, disappearances, and perpetual fear all served as a moral construct for the case of invasion. Many opponents of the war stand their arguments on legal basis; perhaps if the popularity of the war had been addressed with more of a slant toward the humanitarian and freedom side, then acceptance would have been more forthcoming. It can be claimed that this piece of the argument was largely achieved. Democratic elections have taken place in Iraq since the 2003 conflict, malnutrition is a quarter of what it was under Saddam, profits from oil are filtering back to the Iraqi people, and the country has national infrastructures that did not exist prior.

Regrettably, these successes are largely overshadowed by the post-war insurgency and the rise of Da'ash (Islamic State terrorists). Possibly these two manifestations were empowered - in part - due to an Iraqi culture that does not yet comprehend the philosophies of freedom and the rule of law, a culture that accepts violence as the ultimate authority. As Richard Cobden exemplified in a speech to the House of Commons in 1850,

'A people which wants a saviour, which does not possess an earnest pledge of freedom in its own heart is not yet ready to be free'.

So why did we invade Iraq? Allied to the American philosophies that developed from the 9/11 attacks and the swift and thus-far successful operations during the invasion of Afghanistan between 2001 and 2003, is that a conviction developed within the Bush administration, a conviction that began to emphasise a faith in American power and their duty to spread the American ideology. Perhaps the administration was caught up in a narrative of their own making, a narrative that is partly based on a perceived American character, a vision of 'calling' that is founded, in part, on a powerful moral crusade, a crusade that has been emphasised through generations of culture, art and proselytization.

Over the years, presidential phrases such as 'Day of infamy', 'Evil Empire', and 'Axis of evil' encourage the concept that America is as much a cause as it is a nation. Perhaps this narrative was strengthened by the American media and therefore, by default, the American public. If we take all this as the case then the reason for the war was war, an expression of adversity, an enactment of American power ideals, American identity, and that the drive within these milieus was the invasion of Iraq in 2003.

There is nothing new about contractors supporting military operations. In fact, the utilisation of contractors is older than most armies. Yet, from the mid-1800s to the end of the Cold-War, militaries were presumed - and to a greater extent supposed - to be self-sufficient. Large conscripted militaries centred their doctrines on bloc-centric industrialised warfare. As Tonkin has identified in her second paradigm shift away from mercenaries, contractors played a minor part in the logistical workings of NATO and Warsaw-Pact states. By the twenty-first century, Western military forces were undergoing significant changes in how they were organised for operations - streamlined, smaller, professional, mobile forces, began to concentrate the core capabilities of conflict operations. The intervention in Afghanistan became the testing/proving ground for contractor support to US and UK militaries.

Since the end of the Cold War the scope and challenges facing military forces are more complex and multi-faceted. The paradigm of how militaries functioned in the Cold War is no longer relevant now. Socio-politics, economic, and technical factors, have played various parts in creating a defunct Cold War doctrine. Indeed, the enemies of the contemporary modern state have ensured that the supposed conventional warfare that was once attached to the psyche of the people who lived in the Cold War Period are no longer applicable to the way modern warfare operations are conducted. In other words, the change in enemy forces has forced the West to re-think its war fighting strategies.

This is nothing new: consider the British Army in the North American wars of independence, where they conducted warfare with old-style tactics that were non-applicable. The failures of forming square in compact forestry whilst wearing red tunics led to the creation of the light-armed troops - dressed in brown and russet green - using more accurate rifled (as opposed to muskets) weaponry. So it is with the twenty-first century, where the tactics in response to a large mechanised and armoured Soviet force are invalid against such enemies as Al-Qaeda, the Taliban, Iraqi insurgents, and proxy militias. Bloc-centric industrialised military forces are obsolete (at least for now); the actuality is that contractor support is now an integral part of the current military force structure.

Increased commitments, downsizing, and a vacuum in certain skills have led to contractors being invited to enable the military deployment, and made contractors a key component of the modern force structure. Indeed, a failure to accept the inevitable frameworks of the modern military may lead to neglect and inertia in military oversight and responsibility to contractors. Perhaps the blockades that observers place to the obstruction of contractor usage are an attribute of an emotional attachment to the Cold War-centric military model.

The core capabilities, such as war fighting, are tasks which must be retained by State military functions - for now. So what of armed PMC contactors in a war zone? Firstly, armed contractors are not mercenaries: their legal status sets them apart from this group by numerous degrees (actually *A mercenary shall not have the right to be a combatant or a prisoner of war*' as defined by the Geneva Convention, Article 47, Protocol I - paradoxically, this makes groups such as insurgents, and terrorists closer in definition to that of 'mercenary'). Indeed, protective security - even when conducted in an intense combat theatre of war - is still deemed separate from regular warfare. Decision-makers must recognise that PMC contractors do not belong to their military; this differential is extremely important if they are intended to be utilised in warfare and stabilisation projects in the future, as any attempt to do so by the industry, or by political and military decision makers, could end in problems for all parties, not least of all the undermining of the military's operations and political objectives.

PMCs in Iraq displayed what the industry could realistically deliver. However, phenomenal success rates were often only enabled by their narrow contract and task parameters - parameters that did not necessarily complement the overall mission of the wider coalition. Iraq also illustrated the need for standardisation, oversight, and regulation within the PMC industry. The standards of varying PMCs in the early days of the Iraq insurgency varied immensely, from 'contractors' whom did not have contracts, to those that had signed explicitly detailed contracts defining the scope, parameters, legal status, and code of conduct whilst deployed under the corporate banner of the PMC and their clients.

The wars in Iraq and Afghanistan also exemplified the changing approaches to non-combatant immunity, for many a civilian who ventured into a combat and hostile environment - such as humanitarian groups, NGOs, corporate staff, or journalists - during the Cold War period had their positions as non-combatants accepted by many armies, and even insurgent groups. This situation has changed in the modern era of Iraq and Afghanistan, where everyone is a potential target. Public security organisations are not capable of safeguarding every threat that manifests itself in 21st-century conflict, and due to the new 'core-capabilities' structure of Western militaries, they are now poorly placed to do this. Therefore, when an organisation has to send staff to a hostile environment (or have assets in that environment protected) a PMC is often the enabler of that organisation.

Regulation and oversight have been a main area of critique for the disablers

265

of PMC use, and recent armed conflicts have challenged the conventional wisdom that military and security functions should only reside in public forces. Some may consider this to reduce the State's ability to control violence and ensure accountability for misconduct in a conflict environment. However, the widespread use of PMCs has not undermined the capacity of States to control violence in the international gamut. In fact, certain states - such as the US and UK - have at their disposal the capability to apply substantial influence over PMCs in conflict locations. Influence that is available to instigate any applicable laws in order to regulate a PMC and its contractors. The hiring state, the host state, and the home state of the PMC are actually in a predominantly strong position to steer PMC conduct in a conflict location. Moreover, international law imposes a wide range of obligations on these States to enforce and oversee the behaviour of PMCs; this demonstrates the given international responsibility of all these States to manage the actions of the PMC. Privatisation is inherently a public act, therefore, it is the State's obligation to oversee the conduct and regulation of the PMC, and ensure that it is seen as transparent and within the structures of the laws of armed conflict, international law, and international humanitarian law. Indeed, the laws exist - the obligation now lies with the state to implement, promote, and enforce the existing laws, creating cultures of professionalism at state and international level.

Hostile environments have in the 21st-century become extremely volatile places, some PMCs have managed this environment well, and others have shown less adaptability. Although many an observer has promoted the use of PMCs and their capabilities, they do not by any means hold all the answers to conflict environments, for the most desirable outcomes the answer must be a holistic approach that integrates all entities working in close proximity within a hostile setting. This lack of integration in places such as Iraq has often been due to the occupying forces inability to fully integrate PMCs into the overall operational plan, PMCs in Iraq were treated in an ad-hoc manner because they were seen as a bolt-on accessory to ongoing operations.

Contractors retain a valuable resource for those entities that decide to utilise them, both public and private. PMCs have access to pools of talent, expert knowledge, and commercial experience that are often not available in the military and public sectors. They also offer decision makers and commanders flexibility in their tasks and alternative options that may not be readily available from the public sector. Conversely, when deployed in theatres alongside the military, they can make a commander's job more complex, especially if there was not an initial plan to include them in the operational sphere. The point is that the paradigm of deployed forces has changed: militaries, and contractors must - and will - be joined at the hip for many years to come. Indeed, for the US and UK militaries in particular, PMCs are now a part of the deployment structure and require therefore to be integrated at the ground stages of planning and further up to the geo-strategic level.

In a peculiar paradox, it is the culture and social construction surrounding PMCs that presents one of their greatest challenges. The utilisation of PMCs has evolved and developed, their capabilities are readily accepted by many an analyst, they have a legal status within the international realm, and an ethical mandate akin to any public force or corporate organisation. Yet, it is still old-style attitudes and ignorance that the industry must combat - attitudes that are inextricably attached to the Cold War, attitudes that conjure up images of mercenaries in 1960s Africa, attitudes that are ignorant of the laws and legislation that cover the industry, and attitudes that fail to accept that PMCs are now a key aspect of the modern military deployment. There is perhaps even a replacement in future conflict and post-conflict reconstruction projects.

The paradox is that an institutional change has happened in reality, but that change has not yet happened in people's minds. Consider the words of Kupcu and Cohen who illustrate this challenge to the industry:

'*A culture shift is required in which civilian and military leaders take steps to fully integrate private contractors, not only into the force structure but into mission requirements. Without this institutionalised change, the problems we have experienced in Iraq and Afghanistan will continue, significantly retarding the militaries ability to adjust to the evolving security challenges of the 21st century*'.

The point is that contractor utilisation in the twenty-first century battlefield must be considered a strategic activity and integrated into all levels of planning - indeed, ignore them and one may risk operational failure.

EPILOGUE

2015...

Off the coast of East Africa. I'm standing on the bridge of one of the largest oil tankers in the world. I'm watching two dots on the radar, slowly flashing, each blip bringing the dots closer to our vessel. The crew are well drilled; at the sound of the alarm they have assembled inside a pre-installed 'citadel' deep in the bowls of the ship. All that's left on the bridge are myself, my two other security team members, a pilot, and the captain of the ship.

My radio crackles into action, it's one of my team outside on the bridge wings.

'I see them, two small boats approaching'.
'Okay, stand by', I reply.

The captain, a small Indian man - all 5ft of him - has drifted over to the windows trying to get a better look through his binoculars. I tell him to get away from the windows and stand at the back of the bridge, no time for formalities and politeness now. As he turns he catches my eye and mouths two words to me - 'Somali pirates'. I'm not sure if this is a question, a statement, or if he's talking to himself.

I slide the door of the bridge open and go outside, the heat hits me and I'm instantly dripping. I'm carrying a Styr Maritime Scout bolt-action rifle in my right hand, and I'm wearing body Armor with a small grab bag slung over my shoulder carrying extra magazines.

I reach up to the back of my head and click the record button on my head cam. My colleague sees me approaching and gives me a target indication - the good old four fingered point - I see them immediately, two skiffs closing in fast.

With about 400 meters to go one of the skiffs pulls up and slows down paralleling our ships bearing. The second skiff continues on a direct approach. I grab the binoculars and have a look, I don't see weapons, grappling hooks, or ladders, but that doesn't mean they're not concealed. However, I do see black faces, five or six of them, and they're traveling way to fast to be fishing.

I continue to observe for the next few minutes, I feel the ship move and vibrate as the pilot begins his countering manoeuvres.

That's close enough I think to myself. It's time to send them a message. I take a stooped un-supported fire position behind the water drums we've placed on the bridge wings, in my peripheral vision I see my team mate raising his rifle into the air, he's not pointing it, he's showing it in a side-on view. Showing them who we are, and what we've got.

It makes no difference, at about 300 meters the skiff slows and changes direction. It's now paralleling us, a tactic I've seen before. Since the proliferation of armed PMCs in this part of the industry the pirates have learnt to be savvier, no more high speed approaches with guns blazing, this is what we call a soft approach or a probe.

With my right hand I pull the bolt up and back, I then push it half way forward - a quick look in the chamber to see that a round has indeed been picked up - then I push the bolt handle fully forward and snap it down.

I'm in an elevated position, high up on the bridge wings looking down to sea-level; two decades ago I learned how my POA (Point of Aim) changes when firing from an elevated position. I could never have imagined that all those live 'Sanger' shoots in Northern Ireland would have benefited me in the here-and-now, halfway around the world, in the middle of the ocean, against Somalian pirates.

Placing the butt into my shoulder, I take a standing aiming position. My Oakley's are covered in sweat, I throw them aside and try again. This time it's better, I have an excellent sight picture. I push my cap back on my head slightly to make more room for the scope.

I place my right thumb on the top of the butt to the rear of the scope and find the small plastic roller disc built into the weapon's mechanism - the safety catch. I take aim, placing the scope's crosshairs on the engine of the small skiff. With my thumb I gently roll back the plastic disc to expose a small red dot on the safety catch, I check my aim and gently place my index finger on the trigger…

~

Two days later I'm in South Africa trying to explain to a Customs official why my ammo count is low. 'But you declared this amount when you embarked', he says. I speak slowly and attempt to explain that some of the rounds were fired at sea, I don't say in what context but it seems to dawn on him what I'm trying to say.

After a couple of hours waiting and explaining to a handful of different officials, they reluctantly sign my paperwork and I hand over my weapons and equipment to their armoury.

I walk back outside with my fixer and head for his pick-up. 'Are we done'? I ask. 'Yup, I'm taking you to the hotel now, I'll let you know when your flight tickets are ready'.

I enter the hotel room, throw my bags into the corner and dump myself onto the double bed. I pull my phone out my pocket with a slip of paper that the receptionist gave me, and carefully tap in the password and username for the internet Wi-Fi. It takes time to register so I decide to take a quick shower while waiting, I'm looking forward to seeing the pictures of the children that Nikki will have sent me. Our new daughter, Georgia, is in her first year of school now. I turn the TV on for some background noise and head for the shower.

Fifteen minutes later I emerge feeling refreshed, I check my phone. I have the obligatory messages and pictures form Nikki that I was expecting, along with one very unusual message - but it's the one-hundred plus notifications that has my eyebrows raised.

Emails, social media messages, text messages, all from lads I knew back in the battalion, some still serving, some out in the civilian world, some on the PMC circuit. All the messages have the same kind of narrative - 'Robbo, I've had two suits turn up at my house asking questions about you in Iraq' or 'Mate, there's two investigators going round battalion trying to find info on you from Iraq in 03'.

Reference: IHAT 135
Date:

Dear Gary

Firstly let me introduce myself. I am a Civilian Investigator within the Iraq Historic Allegations Team (IHAT) based in Wiltshire. IHAT was set up by the British Government in March 2010, to assist the Secretary of State for Defence to investigate incidents arising from Op Telic, in line with his obligations under the European Convention of Human Rights, (ECHR).

The investigative team I work with within this organisation, has been tasked to examine a shooting that occurred on the ▮▮▮▮▮▮▮▮ 2003, in Basra, involving a unit from 2nd Battalion Light Infantry, (2LI). It is believed that you were serving with 2 LI at this time, and may have information relevant to the Investigation.

The intention of the investigation is to provide clarity and transparency as to the circumstances surrounding the shooting.

Please contact either of us on either of the numbers listed below when we can discuss the matter further: it may be the case that following our conversation that there is no reason for any further involvement.

Yours Sincerely

Neale Whittick

Civilian Investigator
Iraq Historic Allegations Team
Trenchard Lines, Upavon, Wiltshire, SN9 6BE

Tel. (Direct):   *01980 615828*
Mobile 07717484743
Email   *neale.whittickn100@mod.uk*

Alternatively   *Elizabeth Stewart*
Tel. (Direct):   *01980 615828*
Mobile   *07891691128*
Email: *elizabeth.stewart103@mod.uk*

Hi Gary. I called on Monday 18th August. You are obviously the main witness to this incident so because I have no contact number for you I am leaving this letter. I have already got statements from numerous soldiers attached to 'C' coy at this time and so I don't want you to worry about this, we are just going through the process to establish the full facts. Elizabeth

271

I give Nikki a call, fuck the roaming costs. We exchange pleasantries and I ask about the kids, all is well. Then she goes onto explain about a letter we've had through the door, no stamp or address, 'They must have been to the house while I was out' she explains. 'They've been to your dad's house too, he told them you were abroad.'

She reads the letter to me, it's from a detective working for IHAT - the Iraq Historic Allegations Team. They want to talk to me about the gunman I killed in Basra back in 2003. It says they are treating me as a witness for now but would like to see me as soon as possible. I tell Nikki not to worry about it and that I'll deal with it, she says she'll send me a snapshot of the letter. At first I decide to ignore them, but it plays on my mind for the next day or so.

I've checked in my bags at Johannesburg Airport, there's a few hours to wait until my flight, and as I sit down in Starbucks with a coffee my curiosity gets the better of me.

I pull out my phone and take off the back cover, carefully I take out my UK sim card and replace it with an Indian one (If I don't like what they've got to say I can throw this sim away and they can't call me back - old school Op-Sec). I replace the battery and cover, turn on the phone and check the credit - there's enough for a short international call.

I dial the number on the IHAT letter, no answer. A couple of minutes later the phone rings, I answer it knowing it'll be them calling me back. It's a woman's voice.

'Hello, this is Liz Stewart'
'Hello, this is Gary Roberts'

There's a long pause of silence, 'Hi Gary, well we've been looking for you for the last ten months or so', she says.

She goes on over a few minutes explaining how they want me to make a statement on camera so that they can close the case - I'm suspicious of her overly friendly attitude. I tell her I'm still overseas and I'll let her know when I'm back in the UK.

The next day I'm back home and on the phone to a military law specialist. He tells me there's no harm in meeting them to hear what they've got to say. But there's no need for me to assist them in their investigations or to give them any information.

In 2010, the UK government set aside £57 million for the investigations into British soldiers doing their jobs in Iraq. Many observers have regarded this as a legalised 'witch-hunt' against UK troops that served in Iraq. The accusations ranging from ill-treatment to unlawful killings have all been fruitless thus far.

It is, however, the cost to taxpayers and that these 'investigations' drag on for years which has stuck in the throats of most observers. Many a journalist has accused the IHAT of being nothing more than a racket for private investigators and the wider legal industry to bank-roll the government contracts to investigate.

Indeed, the MoD pays an Iraqi agent £40,000 per year to gather evidence against UK troops. That money is being paid by the UK taxpayer to assist in the potential prosecution of UK soldiers that had killed insurgents and unlawful combatants. What's worse is that these Iraqi accusers are assisted in legal fees whereas UK veterans are not entitled to legal assistance until such time as they are charged.

So as turns out I'm on the IHAT's hit-list: a confirmed kill from 12 years ago has come back to haunt me. Even though the RMP deemed the shooting at the time lawful and it was also cleared at brigade level, these guys want to investigate it simply for the sake of investigating it.

I meet the investigators, Neale Whittick and Elizabeth Stewart - the woman on the phone. They assume I'm happy to make the statement. But their hopes are soon dashed when I explain that I've taken legal advice, and based on that advice I'm not giving them anything.

They ask a few more casual questions. Turns out the statement I made the day after is missing, and they also can't find the two Army medics that worked on the gunman that day. They've spoke to all the platoon members that were there, and they assure me that everyone's backed me up. Still, there's something I don't trust in their over-the-top friendliness: is it a ruse to get me talking, I wonder? We depart on amicable terms and I feel that that should be the end of it. And it is, I hear nothing from them for next nineteen months.

In September 2016, Nikki gets a call from the IHAT: they're after me again. I tell Nikki to give them my email address. This time they've upped the ante. Unsatisfied, the IHAT have passed my case on to higher echelons. The email says they want to interview me under caution at a police station; they've decided to take the matter further for no other reason than that the Iraqis said so. I read part of the email again:

"Witness statements have been provided by Iraqi civilians present at the time of the incident and, as a result of this the senior management team at IHAT have decided that you should be formally interviewed in relation to what took place on that day"

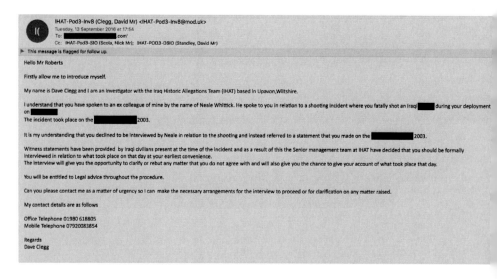

I call the number on the letter, some bloke called Clegg answers. This guy wants to be my best mate as well. He explains that if I don't comply this time I'll be arrested. He says I'll be entitled to legal advice throughout the procedure (I later learn this is bullshit), and that it's my chance to present my side of the story. I listen to him and remain non-committal in my answers. I tell him I'm going to get some legal advice and that he should wait, the line goes silent, then in a forced voice he says 'This isn't going to go away, Gary'. I reiterate my stance and hang up the phone.

One week later, I'm watching Daniel and Georgia doing their track training at the athletics club. My phone rings. It's my lawyer, Alice.

'Hi Gary, I spoke with the IHAT today, and basically - yes, we need to attend the interview with them.'

I listen intently as she explains some of the procedures to me. Then she drops the bombshell…

'They're pushing for a charge of murder'.

Now it's my turn to go silent. Eventually I mouth a very slow Oh-Kaayy.

She tells me not to worry, 'One step at a time' she says. Then she casually mentions that I'm not entitled to legal assistance after all, not until I'm formally charged, and that I'll have to cover her fee myself. Shit just gets better.

Alice arranges a meet with the investigators for the 'disclosure', she plans to collate all the statements and evidence the IHAT have amassed during the investigation. She calls me late in the day. I listen intently as she explains what happened at the meeting.

'I met yesterday with IHAT's David Clegg and David Rees for just over an hour. It was an odd meeting because they did not bring any statements with them, as their superior officers did not want them to be disclosed until just before your interview under caution. It seemed an awfully long way to come just for a chat. They did bring with them a copy of the Battle Group commander's report into the incident. I was not even allowed to take a photocopy of it!'

Our conversation continues and we agree that they're not throwing straight dice, perhaps in the hope of catching me out somehow on the day of the interview.

~

2017...

It's a freezing January morning as I enter Newbury Police Station. I greet Alice, and we're immediately taken through to a small private interview room. Clegg and Rees are both there. Alice gets straight into to them, demanding all the so-called evidence and statements. Clegg hands over file after file, he has a box of paperwork on the floor next to him all labelled up, some of the labels have names I recognise, others are Arabic names - the Iraqi statements.

Alice explains to them that we're refusing to have the video camera pointing at my face during the interview, she thanks them and politely tells them to fuck off for a couple of hours whilst we read through all this paperwork. We sit in silence and read through the witness statements, occasionally conferring on points. I take the soldiers' statements - that of my platoon on the day. Alice takes the Iraqi statements. I recognise all the names on the front of each file, as I begin reading through them. I'm content as all the guys seem to have backed me up, some staunchly, some passively. Alice is scribbling away furiously as she takes notes. Occasionally she breaks the silence with a sardonic laugh; she's obviously finding some of these Iraqi statements amusing.

After about an hour we swap statements, and again we sit in silence. I begin to see what was entertaining Alice. The Iraqi witness statements are, by their own admission, based on hearsay, second hand stories, and they freely admit that they've had the chance to get their heads together to consolidate their story. Some of their accounts are derisory, and they are full of inconsistencies. Alice punctuates the silence sporadically to ask me about some militarism or acronym that she's come across in the soldiers' statements.

By the end I'm pretty sick of reading the same shit over and over, the last couple of statements I skim-read just to get the jist. Alice is done and we go and grab a cup of tea. Back in the interview room, Alice asks me what I think. I think back to my original statement (which is included in the pile of paperwork) from 2003, the one I made the day after the shooting. 'Isn't everything covered in that original statement?' I ask her. 'Yes' she replies, 'That's why I'm going to advise you not to say anything more during the interview'.

Alice spends the next ten-minutes schooling me on how to avoid the traps and tricks these guys will use to get me talking. 'All you have to say is… I've made a statement, and I have nothing to add to it'. She goes on, 'you can just say… No comment, if it's more appropriate'. 'If they go off topic I'll jump in and end that line of questioning'.

Alice is happy that I'm prepared, and she calls the IHAT investigators back in.

After some messing with the video equipment, Clegg clears his throat and asks the three of us if we're ready to start, Alice nods and gives the 'Okay'. Rees leans over and hits the record button. After brief introductions, Clegg goes straight into his spiel…

'Gary Roberts… You do not have to say anything. But it may harm your defence if you do not mention when questioned something which you may later rely on in court. Anything you do say may be given in evidence. Do you understand?'.

'Yes', I reply.
'And are you aware of why we'd like to talk to you today, what we want to ask you questions about?'

I nod… 'Iraq'.

Clegg gets straight into me 'Who told you to write that statement in 2003?'

I open my mouth ready to speak but Alice quickly interjects… 'My client has made a detailed statement on the day after the shooting, and because everything covered in the witness statements is covered in his statement I'm advising him to give no comment during this interview'.

Clegg takes a deep breath, his face slightly red 'Who gave you permission to write a statement in 2003'

'No Comment', I reply.
'Did you write it yourself, or did you dictate it?'.
'"I've made a statement, and I have nothing to add" I reply.
'Was it your CO?'.
'Nothing to add'.

277

'Was it your Platoon Commander?'
'Nothing to add'.
Clegg loosens his tie, and checks his notes...
'What time of day was it?'
'Nothing to add'.
'What was the weather like, clear, overcast?'
'Nothing to add'.
'I see from the mission notes that you'd been on the ground since around 03:00 that morning, were you tired?'.
'Nothing to add'.

Clegg lets out a sigh of exasperation, he checks his notes and decides to up his game...

'So I've seen from your statement that the gunman - well civilian, but we'll call him a gunman for now - was sitting down when you shot him, what part of the AK was he holding, the butt, the barrel...?'.
He's deliberately throwing lies at me now in the hope that I'll rise to it and start correcting him - my statement says nothing close to that. But I'm on to it and I don't bite.

'Nothing to add'. I reply.

Clegg's fat face is getting redder by the minute now, but he cracks on. He changes tack every few questions, one minute he's accusing me of killing the guy out of panic, the next he's saying I shot him to gain some kudos around the battalion. At one point, he tries accuse me of having an ND (Negligent Discharge), I inwardly laugh to myself as I throw him back the usual... 'Nothing to add'.
His next tac is to appeal to the soldier in me, asking me questions he knows I'll want to answer... 'What type of weapon were you using?', 'What's its name?', 'Did you have a sighting system on it, what's the name of the sighting system?'.

'Nothing to add'.
'When did you make ready your weapon?'
'Nothing to add'.
'Who told you to make ready your weapon?'
'Nothing to add'.

'*Why did you shoot him twice?*'
'*Nothing to add*'.
'*Did you shout a warning, if not, why not?*'
'*Nothing to add*'.

I'm feeling more comfortable now and I'm in my stride, I throw each question back at him with a barrage of 'Nothing to adds'.

Again, he changes tack… 'What procedures did you conduct post incident with the captured AK weapons? Did you even know the procedures, *were* there even any procedures?'

Alice interrupts him abruptly: 'If you want to investigate Army procedure, then feel free to open up a separate investigation into that. We're here to talk about the shooting and nothing else, so get back on topic'.

This time I don't hide my wide grin, and Clegg doesn't hide his frustration as he lets out a loud sigh… Go Alice!

Clegg throws out some more bullshit questions for the next thirty minutes. I keep up my mantra of 'Nothing to add'.

Eventually, he takes his glasses of and dabs his fat red face with a tissue, 'That's all I have, no more questions'. Clegg's boyfriend, Rees, closes the interview by reading some formalities verbatim from a file on his lap, then declaring the time and date aloud stops the recording equipment.

Alice doesn't fuck about; she's straight into them, asking them when we'll have closure, when decisions will be made. They're non-committal but assure us we'll know as soon as possible.

Alice and I leave the interview room and walk to the car park. She hands our passes in to the duty police officer as we exit the building. 'I think we'd obliterate them if they decided to take this to trial, but you can never be sure what they'll resolve to do', Alice says. I agree: all those millions spent on this investigation based on some insubstantial Iraqi statements.

We pause on the steps and discuss how I did in the interview; she's happy with how it went. We stroll on toward the car park, deliberating Clegg's interview tactics. Just as we say our goodbyes and are about to go our separate ways, Clegg slams the boot of his car shut a few feet away. Clocking us, he walks over, then holds his hand out. I hesitate for a minute while I decide what to do, then I think fuck it, and shake his hand.

'Thanks for meeting us today, Gary,' he says.

'Yeah ok,' I reply dryly.

But I think to myself - if we ever meet again, I hope it's in the middle of some desert war-zone, 'cos if it is, I'll blow your fucking brains out and I'll leave no witnesses next time...

LESSONS LEARNED

2017...

It's June 1st. I'm back at work. Back on the oil tankers. This time I'm in the Gulf of Oman. I'm stood at the back of the bridge of the NAVIGA8 PROVIDENCE, the pride of the Navig8 fleet. I click open a long black Peli-Case and pull out my HKG3 7.62mm battle rifle. My grab bag of spare magazines is slung over my shoulder and as I make my way to the door, I pull one out and load the G3. I slide the door open to the exterior wings. As the door slides open, three crewmen come sprinting into the bridge and barge past me. The last one stops, a fat lad wearing a boiler suit, hard-hat, and flip flops, he turns to me, "Back-side sir... pirates" he says in his best Indian-English as he frantically points toward the rear of the ship.

I step outside onto the bridge wing and slide the door closed behind me, again the heat hits me, the sea is bright blue and calm, my peripheral hearing subconsciously takes note of the engine rumble in the background as it increases its workload. I'm alone, I'm calm, I've been here before and the knowledge of my experiences relaxes me. I turn and walk towards the rear of the bridge, I don't see the speedboat but I clock the white line it's made in the sea as it heads towards us. I don't feel the need to rush, I have a few minutes before they get too close. I don't do any time-distance-speed calculations for it, I just feel it. Twenty years of soldiering has brought me to this point, twenty years of soldiering has taught me when to shit bricks and when to remain calm, and right now my gut tells me it's the latter.

As I come level with the back of the bridge, a burst of bullets comes flying overhead. I listen to the time lapse between the crack and thump of the air displacement of the rounds and do a quick distance estimate – they're close but not too close. I don't flinch. As I walk I place the G3 on my hip with the barrel pointing upward and cock the first round into the chamber. I don't think they've seen me, they're just trying to scare the bridge crew into stopping the ship so they can board.

I walk across a small gantry towards the funnel, from here I can see the speedboat

approaching from the rear port side. I clock six dark-skinned pirates, and count five AK assault rifles. The sixth is at the rear, steering the engines with a rudder in one hand. In his other hand I notice he is holding a large black box which he's staring at intently, it has a large antenna coming out of the top with a fat bit on the end. This interests me and I wonder if he's holding a scanner, a GPS, or something else. I know the Captain will be on the bridge frantically sending his reports to the authorities, so I assume they are listening.

I turn around and break into a trot as I move to the far side of the funnel. I figure from here I'll have a more side-on view of the pirates. As the pirates disappear from my view, I hear another burst of gunfire go over the top of the bridge.

I appear from the far-rear of the funnel and get my eyes on them again. They're closer. I place my rifle into my shoulder and pull it in tight, I breathe, I slow my breathing, two big breaths then I hold it. Aiming at the black box guy, I slowly squeeze the trigger and put a round straight through his head. He slumps onto some netting in the boat. The guy at the front stands up, AK in hand. I aim and fire again, I clock the round splash into the water. For a split second I think I've missed, then he drops into the boat. The round went straight through him. This time I don't lower the weapon, I turn to the two guys sitting in the boat. The boat has slowed now without its pilot but is still moving forward. One of the sitting guys is scrambling toward the rudder. I slot him in the back between his shoulder-blades, he's in line with the other sitting guy and I quickly shoot him in the chest with minimal readjustment to my firing position. The last two pirates are scrambling to the rear of the boat. I quickly shuffle my feet to accommodate the new angle as they slow down and put one round into the ribs of the first; he goes down. I put another round straight in to the sternum of the last.

The rhythmical chug of the ship's engines continues in its motion. With my gloved-left hand I flick open the cocking handle of the G3 and pull the bolt back slightly. The ejection-opening exposes a few millimetres of the shiny bullet casing. I let the bolt go forward and resume its original position, safe in the knowledge that I have a round in the chamber: I'm good to go. I turn on my heels and walk around the bridge wings. I want to check all around us, make sure they don't have any friends hanging around. That's the problem with working alone - I have to watch my own back. I clock two larger Dhows in the distance, the 'mother' vessels provide a launching point for the speed boats, but they're

low and slow compared to our oil tanker. They'll be over the horizon in no time.

I slide the door to the bridge open and walk inside. The air-con is bliss, the Captain is talking furiously in Indian on channel 16 of the VHF. He pauses and looks at me; he wants to know what's going on. I open my mouth but pause for a spilt second, my mind casts back to the day in Newbury Police Station, I decide to leave the details out of it. "They're gone now", I tell him. "Let's just keep best speed for now and we can start our reporting procedures". He nods a sigh of relief.

The contact lasted no more than half a minute. My report reflects six rounds fired, I didn't expand on where those rounds were aimed or where they landed. No one follows up to check my facts. If my experience in Basrah and with the IHAT investigation has taught me anything, it's don't leave witnesses – no witnesses, no witness statements. Lesson learned.

~

Within a couple of weeks I'm on my way home. Two flights, a train, and a taxi later, and I'm looking forward to opening my front door with the kids jumping all over me when I get in. I pay the driver and walk up my drive. I place the key in the door and open it.

Silence. I walk in, I walk around the rooms. The house is empty, no kids, no Nikki, no furniture, no appliances, no food, no nothing.

She'd left.

Lesson learned.

WEAPONS

AK	AUTOMAT KALASHNIKOV – 7.62X39MM SOVIET ASSAULT RIFLE
PKM	PULEMYOT KALASHNIKOV MODERNIZED – 7.62X54MM SOVIET LIGHT MACHINE GUN
RPK	RUCHNOY PULEMYOT KALASHNIKOV – 7.62X39MM SOVIET ASSAULT RIFLE (LONG-BARRELLED AKM VARIANT)
M4	AMERICAN 5.56X45MM ASSAULT RIFLE
SA80	BRITISH 5.56X45MM ASSAULT RIFLE
M21	SERBIAN 5.56X45MM ASSAULT RIFLE
SLR	BRITISH/BELGIAN NATO VARIANT 7.62X51MM BATTLE RIFLE
GMPG	GENERAL PURPOSE MACHINE GUN 7.62X51MM SUPPORT WEAPON
STYR SCOUT	AUSTRIAN BOLT-ACTION RIFLE 7.62X51MM
RPG	ROCKET-PROPELLED GRENADE
DRAGANOV	SOVIET LONG-RANGE RIFLE – 7.62X54MM
GLOCK 17	AUSTRIAN 9X19MM SELF-LOADING PISTOL
BROWNING HP	BRITISH 9X19MM SELF-LOADING PISTOL
APC	ARMOURED PERSONNEL CARRIER
AFV	ARMOURED FIGHTING VEHICLE
ACOG	ADVANCED COMBAT OPTICAL GUN-SIGHT
SAW/M249/ MINIMI	BELGIAN/NATO VARIANT – 5.56X45MM LIGHT MACHINE GUN